DONAL LENIHAN

MY LIFE IN RUGBY

TRANSWORLD IRELAND

TRANSWORLD IRELAND PUBLISHERS
28 Lower Leeson Street, Dublin 2, Ireland
www.transworldireland.ie

Transworld Ireland is part of the Penguin Random House group of companies
whose addresses can be found at global.penguinrandomhouse.com

First published in the UK and Ireland in 2016
by Transworld Ireland
an imprint of Transworld Publishers

A CIP catalogue record for this book
is available from the British Library.

ISBN 9781848272255

Typeset in 12/16 pt Minion by Jouve (UK), Milton Keynes
Printed and bound in Great Britain by Clays Ltd, Bungay, Suffolk

Penguin Random House is committed to a sustainable
future for our business, our readers and our planet. This book
is made from Forest Stewardship Council® certified paper.

1 3 5 7 9 10 8 6 4 2

To Mary and David and to
the treasured memory of Sarah and John

Contents

1
Listowel

'You're a lock.'

That was all I was told before my first rugby involvement on games day on a Wednesday afternoon at Christian Brothers College in Cork. Incredibly, this was on a pitch that directly bordered Collins Barracks where, unknown to me, my grandfather had been court-martialled and sentenced to death fifty years earlier.

Coming from a Gaelic football background, I didn't have a clue what I was being told. Locks? Weren't they for doors and keys? It's amazing how life can hinge on small decisions.

Growing up in St Luke's Cross on the northside of the city, it was all about playing on the streets, playing hurling and football, batting a sliotar or a ball off the gable end of houses. I was always out with a ball, morning, noon and night.

In primary school in St Patrick's we used to have an hour

and a quarter for lunch. I'd run home, have my dinner and run back to school immediately for a match. There would be a soccer match every day in the yard; we'd play with the same teams for a week before having to go through the selection process again every Monday lunchtime. That was it, five days a week, all rough and tumble. Playing sports was all that mattered. But rugby didn't come into it.

Rugby was a game we never played. We never had a rugby ball and it was not part of our childhood; though I do remember as a kid, when the Five Nations was on the television we'd go out, pretend the soccer ball was a rugby one and start passing, but that was about it. Rugby was never on the agenda until I went to secondary school.

I grew up playing hurling and football for Old Youghal Road in street leagues run by Brian Dillon's Hurling and Football Club, and also had great craic playing for the club for a number of years.

St Patrick's National School was well rated in GAA circles in Cork. My teacher, J. J. Fennessy, was part of the fabric of the scene and he always had great time for me.

My first sporting highlight and subsequent disappointment came at eleven years of age when we reached the final of the Cork city primary schools' competition, only to be beaten. Consolation came with the selection at centre-back for the Cork primary schools' team to play Limerick at the old Athletic Grounds. Had we won the final, I would even have captained Cork as the only St Pa's representative on the team. Captaining teams and being a leader on the field I guess came naturally to me and was to be a constant theme throughout my sporting career.

As a child, my dream was to play Gaelic football for Cork,

but all that changed when I went to Christian Brothers College. One of the main reasons my parents sent me there was because I was very young starting primary school and CBC offered a six-year secondary cycle; most of the other secondary schools in Cork were five-year cycles. It also helped that it was ten minutes down the road from here. As a fee-paying school, Christians, along with Presentation Brothers College, were seen as the snobby schools by many of my classmates.

If my parents had sent me to one of the other five-year-cycle schools I would have played Gaelic football and might never have touched a rugby ball. I'd like to think I would have played football for Cork, maybe even have won a Sam Maguire, but as I walked nervously through the gates of Christians little did I know what lay before me and how everything would change completely.

When J. J. Fennessy learned that I was going to CBC, he talked me up to the Christian Brothers reckoning I had potential to be a great rugby player. Catching, fielding, jumping all came naturally to me and he was always very supportive. He saw something in me.

Leaving the security and familiarity of St Patrick's for CBC was daunting enough but I was lucky that I had Brother Phil O'Reilly as my class master as well as games master. It was he who introduced me to rugby, told me I was a lock before explaining what it meant, and instilled a great love for a game that has been a massive part of my life. On that first Wednesday afternoon, my life changed for ever.

Even if rugby was never in my family, my father, Gerald, does recall trying it out with his great friend John B. Keane, a schoolmate of his growing up together in Listowel, County Kerry, and claims he played for the local club. As with the rest of the kingdom, though, Gaelic football was the sport of choice in Listowel. My father was a fine player and ended up playing wherever his job took him, often under a false name as he was lining out for a few different teams at the same time.

He won a Cork senior county football medal for St Nick's, the sister club of Glen Rovers, playing alongside such legendary figures as future Taoiseach Jack Lynch and the great Christy Ring. I remember when I first made it on to the Irish team, Jack Lynch was a VIP at matches and at the post-match reception under the stand. He would always make a point of coming over to me for a chat. Some within the IRFU were wondering what was going on – what was so special about Lenihan?

My father also boxed for the Glen Boxing Club and was Irish junior heavyweight champion. He got one cap for Ireland at senior level, boxing against Germany. He was a big strong man, very athletic by all accounts, and also won an All Ireland junior football medal with Cork.

Up to when I was twelve years of age, Dad was away for five days a week working wherever his job took him. When I was growing up in primary school, he was always away. It was only in the early 1970s when he became a contracts manager with Rohans in Cork that he was at home during the week.

I remember him coming home on a Friday evening, always with a bag of sweets for me and my two sisters, Jo and Audrey, before heading off at dawn again on a Monday morning. He wouldn't have been going to my games, but it was different then. Nowadays parents drop kids off everywhere and they're all on the sideline. There was no such thing when I was growing up. When I played for Cork primary schools, my mother,

Chris, did go to the match, but unfortunately Dad never saw my one and only appearance in a Cork jersey.

At the time, Gaelic football was my passion and all I wanted to do was play for Cork. I was brought up going to Cork-Kerry matches, national league and Munster championship games in Cork and Killarney.

Although my dad had played for Cork he was a passionate Kerry man, and as a young boy I was a bit confused trying to figure out which he was. One Cork-Kerry clash in the Athletic Grounds stands out, however, and sorted any confusion I may have had as to where his loyalties lay.

Mick O'Dwyer was playing for Kerry and was being marked by Seamus Looney, a great young dual player for Cork. Looney must have been giving Micko a hard time so Kerry switched Mick Gleeson in on him. Within minutes there was a massive digging match and both were sent off. We were sitting on the freezing cold concrete seats in front of the old stand. Gleeson was being helped off around the perimeter of the pitch with the whole of the Cork crowd shouting and roaring at him as he passed. Next thing I know, my father jumps up and starts shouting and clapping furiously. 'Well done Mick Gleeson!' I thought we were going to be killed! It obviously helped that many in the Cork crowd knew he was a heavyweight boxing champion but I didn't appreciate it at the time. Even to this day, if you suggested to him that he was a Cork man, he would take the head off you.

It was my dad's friend John B. Keane who wrote about how close my grandfather John (or Jacko as he was known) came to death at the hands of a firing squad.

It was 19 February 1982, the night before a Triple Crown

decider against Scotland in Lansdowne Road. The hype surrounding the game was like nothing I had ever experienced before. Then again, that wasn't overly surprising given that the match was only my fourth cap.

What was unusual was that, for the likes of the vastly experienced players in the team, decorated men such as Fergus Slattery, Willie Duggan and my Munster room-mate Moss Keane, this game was different. It represented a first real opportunity for them to win a Triple Crown, and you could sense it. Ireland's last Triple Crown had come in 1949, with our one and only Grand Slam the year before. History was beckoning.

Slattery had been robbed of his chance ten years earlier when Wales and Scotland had refused to travel to Dublin because of the escalation of the Troubles in the North. Having beaten both England and France away from home already that season, he was denied a potential Grand Slam.

The Championship was won by Ireland in 1974, but in many ways it was an almost forgotten title. If it wasn't a Triple Crown – the game with Wales was drawn – did it mean as much or get as many headlines? It never stuck in my mind, though the game the following season when the IRFU celebrated their centenary with a match against a World XV in Lansdowne Road stands out clearly.

Myself and one of my closest friends in school, Barry Coleman, got the train to Dublin for the game and we were crammed in on the East Terrace getting a glimpse of our heroes. I'll never forget running on to the pitch at the final whistle and managing to tap Willie John McBride on the arm as the players made their way back to the dressing room. He turned and shook my hand. Who would have believed that this lanky teenager would be playing under Willie John for Ireland and the Lions just a few years later?

I could sense the edge to Moss when we returned to our room before dinner having collected the evening papers in the foyer of the Shelbourne Hotel. The coverage of the match was incredible and unprecedented for a rugby international, with the *Evening Herald* producing an eight-page Triple Crown supplement to preview the game.

Moss passed it over to me as there was an interview by Karl MacGinty with the headline 'Donal Lenihan – Cool, Calm and Collected' adorning the back page. But it was the piece by John B. Keane on page two of the supplement that captured my imagination.

John B. wrote proudly of the Listowel connection going back to my father, Gerald, and grandfather, Jacko, who was arrested for the shooting of Royal Irish Constabulary District Inspector Tobias O'Sullivan in the town in January 1921. I was always told that, while he was an active member of the Listowel Company of Irish Volunteers during the War of Independence, he'd played no part in the murder of the inspector.

The killing of Inspector O'Sullivan had actually been carried out by Con Brosnan, a future Kerry All Ireland-winning captain, and two of his colleagues, Dan Grady and Jack Ahern.

While researching this book, I was introduced to Con Brosnan's son, Jerry, who at eighty-eight years of age was a fount of knowledge on those troubled times. The first thing Jerry showed me when I visited him in the old family home in Moyvane, just a few miles outside Listowel, was a picture of a rugby team. I recognized the setting immediately. It was a British Navy team playing the British Army in Twickenham in

1928, and in the back row stood Con's brother, Michael, who had trained to be a doctor in the British Navy and by all accounts was the first Kerry man to play in Twickenham – certainly the first from Moyvane anyway!

In the aftermath of the killing of Tobias O'Sullivan, my grandfather Jacko was revered in the area as he never squealed on Brosnan or his fellow Volunteers despite being sentenced to death for an atrocity he played no part in.

'Time passed,' wrote John B. 'And then on a never-to-be-forgotten morning he was awakened by his gaolers and ordered to dig his own grave in the prison grounds. When the grave was dug he was told that the date for his execution was a mere forty-eight hours away.'

One night, while my grandfather was being held in Buttevant Barracks, the IRA massacred a dozen British Army men at nearby Headford train station. Six of the dead were brought back to the barracks and the Black and Tans, along with the military, were going nuts around the towns and villages looking for revenge. Jacko and the five others in custody feared for their lives.

A British soldier went into my grandfather's cell that night and whispered, 'Say the rosary, Paddy, I think you are for it.' The soldier handed him a set of rosary beads and said, 'I got this in Palestine, I think a lot about it.'

Jacko was fully expecting to be shot in reprisal but they left him alone and he survived the night. However, for seven days after the ambush, the prisoners were left without food. For the rest of his life Jacko also had terrible back troubles which came from having to sleep on flagstones while in prison.

Later that year, when the Anglo-Irish Treaty was signed, his sentence (along with those of many others) was commuted and he lived to marry, have kids and live out the rest of his days in Listowel, a carpenter by trade. I was nine when he died and I remember him well, bringing me to his local pub in Listowel, sitting me up on the stool with a glass of orange and a bag of Taytos. He would also bring me into his workshop in the back of his house on Charles Street where he would show me an underground hiding place where the IRA guns used to be hidden. Although the RIC often raided the premises they never found his hiding place.

Unfortunately the workshop is gone now, as is McKenna's Timber Yard, which was situated across the road and was where my father would be sent to buy wood for Jacko. There he met and became friendly with an office clerk by the name of John Sexton. Little did they appreciate that, many years down the road, they would be reacquainted when their respective sons, Willie and I, played together for Munster and Ireland. I am sure John Sexton would have been equally proud of the many achievements of his grandson and namesake Johnny, who continues to lead the charge for Leinster and Ireland.

My father completed his apprenticeship as a carpenter under Jacko's direction by the time he was seventeen. His sister Eileen was married to Jack Sullivan, an Irish soldier stationed on Spike Island, so he was sent down there for two-week holidays. He was all set to join up with the rest of his siblings, Breda, Sean, Dinny and twin brother Donal, who had all followed their eldest sister Mai to Huddersfield in England where Mai had trained as a nurse during the Second World War, but he ended up getting a job in Cobh and has lived in Cork ever since.

'Rabble', as Brother Phil O'Reilly was affectionately known, was an iconic figure in Irish Schools rugby and I was so fortunate to have played under him at Christian Brothers College. He was an incredibly innovative coach, way ahead of his time, doing things that are taken for granted now. He delivered eight Munster Senior Cups in ten years for Christians and brought through a huge amount of rugby talent. I went through my whole time at CBC without ever losing a cup match.

We had a culture of winning and seven or eight of us from Christians went on to play together in UCC – University College Cork. Rugby gripped me from the outset. But Schools rugby was alien to my family. They wouldn't have seen me play until I was made captain of CBC's Junior Cup team. At that stage they probably thought they'd better see what all the fuss was about. My father was working permanently in Cork by that time and they'd started going to the Schools games. Overnight, their lives changed too as they followed all the cup games and built up a core of friendships with the parents of the other players.

I played with my friend Barry Coleman all the way through Christians. His father Norman had played for Munster in 1954 against the touring All Blacks and was a great club man with Dolphin for years. When the first ever Irish Schools team, captained by Donal Spring, played in 1974/75 to mark the centenary of the IRFU, he drove us up to Dublin to watch the game. Watching the Schools players in the green of Ireland that day, I started to think that maybe it could also be me playing out there one day. It instilled a desire in me to emulate those players. Playing for Ireland was becoming a goal.

I got a final trial the following year, though I was still only sixteen. I didn't make the cut, but in my final year I became the first from CBC to get selected. That made it even more special. We played Wales in Lansdowne Road and years later my father revealed that of all the games I ever played, the first time I wore a green jersey at any level was the one that stood out the most for him.

Norman Coleman was also there with Barry that day, and at the final whistle he called me to the sideline to shake my hand. I have no doubt that one of the reasons he brought Barry and me to that first ever Schools game was to open our eyes to the possibilities that lay ahead.

When you're playing for an Irish Schools team it starts to dawn on you: maybe I could play for Ireland some day. It sows a seed in you. You wouldn't have many expectations of yourself at that stage. Other fellas, their fathers, brothers, uncles, might have played rugby, but I had no history or background in the game. But then when you're in the Irish Schools set-up you start to think to yourself, 'Maybe I could be doing this, maybe I belong?'

Even after my career took off at full international level, I remained a fanatical supporter of Cork hurling and football teams. During the summer break from rugby I would travel to all the Cork matches, but you would always get some gombeen shouting at you, 'Aren't you at the wrong game?' Yeah, right.

It would drive me mad that some within the GAA would see themselves as being more Irish than we, as rugby players, were. Often it was people on the periphery that would be lobbing in the odd little comment. One incident in particular really hit home, when we stopped off in a watering hole in Mitchelstown on the way back from one of the greatest Munster hurling finals Semple Stadium had ever seen. But I'll tell you that story later.

By the time of that incident my Gaelic football dreams had been left far behind in my childhood. I was captain of Ireland. I'd won Triple Crowns, played for the Lions and appeared in a World Cup. And I'd played a lot of games since turning out for Irish Schools, with both heartbreak and celebrations in between.

2

Proving Myself

Although I got my first Ireland cap against Australia in November 1981, I had been invited to go on the tour to South Africa earlier that year, in the summer. I couldn't and didn't go because I was doing my finals in UCC and I had to get an honours degree for the job I was hoping to get in commercial banking. People can talk, saying it was for all kinds of political reasons and all of that, but that is the plain truth.

There were a lot of issues and a lot of fall-out because of that tour, with apartheid still rife in South Africa, and quite a few of the players had to leave Ireland through the back door, assembling in London. If I hadn't had my finals, would I have travelled with them if selected? To be honest, yes I would have. I was only twenty-one at the time and all you think at that age is, 'God, I'm missing out on an opportunity of a lifetime.' You don't think of the political ramifications. I did go to South

Africa in June 1982 for the opening of Ellis Park in Johannesburg with a Five Nations team that was managed by Syd Millar and captained by Fergus Slattery.

There were quite a few protests against the Irish tour from the Church and the political establishment and a number of players, including Moss Keane and Tony Ward, made themselves unavailable. Moss was working for the Department of Agriculture at the time and he made up his own mind not to go, while Wardy had been soured by what he saw when touring with the British and Irish Lions the previous year.

In the end, the team actually did quite well in the two Tests, losing both narrowly. Brendan Foley played in the second row with Jerry Holland, who I played with in UCC. That was his first cap, but to be fair, I never thought, 'I've lost the opportunity,' or that it was gone. I was delighted for Jerry, not only as we had played together but because we were also very close friends.

I remember calling to his house in Sunday's Well which peered over the home of UCC rugby down the Mardyke, where we had so often trained and played together, and being proud of him. He showed me his Irish jersey and the Springbok one worn by his opposite number Louis Moolman, with whom he'd swapped shirts.

At twenty-one I didn't think I would be playing for Ireland just yet. That thought was way down the road. It turned out, though, that I got selected for that next international against Australia, ironically at Jerry's expense. It was brilliant to be chosen but even then the circumstances were a bit strange.

In those days when you were selected for your first cap, it was a tradition that you didn't play the weekend before in case you got injured and you might never be picked again. But in my case, Munster were playing Australia on the Tuesday in

Musgrave Park. Although I had been selected the previous week for the Irish team, there was never any question of me not playing for Munster.

These games were extra special because overseas sides didn't travel with anything like the regularity they do now. Munster played New Zealand in 1973, '74 and '78 but then didn't play them again until 1989, so there was a massive gap there. Obviously now in the professional era they need the money so they're all coming up every autumn.

That 1981 Munster side still had a lot of the guys who had played against and beaten the All Blacks in '78. Ginger McLoughlin, Colm Tucker, Brendan Foley, Christy Cantillan and Tony Ward were all still on board and they weren't overawed to be playing the Aussies.

Musgrave Park was packed to capacity and the expectation was 'We're going to win this'. Munster struggled to win inter-provincials but our record against touring teams was always good. With the intense rivalry that existed between the likes of Shannon, Cork Constitution, Garryowen and Young Munsters there was a bit of an attitude of 'don't tell him what you're doing' during preparations for inter-pros, but that was all gone when you played against touring sides; otherwise you could be destroyed. Munster's proud history against tourists dictated that you had to put your best foot forward. That was the catalyst that brought Cork and Limerick together.

You were always conscious of what went before you. We'd be told about '63, when Munster lost narrowly (6-3) to the All Blacks, and the '67 side that beat Australia in Musgrave Park. You had the close shaves as well. We got a half-day from CBC to go to Musgrave Park for the game in '73 when New Zealand got a kick in the last minute of the game to draw 3-3.

In many respects playing for Munster was a good thing for me because my international debut at the weekend was the last thing on my mind. Peter McLean was playing in the second row for Australia in Cork, and was also a certainty to be picked for the Test on Saturday, so I was going to be facing a quality international twice in five days.

I don't know if it was the innocence of youth or whatever, but I never worried about the game. I never worried about it at all. I just got on with it, and after we won, 15-6, everybody was going ballistic. There was a dinner afterwards so I went home to get changed and my father dropped me back in for the reception where there were huge celebrations going on. All I was thinking was, 'I'm not going to have a pint in here tonight because I have an international coming up.'

After beating the Aussies the celebrations went on in Cork all night, but I was home early, thinking only of Saturday and running out for my first cap. I went to Dublin on the Thursday morning and was put rooming with Wardy, which I thought was a bit strange. Rooming selection was very important in those days because you spent so little time together – that was how you got to know a fellow. But here was me, a young second row, now rooming with the star out-half.

The thing is, I never felt out of place. Quite the opposite in fact. I suppose I was lucky in that. I never got nervous before games. Never had butterflies. I couldn't wait to get out there. That was my attitude. There were other guys like Brendan Foley from that Munster game on the Tuesday who I was playing with on the Saturday. That was a big help.

When I got opportunities early in my career it was because Moss Keane was injured. I also played with Brendan in my first ever inter-pro, against Ulster in Thomond Park the previous season. We beat Ulster that day but Moss was fit for the Leinster game in Lansdowne Road the following week and, quite rightly, was selected with Brendan. I wasn't even a togged-out sub: second rows rarely were back then as you could only carry three forwards on a five-man bench. I was asked to travel with the party, however, and I received a great boost later that evening.

An Ireland B team was selected to play England in Twickenham and I was picked in the second row with Jerry Holland and another former UCC colleague, Anthony O'Leary, chosen to captain the team from No. 8. Munster were well beaten that day against Leinster. As a consequence I was selected in the second row for the final inter-pro of the season against Connacht with A. N. Other announced as my partner. Incredibly, the selectors were going to pick one from Moss Keane and Brendan Foley, which was an extraordinary position for me. I was just a month past my twenty-first birthday and they were the two Irish second rows at the time. In the end, Brendan was picked and, in a bizarre compromise, Moss was parked on the bench.

Moss, though, was always fantastic to me. There was the Kerry connection through my dad and the UCC connection as well. Moss loved his time in college in Cork and was eternally grateful for his introduction to rugby in UCC. He also knew my uncle Sean in Dublin as they were neighbours in Rathfarnham.

Brendan Foley was the one who lost out in the end because he would have been on that Triple Crown-winning side in 1982 only for me coming on the scene, but again, it was never an issue. UCC and Shannon were big rivals at the time and we often clashed, the young buck and the experienced pro, but we had a good relationship.

I can still recall how, on my debut, this young lad was brought into the dressing room after the game and sat down between us. He was eight years old at the time, waving his Irish flag. It was the first time I met Anthony Foley. Brendan was in the second row for Munster's greatest day against the All Blacks and then Anthony was captain the first time Munster lifted the Heineken Cup. It's passed on from generation to generation.

Coming into the Ireland team in 1981, I was extremely lucky because seven of the eight forwards had played together in an outstanding two-Test series win in Australia in 1979, beating the Wallabies convincingly 27-12 in the first Test and 9-3 in the second. It was one of Ireland's most successful tours, which also saw the debut of Ciaran Fitzgerald.

On the back of that successful trip, Ireland were favourites for the 1980 Five Nations Championship. I played for the Irish Universities against our English counterparts on the Thursday in London, but we were the only Irish side to win on that first Five Nations weekend. Standing on the terrace in Twickenham for the first match of the 1980 season, little did I appreciate that the next time Ireland played here, I would have an altogether better vantage point. Ireland were expected to win handsomely that day, and win the Championship, but England beat them and went on to win the Grand Slam, with Ireland runners-up.

Despite then losing all four games in the 1981 Five Nations, as well as those two summer Tests in South Africa, there was a nucleus of a very good Irish team there. It was described affectionately as Dad's Army. I was the only concession to youth in the forwards and there was definitely a sense that you had to prove yourself. There was Phil Orr, Ciaran Fitzgerald, Ginger McLoughlin, Moss Keane, John O'Driscoll, Willie Duggan and

Fergus Slattery. Moss quipped that my arrival brought the average age of the second row down to lower than that of the half-backs, so he was quite happy. By the time we finished our careers, all of that pack had played for the Lions at one point or another so it was an extremely experienced group.

On the weekends building up to internationals you trained on a Sunday morning, with the fellas from outside Dublin put up in the Shelbourne Hotel the night before. For the training weekends leading up to my debut against Australia, the IRFU, in their wisdom, had put me sharing a room with hard-man Willie Duggan.

I was tucked up in bed early, getting myself ready for my first Ireland training session, when in comes Duggan in the middle of the night, shaking me like a madman in my bed as he rolled into the room. 'Jesus Christ,' I thought to myself as I tried to get back to sleep. 'This is my introduction to Irish rugby at the senior level.'

The following week I decided I had to give him a taste of his own medicine. Arriving in later than him I repeated the dose, just to lay a marker. He only laughed at me, but after that we got on really well. I always liked Willie and loved playing with him. He was a rock and identified with the Munster mentality.

If you were rooming with Moss Keane then getting to sleep was another thing altogether. Moss was such a larger-than-life character. He was eleven years older than me, and it was almost like he took me under his wing. When we trained, we trained hard. But the whole experience off the field was nearly a laugh a minute.

I was proud that, in my time with that brilliant pack of forwards over three years, I never missed a game and accumulated thirteen caps. That was a lifetime on the Irish team for some players. You'd get thirteen caps in a season now. Moss Finn, Michael Kiernan and myself would always travel together to Dublin. We were the three Cork players on the team but we'd be wondering and asking ourselves, 'We have nine caps now, have we made it yet?' Twenty caps in those days was a huge milestone. Every cap was treasured.

There's always a huge sense of excitement for the first international of the year. You come in at lunchtime, have your meal and everyone's together. You're in the centre of Dublin, in Stephen's Green, the team is being recognized and there's a buzz around the place.

It's special because there's a routine there. You have your lunch on the Thursday. You train on the Thursday afternoon and then go to the pictures that night. We always had two pints on the Friday before a match in Dublin. Sean Lynch had a pub just off Stephen's Green and for all the forwards, that was the ritual. Just the forwards; the backs were never invited. It wasn't compulsory, but you always went. If you wanted to have a bottle of water or an orange that was fine, but we always had two pints in the snug.

Sean Lynch had played for Ireland and was on the Lions team that beat New Zealand in '71. The minute he'd see us coming in, the snug was organized. There were always two old dears from the flats around the corner who'd be in there having their glass of Guinness. 'Jesus, the boys are in again tonight. How will you do tomorrow, lads?'

It was like a collective therapy session for us as we sat around just talking and relaxing. You didn't have that much time to bring people together, so this was all part of the team bonding, getting to know people, being comfortable in your own skin. You'd be chatting about the game and the opposition and some fellow might have noticed something to watch out for. At that time you weren't stuck watching the other team, analysing them to death.

In terms of tactics, it was nothing like what you have now. You had your set-piece, your scrum, and you'd organize your line-out calls and variations. The line-out was a lot different in those days and getting off the ground was the biggest challenge. We used to cut the line-outs a lot, and you'd have three-man, four-man options. There was a lot of variation.

We didn't have a forwards coach so Ciaran Fitzgerald would have been the driver of it, in conjunction with Tommy Kiernan. There was no assistant coach, but with all the experience in that team the forwards were, in effect, running themselves. Far more games were won rather than lost as a result of those think-tanks in Sean Lynch's snug on those Friday nights.

Our set-piece was very strong but we also had a fantastic back row. Fergus Slattery, Willie Duggan and John O'Driscoll were individually excellent and collectively outstanding. O'Driscoll was a player's player who made two Lions tours but never attracted much public attention. Duggan revelled in the myths flying around Dublin that he wasn't fit and that he didn't train. The fact that he always appeared to have a fag hanging out of his mouth didn't help matters, but Duggan always trained – you wouldn't survive at that level otherwise. But he was just hard, and was also a very effective line-out operator; he was a very intelligent guy who just took no messing and was great to have on your team. There's always that time in the dressing room when you look around just before taking the field. Seeing him there, you always felt, going out, that you had a chance.

Moss Keane was different. Moss was great for me. I think he

recognized that we could complement each other and that I was good for him. For example, I was able to move around the line, wherever I wanted to jump. That was my call. Now you wouldn't always get a senior second row bowing to what the junior fellow wanted, but the quid pro quo was I always had to pick up their best man on their throw, so that took the pressure off him in other ways.

Playing with him, putting your arm around him going into a scrum, you felt ten foot tall. The strength of the man – he was a colossus. He just had a presence about him. He was such a unique character in so many ways. He was the focal point that brought the team together.

He liked to play the idiot at times. I remember when we roomed together it almost became a ritual that he'd open the window and roar and shout like a foghorn. There were all these offices in behind the Shelbourne, and he used to bellow out to them like a rhinoceros.

Moss was into agriculture and science, incredibly intelligent and way ahead of his time in so many ways. He had his own routine, and was into holistic medicine and all that type of thing. He'd have these pollen tablets, garlic pills and a range of different concoctions on the locker at the side of the bed. On a Thursday he would unveil this parcel with six eggs wrapped up in newspaper and he'd have two raw eggs in a drop of milk every morning. 'Christ, Lenihan, look at those,' he'd say. 'They're magnificent, the shit is still hanging off them.' I'd be in stitches.

He was, as I said, larger than life. I always felt he acted the gombeen at times to take the pressure off. I certainly never felt under any pressure before a match when I was rooming with him because I couldn't wait to get to the Shelbourne to hang out with him. Michael Kiernan and Moss Finn would always be calling in to share the craic. Our bedroom was a hive of activity. He was just brilliant for that team. Ciaran Fitzgerald was the technical leader while Moss was the personality that brought everyone together. Everybody loved him.

That night before my first international I slept soundly. I was excited and looking forward to the challenge of the game. My first cap, wearing the green, standing for the anthem, and seeing the crowd in Lansdowne. It helped, of course, that I knew what to expect – or at least I thought I did, having played against Australia only a few days earlier. However, as I was soon to find out, international Test matches are an entirely different matter.

On the Saturday morning, matchday, the team would assemble after breakfast and go across the road to Stephen's Green for a walkabout and a bit of fresh air. The whole team would come together, you'd walk around Stephen's Green, the backs would pass a few balls and the forwards would go through line-out variations. That was the start of the day. Of course, people are out on a Saturday morning in Dublin and, seeing the team, they'd stop and watch. Suddenly your concentration levels would go up. You wouldn't want to be seen to be missing the ball. It's a great way of focusing.

After that you get some lunch. Then you go into your room and get a half hour to yourself before the team meeting, which was always on the first floor of the Shelbourne. At that meeting, it starts to sink in – 'this is for real'. You come out from that meeting pumped up and ready for battle. Then, walking down the stairs and into the hotel foyer, you're hit by a wall of people clapping and cheering you on to the team bus.

It's funny, the more things change, the more they stay the same. The team is now back in the Shelbourne after years of being based in a number of different hotels around the city. I was staying there before the Australia Test in 2015 and it was like a trip down memory lane. The fans were back at base camp too and were still clapping the team as they came down those stairs.

That day in November 1981 took me back to my school days when I first got a taste of rugby and saw the players being hailed as heroes by their mates as they walked through the school hall. Now here I was playing for my country being applauded by my fellow countrymen as I made my way down and out of the Shelbourne.

Driving for the first time down Baggot Street with a police escort, sirens blaring and more people cheering you on the streets – it's heady stuff. Then there are the private moments. They don't change regardless. This is your own personal time before the storm of the game hits you.

I'm looking out the window as we pass seamlessly through the city streets, seeing the fans in the pubs and the crowds gearing themselves up, and now I'm thinking, 'Yep, this is it, I'd better perform today.' But there are no butterflies. Just looking forward to proving myself. You'd have other fellas inside the jacks vomiting five minutes before going on to the field, but people are just made differently. Me, I can't wait to get out there and get on with things after the prolonged build-up. When you get older and the old bits start falling off, you know the pitfalls and you look at things slightly differently, thinking, 'I'm not going to get exposed here.' But when you're younger, you relish it and want to show what you're made of.

Nerves were just never an issue for me. I suppose it's like

everything in life: the more preparation you do, the less nervous you are. But I just never thought about it. It was never a case of 'Oh, I can't wait to get this thing out of the way', or 'I can't wait till it's over'. I wasn't one to over-analyse things. Just get on with it and prove what you're capable of – that's my philosophy.

As a kid learning the game, I never had any self-doubts either. I captained most of the teams I played on from junior up to senior Schools level and I never lost a Schools cup match. One senior Schools cup final required a drop-goal in the ninth minute of injury time to see us over the line, but we got there eventually thanks to Alex O'Regan's superb footballing brain.

I also played in an outstanding UCC team during my college years, once beating Shannon 18-3 in a Munster Cup final when we were supposed to be annihilated. This was Shannon with Ginger McLoughlin, with Brendan Foley, with Colm Tucker, a Lion in South Africa the previous season. They hammered everyone, but we beat them with a bunch of twenty-one-year-olds. We were winning Munster Senior Leagues and Senior Cups when UCC hadn't won them since the 1960s with the likes of Tom Kiernan, Paddy McGrath and Jerry Welsh, who were all Irish internationals. During our time in UCC in the late seventies and early eighties we had an annual win ratio of over 80 per cent, which is exceptional.

There was a nucleus of talented young players playing right across all of the university sides in Ireland at the time. They were confident in themselves and their playing ability, and that resonated right through to the team that would win another Triple Crown in 1985. Eight or nine of us had played together either at Irish Schools or Irish Universities level. We had grown up playing and winning together. Success breeds success.

On the pitch in Lansdowne against the Australians, I think, as debuts go, I played quite well. It was a way more physical game than the Munster one earlier in the week, played at a higher pace and intensity. We destroyed them in the scrum, and there was a fair bit of madness in those days. They had one fellow who was starting to create a bit of hassle and Willie Duggan decided he needed to be sorted out. Five minutes later, all you heard was this massive thump and this guy is prostrate on the ground.

Some of the stuff that went on in games was not only madness, it could be dangerous. You just didn't have the same number of cameras on you as nowadays. I soon appreciated that you were just at a different level of physicality and the players were bigger and stronger at that level. Plus they were more experienced. You played at club level and you might have one or two internationals in the game. Now everybody was at the same level, and the Australians were all athletes anyway. Their whole culture was geared towards running and being fit, and a healthy lifestyle.

During the fracas I wasn't sure what the sound was that I heard, all I knew was this fellow was prostrate and the hassle had been sorted out. I remember thinking, 'Jesus, we're at a different level here all right.' But by the final whistle, we'd lost, 16-12. The team didn't play particularly well, even though we probably should have won the game.

There was nothing in the game that made me think I couldn't play at this level, though. In fact, the opposite. I couldn't wait to get on to the pitch the next time. When you got a smell of it, you wanted more. And now I had a better idea of what to expect.

3

'We can go into work with our heads held high'

The November internationals were always seen as great preparation for the Five Nations Championship in the New Year. The Five Nations was everything. It was the ultimate goal, and you built up gradually to it through the inter-provincial series. The final trial was held just after Christmas. Everything was geared towards being right for those games. The colour, the atmosphere, the crowds. It was every bit as big then as it is now.

There wasn't much hope or expectation on us going into the opening game of the 1982 campaign, against Wales. But there had been a couple of key changes from the team I'd made my debut with the previous November. Ginger McLoughlin came into the front row while Moss Keane had recovered from injury and was back in the second row with me. There was a change of captaincy as well when Ciaran Fitzgerald was given that honour for the first time.

Ollie Campbell had also recovered from injury and was back at out-half. Campbell was hitting his peak at that stage. Unfortunately he got sick in '84 and also missed all the '85 campaign as well. With Campbell fit, the Ward v. Campbell selection issue became huge. You couldn't get a taxi anywhere in Dublin without the driver saying to you, 'I want to ask you one thing.' And you knew what was coming. It was everywhere you went. Would you pick Tony Ward or Ollie Campbell? It was very hard for Wardy, even though Campbell was the better fit for that team.

Wardy was a mercurial player, a very talented individual. He was flashy. He was flamboyant. To this day I'm very friendly with him and enjoy his company. But he's quite a shy and reserved individual in many ways and was left scarred by the controversy surrounding that time.

Ollie Campbell was a class player. Defensively, he was the Jonny Wilkinson of his time. His line-kicking and place-kicking were ideal for the team we had, because we had a very strong pack of forwards. We also had an outstanding back row. The outside backs were of a younger vintage, with Moss Finn and Trevor Ringland excelling. Michael Kiernan came in when David Irwin broke his leg against Wales and fitted in seamlessly. Hugo MacNeill was full-back and Paul Dean was in the centre then, with Robbie McGrath feeding Campbell from scrum-half.

It was just a completely different mix. When the younger guys came in, it put the finishing touches to the team. The balance in that team was excellent. You could play two different types of game, and Campbell was the guy who had the capacity to change the way you played. He did the right thing at the right time all the time and we had players who were able to take the opportunities when they arose. The catalyst was to be the opening game of the Five Nations against Wales.

Lansdowne Road looked crap when it was empty, but when it was full it was brilliant because everybody was on top of you. The team bus would pull into the car park and the same faces would be there to greet you and wish you luck. Then, down the steps into the dressing room, forwards on the left, backs on the right. Putting my bag down beside Moss Keane's, the number 5 hanging proudly on its hook, waiting for me.

There was no warm-up on the pitch in those days so you'd go out for a walk beforehand. The old Lansdowne Road had these steps leading you on to the pitch, as if coming up from a dungeon and then out into the bright daylight and the noise. As you came out in your civvies, everyone on the terraces was in position already and waiting. There were these wooden seats right on the edge of the pitch and the supporters were actually within touching distance. I think it's awful now that when teams come out there are very few seated in the stands, they're all still in the bars. Walking around the field, you'd be testing the wind with the hookers to see how it might affect or influence the line-out calls. It was all about concentrating, preparing, focusing.

Back in to change, stretch and get ready. Slipping the green jersey on. The shamrock crest. Ireland. Pride, excitement – keep your focus. Show them what you can do. Then, last words. The fire in the belly, the clip-clop of studs on the floor, racing back up those steps and into the roar of the crowd.

The people on the far side in the East Stand would see you coming and it was almost a ripple effect as the roar made its way around the ground. Wales were standing there waiting. Officials met, the President's hand was shaken, and the first words of 'Amhrán na bhFiann' rang out. Such a proud moment with my mother and father in the stand.

Protocol over, getting into position, standing to receive the kick-off. Full-throated roars from the crowd – they're almost a part of it as Fitzy shouts his encouragement and the ref blows his whistle. You can prepare all you like, but until you go through it and experience the intensity and ferocity of the Five Nations, it will never match up.

Coming off the back of four losses from the last campaign, nobody was giving us much of a chance, but with Ollie Campbell back and young blood mixed in with the experienced heads, Wales were taken by surprise and we won 20-12. We were up and running.

The Five Nations was different to my international debut, where the outcome of the game nearly became irrelevant. It almost sails beyond you in that the most important thing is to get out on to the field, to get your first cap for Ireland under your belt and to experience the day. It's a huge moment. A proud moment for yourself and your extended family. And the result? That's almost secondary as you're caught up in the emotion of the day.

The Five Nations Championship is a lot different, and the fact that we launched our 1982 campaign with a win made it even more special. An Irish team hadn't experienced a victory in an awful long time. Even though the team was a very good side, they had been on a seven-game losing streak, albeit that every match of the previous year's Five Nations was lost by a maximum of one score.

That day against Wales, it all seemed to click. Campbell was superb. He was the one who made the break in the first half off a scrum for Moss Finn's score. Moss got two tries in the game which was a huge thing, even though he got concussed, spent the night under observation in hospital, and couldn't remember a thing afterwards! The third Cork man, Michael Kiernan, came on as well and won his first cap so it was a great day for rugby in Cork especially. Trevor Ringland also got a great score in the corner, and as a collective, the forwards were superb too that day. Sadly, though, David Irwin broke his leg in the second half which put a dampener on things.

Atmosphere-wise it was an incredible buzz because the crowd could sense that we were getting off to a winning start. It was the first time in a long time that Lansdowne Road was rocking.

It was the win that had been coming for so long because the team had been there or thereabouts, and once it arrived the campaign just took off. The injection of some of the younger players added freshness to the team and gave them that push that saw them winning games now instead of losing narrowly.

Playing against England next in Twickenham was the big one. I was rooming with Moss Keane, and a few of us went out for a drink on the Thursday night to relax. Con Murphy, the iconic doctor to Cork hurling and football teams since 1976, and a great friend of Moss since their UCC days, was there, along with another former UCC colleague, Pat Parfrey, who was capped by Ireland against New Zealand in 1974. The last link to UCC was provided by Moss Finn who was in great form after scoring two tries in the opener against Wales, even if he had no recollection of scoring either. We told him he played better when he didn't know what he was doing.

Like his namesake in the second row, Moss Finn was a great character, a great player who often suffered due to his versatility. An out-half by trade, he was a magnificent athlete, was extremely powerful and had great pace. As a consequence he often found himself on the wing. I would describe him as a reluctant winger. I remember congratulating him after Munster beat New Zealand in that famous outing in Thomond Park, and his immediate reaction summed up his feeling about playing on the wing. 'Christ,' he said, 'I did nothing. I only touched the ball twice and that was to hand it to Pa Whelan to throw it into the line-out.'

Pat Parfrey was a doctor in London and was an integral part of the rugby set-up in London Irish. He told us that England were raging favourites and had a great team.

Here we were, five UCC lads in the heart of London. We only had two pints but the conversation was stimulating and helped shift the focus from my first ever away international. I was thinking, 'This is great craic.' The expectation level wasn't huge at all.

I had played in Twickenham in that B international two years earlier, which also helped. Twickenham was a brilliant stadium because it was just so old-world. The dressing rooms were all timber and you had these individual baths in the shower area. I think some of them are still there – maybe in the museum now.

A bit like Lansdowne Road, you came up a couple of steps on to the pitch and the surface was just magnificent. It was like a carpet, and really fast. Plus you had these old timber stands that were right on top of the field. You really felt you were on stage in Twickenham.

I never found it intimidating, just different. The most intimidating place would have been the Parc des Princes which was an incredible stadium. How the French Rugby Federation ever left that place is beyond me. The new Stade de France is lovely with clean, open space, but it's nothing in comparison.

We had no inhibitions playing against England that day. We were always ahead by a few points, and though Mike Slemen got a try for them with the last move of the game, we won by a point in the end. Nobody had expected anything but we beat them, and that famous Ginger McLoughlin try where he seemed to drag half the English team over the line with him has gone down in Irish rugby folklore.

Coming into the dressing room afterwards it kind of dawned on somebody, almost by accident, 'Jesus lads, we're playing for a Triple Crown in two weeks' time.'

How did we get here?

I'll never forget Moss Keane taking me aside after the game. There was an old bar in Twickenham itself and he was meeting some friends there, so he dragged me along, just the two of us. Moss stood out like a beacon. This was the early eighties, recession Ireland, and people having to go to England for work. The number of fellows who came up to us was unbelievable and obviously everybody knew Moss. He just attracted the world on top of you. One man came up – he had a suit on with a cap – and was just thanking us over and over. 'You have no idea what this means to us,' he told us. 'We can go into work with our heads held high now.'

That stuck with me. It was difficult at times being Irish over there, and giving the Irish people something to be proud of meant a lot.

Now, all of a sudden, we were playing Scotland for a Triple Crown. The build-up to the game was off the scale. We trained in Merrion Road at the Wanderers club ground on the Sunday before and over a thousand people turned up just to see the session. It was crazy stuff.

Tommy Kiernan was putting us through our paces with a

particularly long warm-up routine. We were doing laps, sprinting, laps, more sprinting, and Willie Duggan, who had obviously been out the night before, goes up to Tommy and says, 'Tommy, unless you want me to puke in front of all these people, you'd better stop this very soon or get out of the way.' Mercifully, Tommy ended that part of the session soon afterwards.

Training on the Sunday, back to work Monday, Tuesday, Wednesday . . . you couldn't wait to get up to Dublin on the Thursday. And then the Shelbourne became the focal point for everyone. There was a general election campaign on at the time and I remember Willie John McBride coming down from the North, being interviewed about the game and saying, 'I hear you're running some kind of an election as a sideshow to this game?' Nobody was interested in the politics. We were the only show in town it seemed, and history was in the making here.

We were confident enough going into that match. Scotland were a very good side but we had enough players of experience to know what needed to be done. It wasn't a great game. We went 6-0 up and were dominating, but Scotland came back with a try (four points in those days) under the posts. The crowd went silent. Suddenly it was 6-6. But then they started to concede penalties and Ollie kicked everything. He kicked six penalties and dropped a goal to win it 21-12 for a comprehensive enough victory in the end.

With ten minutes to go we knew we were about to achieve something incredibly rare and worthwhile. Finding the stadium clock – 4.15 p.m. – and working out how much time was left in the game. Knowing we were going to do it, the crowd broke into song, and outside Wales I'd say Lansdowne Road was the only other venue where you would get that singing from the stands and terraces. 'Cockles and Mussels' was huge with the Lansdowne crowd.

'Singing cockles and mussels, alive, alive-oh!'

'I can't believe my luck,' I thought to myself. 'This is only my fourth cap and we're going to win the Triple Crown and the Five Nations Championship.'

At one stage, at a 22 drop-out, I glanced across at Moss Keane and Phil Orr and caught their eye. There was just this smile. They had waited for this for a long time. It is rare that you can actually enjoy something before it's over, but we knew.

When the final whistle blew it was sheer joy and exuberance, but within seconds your priority is to run off the pitch because you are going to be mobbed. There was no presentation and we didn't get any medals to put over our heads. There were no fireworks blowing up in the stadium. We just ran for the safety of the dressing room.

Our celebrations kicked off in O'Donoghue's pub on Baggot Street that night. Before the official dinner, we got into our black tie dress suits and headed for upstairs in O'Donoghue's. That was special. That was when you felt you had achieved something unique together.

We celebrated like only the Irish could, and subsequently made a balls of it in our last match against the French, leaving a Grand Slam behind us.

With only five teams in the tournament, the Five Nations fixture list meant that every team had a blank weekend. Ours was two weeks after we had won the Triple Crown, so it was a month to our next game. Of course, in the meantime there were receptions and a few club dinners to attend. We were invited here, there and everywhere, and because Ireland hadn't won a Triple Crown in thirty-three years the Grand Slam was almost incidental.

If you talk about regrets, that would definitely be one. If we had been playing France two weeks later, I'm convinced we would have beaten them, even in Paris. The focus would have been there, we'd have had the continuity. Even if that four-week break had come earlier in the tournament, I think we'd have still managed it, but after winning the Triple Crown we had achieved something historic and our heads were elsewhere.

France had gone badly that year so they recalled four or five seasoned performers for the game, and they just literally kicked the shit out of us for eighty minutes. It was the dirtiest game I ever played in.

It was my first time playing against France and, as I found out subsequently, playing them in Paris is completely different to playing them in Dublin. They were definitely a different beast. There was a vacant stare in their eyes with a madness in them. The French players were coming out of their dressing room with blood streaming out of their noses. They had been beating the shit out of each other before they came out and then were just completely over the top on the pitch.

Since then there have been allegations of amphetamine use by the French in the 1980s. On the basis of what I experienced, I wouldn't be surprised. I just remember mayhem on the field, boots flying everywhere. If you were on the ground, on the wrong side of a ruck, you were a legitimate target.

The first scrum of the game set the tone. On a pre-arranged call they effected a quick wheel, dropped it, and the whole French scrum came in over the top of us. It was like being spat out the end of a combine harvester. To add insult to injury they were awarded the penalty.

I looked at Moss Keane.

'What the fuck was that?'

The only time in my entire international career I felt 'Jesus, I could get killed here' was in that game. At one point I was lying on the ground, caught in the bottom of a ruck with my hands pinned and my head sticking out. I saw one of their second rows coming towards me and he only had one thing on his mind. As far as he was concerned, I was a legitimate target. After all, French club rugby back then was just one continuous brawl. I could see it coming and I thought, 'This is it, you've heard about it, brace yourself.' But somehow, by the grace of God, I managed to wriggle my head out of the way at the last second.

It was a sour way to end the campaign, with a 22-9 defeat and too many cuts and bruises, but still, we had won a Triple Crown, the first since 1949 and only the fifth in Irish rugby history. What a way to start my international career.

For the next few years against the French, though, that game set the ground rules. We would be ready. I remember their nuggety prop Robert Paparemborde, a brilliant scrummager, being on the receiving end of an unmerciful shoeing the following year in Dublin. He finished the game swathed in bandages with blood pouring out of his head.

Off the pitch, the different parts of my life were also falling into place. I started with ICC, the Industrial Credit Corporation, Ireland's semi-state bank, in June 1982. Three months later Mary and I were married in Cork, a week after touring Romania with Munster. Just prior to that trip I also officially confirmed that I would be joining Cork Constitution when my time with UCC was up.

There was a bit of pressure on me to choose a club in Cork

and I was friendly with a lot of people in Dolphin, but in reality I was always leaning towards Cork Con. The fact that I had five Ireland caps already not only meant that I was in demand, it also offered me a degree of independence. It also helped that Con had a number of more established representative players and that meant the burden of responsibility would be shared across a stronger playing base. The likes of Christy Cantillan, Greg Barrett and Moss Finn who were in the Munster team that beat the All Blacks, were senior players in Cork at the time. Two of my UCC team-mates – Packie Derham, the hooker I would play with for all of my fifteen years of club rugby and the best line-out thrower I ever encountered, and John Barry, a lifelong friend since our schooldays together in St Patrick's – were also moving on. We decided that where one went, all three of us would go, so we joined Cork Con together.

Having settled into married life, a career in finance and club rugby in Cork Con, who had a long tradition and history of competing at the highest level in Munster rugby, I couldn't have been happier and was looking forward to another season on the international stage. After the heroics of 1982, the next year saw basically the same Irish team, and we continued from where we left off, starting with a win away to Scotland. The Scots were fancied, but winning 15-13 in Edinburgh was the perfect start for us. Ginger McLoughlin was initially dropped for the game but his replacement Mick Fitzpatrick ripped his groin and Ginger was brought back in. Annoyed at being the only change to the pack in the first place, Ginger had a stormer in Murrayfield and made his point.

We didn't have another international for a month so the following Saturday I was up in Dublin for a 'friendly' with Cork Con against Lansdowne. Outside the Munster Cup the biggest games on Cork Con's fixture list were against Lansdowne and Wanderers at Lansdowne Road. In the days before the advent of the All Ireland League you relished the chance to take on the Leinster league or cup holders, and Lansdowne were the best team in Leinster at that stage. There was a healthy rivalry between Cork Con and Lansdowne.

Moss Keane was playing for Lansdowne and of course, Moss being Moss, he was trying to climb all over me and take me out at every line-out. There comes a point in those games when you have to stand up, but as I went to hit him a dig, I caught the back of our prop Finian O'Driscoll's head – a bad mistake. I felt something crack in my hand. Moss was looking at me about to laugh, but then the seriousness of the situation kind of dawned on him and me.

I was taken to hospital, X-rayed, and told that the bone was broken. If Ireland had an international the following Saturday I'd have been ruled out, and it would still be touch and go to make the France game in three weeks' time. Not only that but the Lions was also becoming a real possibility for me, so a lot was at stake. I couldn't take part in the training sessions leading up to the France game, and on the Thursday before the match Mick Molloy, the Irish team doctor and my UCC coach – a man who has been a huge influence on my rugby career – made a little cast that I was able to put over the outside of my hand.

On the day of the match one of our medical specialists, Joe Gallagher, wasn't 100 per cent happy with it but we were two hours before kick-off so I basically told him to piss off. I was playing, that was it.

I had to strap my hand and present it to the referee, but I then got it re-strapped afterwards with this brace inside it; and then somebody came up with the bright idea that, since the

French would target me, I should strap both hands. That was great, only for the fact that the French now opted to stand on either hand any time the opportunity presented itself.

It was another pitched battle that day but we beat them 22-16. It was a massively physical game but thankfully I got through it and could now focus on the rest of the campaign.

Wales in Cardiff proved a big barrier once again, though. Beating them at home in '82 had set us on the road to great things, but Irish teams appeared to have a hang-up playing Wales in Cardiff – a legacy of some big defeats at the hands of their mercurial teams from the seventies. I'd noticed it when I first came into the Irish set-up. There were still some players from that incredible Welsh side playing – Geoff Wheel in the second row for one – and there was this aura about them still, especially in their capital city. Fergus Slattery, Willie Duggan, Moss Keane, Phil Orr, none of them had ever won against Wales at the Arms Park, and though we were well in the game, they scored two opportunist tries which turned the game and saw us beaten 23-9.

To be fair, the selectors kept faith in the team and were rewarded when we beat England 25-15 at Lansdowne Road in mid-March. With three wins out of four we ended up sharing the Championship with France, but there was no Triple Crown this time. Again we were so close to something historic. We were only one game away from consecutive Triple Crowns and only a second ever Grand Slam.

I had completed two seasons at international level now and had a Triple Crown and Championship to show for it. Success, I thought, would be perennial – and now I also had a mouth-watering Lions tour to New Zealand in the summer to look forward to.

It seemed nothing could go wrong in my rugby career.

4

'I feel like declaring myself'

Captaining your country is undoubtedly the biggest single honour in the game, but Lions selection was and remains a massive achievement, even if a modern-day Lions tour has almost become a bit of a circus. The number of support staff swanning around in a coveted Lions blazer, doing a lap of honour after clinching the series in Sydney in 2013, was a bit cringe-worthy – especially as the vast majority were from the Lions marketing company.

The Lions in my time was very much player-driven. There was no great public consciousness of Lions tours because you were on the other side of the world and it didn't matter that much to anyone outside the touring party whether you won or lost. Having said that, there was a real mystique and aura about the Lions because of the legendary rugby figures and history that had been built up over the years.

My first real exposure to Lions rugby came with the 1971 party that won the series in New Zealand for the one and only time to date. I had just got into CBC and was playing for the school's U13 team. Rugby as a sport was coming on to my radar. We were brought down to the hall where they were showing this black and white cine camera coverage of the Lions tour. With a number of Irish players on board, such as Willie John McBride and Mike Gibson, there was strong interest in watching how the tourists finally overcame the mighty All Blacks.

That Lions team was legendary, playing outstanding rugby with the famous Welsh backs of that era: Gareth Edwards, Barry John, Gerald Davies, John Dawes and J. P. R. Williams. They were superstars in our eyes.

That '71 team formed the backbone for the 1974 'Invincibles' who went to South Africa and won twenty-one of the twenty-two games they played. It was incredible stuff. The fascination with the Lions for me came from watching those two teams.

Because of those back-to-back successes, by the time the 1977 Lions team went to New Zealand you were getting more news and coverage around the matches. I was in sixth year in school by then and would stay up until three in the morning with my great schoolmates Barry Coleman and Brian Oliver, craning to listen to the crackly BBC commentary on the radio in the Coleman household. The Lions were a world away, visiting outposts in a frontier-land; it was thrilling, exciting and exotic trying to tune in to hear how they were doing. Little did I appreciate that six years down the road, when the Lions would once again head off to New Zealand, I would be selected to take part in such a wonderful adventure.

I had been ever-present on the Irish side since my debut, was playing well and knew my name was being strongly mentioned for the 1983 tour. When the squad was finally announced I had made the cut, along with seven other Irish players, including Ciaran Fitzgerald as captain. It was a huge honour for me personally and also showed what a strong position Irish rugby was in to have so many of our players picked in a party of only thirty players.

To celebrate the achievement, the night the squad was announced there was a big gathering at rugby's most famous watering hole in Cork, the Western Star. Given that Michael Kiernan was also selected, for once Cork Con and Dolphin were united in celebration, with players and officials from both clubs coming together to mark the occasion. Michael was far more immersed in the history of the Lions given that his famous uncle Tom Kiernan had captained the Lions tour party to South Africa in 1968, while another uncle, Mick Lane, had also played for the Lions, in 1950. Suffice to say, the closest the Lenihans from Listowel ever got to the Lions up to then was in Dublin zoo!

A few weeks later, with the Lions assembling in London, Mick and I headed off from Cork airport after waving goodbye to our extended family and friends. For the next three months we were off on the rugby adventure of a lifetime. Mick and I couldn't wait.

Arriving at our London hotel, the reality of the situation hit us when we were given our Lions gear and were presented with the famous blazer. I can still recall meeting up with all the players from Wales, Scotland and England for the first time, just prior to the opening team meeting. Willie John McBride, who was team manager and an iconic figure in Lions rugby, stood up to speak about what it meant to be a Lion. It was awe-inspiring stuff. There was then a series of medicals to be undertaken throughout the afternoon by the team doctor, Donald MacLeod. That evening we had a reception to attend at the New Zealand Embassy and we were all decked out in our Lions number ones for the first time. That was special. The tour party was already forming an identity.

The medicals were being carried out that day just to give you the once-over before heading off. None of the other players even bothered to comment about them so the fact that I was the very last to be examined, around nine p.m., didn't make me register any specific anxiety.

Next thing I knew, Dr MacLeod, after checking me out, said he had found a hernia. I had noticed a small bit of swelling in the weeks prior to leaving home but thought nothing of it. It turned out that if I had been examined any time earlier in the day some of the fluids that were seeping through this tear in the muscle wouldn't have been there and I would have been cleared to travel.

'I'm afraid you have a hernia, Donal,' the doc told me flatly. 'This is a serious issue. We can't take you on tour.'

I was looking at him, saying, 'Are you joking?'

What happened after that was cruel in the extreme, leaving me with a very sour taste about how I was treated. I was subsequently sent back to my room and told not to contact anyone. I was sharing with the English second row Steve Boyle and told him I had a problem. I did manage to get a hearing in Willie John's room but he told me straight out that I was going home. To be fair, he did ring Mick Molloy. He and Mick had manned the second row for Ireland on numerous occasions, and as Mick was not only the IRFU's team doctor but my former coach from UCC, I thought I might get a lifeline. But Willie John was under pressure to support his team doctor in the first crisis point of what was to prove to be a difficult tour.

I was just in complete shock. The Lions was something I'd worked towards for the last two years. I'd already said goodbye to my family and friends and been sent off with the cheers of all at Cork Constitution ringing in my ears. And now this. Suddenly I was being told it was over before it had even started. What I should have done was insist on a second opinion the following day, but I was young and inexperienced.

Then Ciaran Fitzgerald, as tour captain, joined Willie John in the room.

'Look, I'm sorry, but this is the situation,' Willie John told Ciaran.

Fitzgerald then insisted on talking to Mick Molloy on the phone, and in the midst of all this madness I could hear him saying, 'I feel like declaring myself.'

'What does he mean by that?' I thought to myself. 'What's that all about?' It just stuck in my head.

But that was it, there was nothing more to be done, I was going home. My Lions dream was over within twenty-four hours. The worst of it was being told that I had to be gone out of the hotel by 6.30 a.m. because they felt my departure would be upsetting to the other Irish players. I was to be gone before the team assembled in the morning. Again, what I should have done was insist on speaking to my Irish team-mates John O'Driscoll and David Irwin, both of whom were doctors, to buy some time. But I wasn't allowed to talk to anyone.

It was about midnight when I returned to my room having to face the prospect of packing my bags again. I picked up my Lions blazer, hard-earned ever since I had come on to the

Ireland team two seasons ago. 'Fuck this,' I said to myself. 'I've earned my blazer.' And I packed it in my bag to take home with me, a reminder of what might have been.

I'll never forget the feeling of despair and disappointment as I left the hotel on my own first thing the next morning. As I got into a black taxi to head to Heathrow I was really bitter about the way the whole thing had been done. I flew into Cork airport, and as I came down the steps of the aeroplane Mark Woods, a young reporter from the *Cork Examiner*, was waiting on the tarmac for me.

'How does this compare with missing the Munster Cup final for Cork Con?' he asked me.

Con had beaten Shannon in the final a few days earlier but the Lions management had refused permission for me to play.

I looked at him in astonishment, thinking, 'Are you taking the piss out of me?' I think he realized then just how devastating and upsetting the whole thing was for me.

Far more understanding was stalwart Cork Con president George O'Connell who put his arm around me and said, 'Don't worry, Donal, there will be plenty more Lions tours for you.'

Mick Molloy decided I should get operated on immediately and gave me hope that I could recover in time to go on standby if any of the second rows got injured. I was out of the hospital in a couple of days when Con Murphy and Moss Finn took me out for a few pints to watch the opening game of the tour in Rosie's pub in Carrigaline.

Watching that match, all I could think was, 'I should have been there.' The next tour wouldn't be for another three years and because it was scheduled to be in South Africa there was a strong chance it wouldn't go ahead due to the apartheid regime. I could be looking at six years down the line before another tour. Who knows what might happen by then? Had I missed my chance?

At one stage during the highlights of that Lions game, Con went to the toilet and Moss told me that Moss Keane had rung him and asked him if I had declared myself.

'What do you mean by that?' Moss asked him.

'Sure, everybody in Dublin knows that Ciaran Fitzgerald has a hernia the size of a tennis ball,' he'd replied.

It hit me straight away then what Fitzy had said on the phone in Willie John's room: 'I feel like declaring myself.'

Apparently you can push a hernia back in so that when you go in for a medical you can disguise the fact that you have it, and Fitzy had been coached in how to do that. If I had known, I could have done what he did. It hit me for six.

Dr Con rejoined us and took one look at my face.

'You told him, didn't you?' he said, turning to Moss.

I've always had huge admiration for Ciaran Fitzgerald. Knowing that he was contemplating sacrificing his captaincy of the Lions to try and make a point or help me out of trouble, it said everything about him.

As the tour progressed, I was getting myself back to full fitness while keeping an eye on the match reports and TV footage. After the second Test, which the Lions lost 9-0, Bob Norster had a problem with his back, and the next thing I get a phone call on a Sunday morning from Mick Molloy telling me that Willie John had been on to him with a request for me to rejoin the squad. There were still six matches of the tour left and I was getting another chance.

Myself, Ginger McLoughlin and England captain and scrum-half Steve Smith had all been called up as injury replacements. Flying to the other side of the world with Ginger, who was an eccentric character at the best of times, was an adventure in itself. Somehow we kept losing him wherever we stopped off. In Los Angeles there was no sign of him. Steve and I were looking all over the airport for him. The place was being renovated at the time and we spotted this crowd gathered on one of the concourses with scaffolding everywhere. Right in the middle of them all was Ginger doing press-ups and pull-ups on the scaffolding bars, entertaining a group of Lions supporters who, like us, were travelling to New Zealand.

'Eh, Ginger,' I said, trying to get his attention in the middle of the cheering crowd, 'we have to get going, we have a flight to catch.'

The last leg of a mammoth journey saw us on a domestic flight from Auckland to Christchurch. When we arrived at the hotel and met up with all the Irish lads we hadn't seen in weeks, we finally got to take that picture of the nine of us together in our Lions gear.

The Lions lost 22-20 to Canterbury later that day and Fitzy was on the subs bench with Scotland's Colin Deans starting. After the game, Ginger, Smithy and I were told by Lions coach Jim Telfer to go for a run with the subs. So there I was for my first ever run out in New Zealand, excited just to have made the journey after everything I had been through, when Fitzy called me aside to work with him in a few line-out drills. He had been the target of some pretty vicious attacks from sections of the British media from the outset of the tour, and it was getting to him. The bond between a jumper and his hooker is crucial and I always had a very good working relationship with Fitzy. Given all the crap he was getting in the media at the time, I think he was thrilled to see a familiar face, someone he trusted. He was under such pressure it was almost a relief for him to have someone there who had no issues with his technique. We spent twenty minutes working together in a corner of Lancaster Park that afternoon. Afterwards I jogged back to the dressing room wondering what all the fuss was about.

The Lions were playing the third Test in Dunedin in three days' time so I had no chance of making that. I hadn't played a game in over eight weeks. They lost the match 15-8 so the series was decided even before I got to make my Lions debut.

Four days later there was a game against Hawke's Bay in Napier for which I was selected. 'Finally I'm getting a game,' I thought to myself. 'I'm going to be a Lion after all.' When Donald MacLeod the team doctor said he wanted to do another medical examination on me the day before the game I contemplated clocking him in the privacy of his room but thought better of it.

We won a tight game 25-19 and I set up the drop-goal for John Rutherford from a forward drive with fifteen minutes to go that put us into the lead for the first time. Given that I hadn't played for so long and was up against an All Black second row in Graeme Higginson, I was pleased with how it went.

Even more so when I was picked for the next game the following Saturday against Counties in Pukekohe. Mick Kiernan was also in the side for that game so we got to play together for the Lions after all. We won that 25-16, and there was growing speculation amongst the press that I was in line for the most spectacular recovery of all – selection for the final Test. It wasn't to be, however: Steve Bainbridge, who had been the one to benefit from my medical disaster back in London, was picked once again along with Maurice Colclough in the second row. I wasn't really that surprised as I had so little rugby under my belt, and as second rows didn't man the replacements bench back then, there was to be no Test appearance for me in the end.

We lost that final Test 38-6, the worst defeat of the entire tour, resulting in a 4-0 series whitewash. But for me, given everything that had happened, just to have got out there and played a part in the last three weeks of the tour was a satisfying feeling. The blazer I'd taken home with me now finally meant something, even if there would be more memorable Lions tours to come.

Despite the pressure he was under from the outset, Fitzy carried himself magnificently on that tour. He had been outstanding for Ireland, both as a player and captain, throughout the 1982 and 1983 Five Nations campaigns, and had earned the right to lead the Lions. The problem was, parts of the English press wanted Leicester hooker Peter Wheeler in the squad and Scotland's Colin Deans in the Test side and that created tension within the management group.

One night two years later, when Ireland were on tour in Japan, after a few pints, myself, Michael Kiernan and Fitzy finished the night in the captain's room. 'Fitzy,' we asked, with plenty of Dutch courage now, 'we're two years on from the Lions. Tell us what was really happening behind closed doors with you and the management.'

And he told us everything – the truth, the ins and outs, what was said and the private conversations that were had. But when myself and Kiernan woke up the following morning we couldn't remember a thing he had said – nothing at all!

5

Ball Work and Brain Transplants

This was an Ireland team at its peak. To contribute eight out of thirty players picked for the Lions was a huge number – and that was excluding Fergus Slattery, who was unavailable, as was Willie Duggan, who had his own electrical business to run. While it was a great honour to be selected for the Lions, it was also very difficult if you were self-employed, as Willie knew all too well.

But then, in 1984, the wheels came off for Ireland. Many of the team were in their early to mid-thirties at that stage and had decided to give it one more year. After the successes of 1982 and 1983, who could blame them? We also had a new coach as Tom Kiernan's three years were up and the great Willie John McBride came in.

Willie John enjoyed a huge standing in world rugby but he

inherited a team fast approaching its sell-by date. As we'd had no international since defeating England in Dublin the previous March (there was no autumn game in 1983), he was also probably reluctant to make any radical changes, and for fellas at that stage of their careers the ten-month break was too long.

France in Paris was our opening match of the 1984 Championship. If we had played on the Friday night we'd have won by 20 points after the team meeting we had. After the bloodbaths of the previous two years, we were ready for them. Unfortunately, while we were prepared for the fight, just waiting to get stuck into them, they reverted to their more traditional style and started running the ball all over the pitch. Next thing we knew we were 15 points down before we realized, 'Looks like there's going to be no fight today. They're playing rugby instead.' By that stage we were on the back foot and lost 25-12.

The following year, though, the mayhem against the French started again and another filthy game ensued. When I see some of the offences that players get yellow cards for nowadays, it makes you think that there would be nobody left on the field if they'd been in operation against the French in those days. It was definitely more Wild West then. Eventually French prop Jean-Pierre Garuat was sent off for gouging John O'Driscoll.

But that's just the way it was. Professionalism has transformed the sport over the last twenty years, and it is undoubtedly a far better game now in so many respects. Rugby in those amateur days was a players' game. It wasn't really a fans' game. You weren't there for entertainment. You had three times as many scrums as you have now, though to be fair, you had very few resets, certainly far fewer than you see now. The line-out was a dogfest with fellows leading with their elbows, trying to take you out in the air. Certain teams would be coming in underneath you and getting away with it. You'd be sent off straight away now for that, but it was a regular occurrence then.

On the plus side, defences were nothing like as organized and there was far more space available. Consequently some of the running and handling was top quality. But the game was nothing like as physical as it is now. The players just weren't as big. Some of the backs playing now are bigger and heavier than many of the forwards from thirty years ago. While the game was dirtier, it wasn't as physically intense. You weren't taking the type of hits players take routinely now. I can understand when some of the current players tell you that it can take three days to fully recover from some international games. We didn't have to endure the massive collisions they must take for granted in every game. That level of hitting just wasn't there.

I went through nine years of international rugby without picking up any really serious injury, and never missed a big game. Eventually, however, like many of my contemporaries, the game exacted its toll. I had two new hips by the time I hit forty-five, and in truth could have done with them at least five years earlier. My knees are in trouble also, but so be it.

After the defeat to France in January 1984, Ginger McLoughlin was dropped and didn't play for Ireland again. Then at the beginning of February we lost 18-9 to Wales at home and lots of changes started. Ciaran Fitzgerald was dropped for the England game, and that tore the heart out of the team. It was a terrible decision. We lost 12-9 in Twickenham, and after that the end was nigh for a lot of players who had given sterling service to Irish rugby for close on a decade.

Our last game of the Championship was against Scotland in Dublin. They were going for the Grand Slam and we got hammered 32-9. By that stage Ollie Campbell was out again, this time with an illness the doctors were having trouble diagnosing. It was a year that started badly and got worse as it went on.

While the core of that team was retiring and leaving a historic legacy behind them, Willie John also moved on after only a year in charge, albeit in controversial circumstances. Having been a sub selector in '84 (what a nonentity of a job that was) after putting his name forward for the coaching job that year, Mick Doyle, now a full selector, went forward once more in a direct head to head with McBride who was looking to continue his tenure. As always the appointment would be decided by the national selectors.

On that selection panel, McBride had the support of fellow Ulster man Jim Donaldson, while Doyle had a vote himself and that of his right-hand man in Leinster's Mick Cuddy. The deciding vote would therefore come down to Munster's Jim Kiernan, who had been unexpectedly appointed, replacing fellow Munster man Benny O'Dowd. Kiernan's casting vote went to Doyle, and McBride was gone as Irish coach after just one year.

It was unusual that a coach didn't finish his three-year term, and for McBride to be out after only one season led to cries of machinations and skulduggery in the press. In truth, Willie John hadn't impressed as coach and the vast majority of the players at the time felt that Kiernan made the right call, and that was confirmed by subsequent events. In the end it was generally agreed that Mick Doyle, who had guided Leinster to three inter-provincial titles in a row, was the best coach in the country and should be given the chance to prove himself at international level. It was a bit awkward as Willie John had returned as Lions manager and was still on the selection panel, but to his credit he bit his tongue and stayed in situ. That can't have been easy for him.

It wasn't going to be an easy task for Doyle either, trying to rejuvenate the team and bring in new blood. If he had got the job the season before it would have been a poisoned chalice, but Doyle was the right man in the right place at the right time for us. I don't think anybody else would have got a Championship or a Triple Crown out of that group at that point in time.

While his approach with Ireland was to run the ball at every opportunity, his Leinster team had won playing dour ten-man rugby, so it wasn't as if he had this universal philosophy. Leinster had a very strong pack, they had very good half-backs, and Doyler played that way. He got the best out of them in classic good management style. Doyler had a vision that nobody else had at that time. He was intelligent, he had great charisma, and he was a gregarious character. He knew how to get into fellows' heads.

From the outset he said that Ireland were going to run everything. He put it out there that we were going to run and move the ball at every opportunity, and to deliver on that said something about the man. England's coach, Dick Greenwood, declared that Irish rugby would need a brain transplant for it to happen. But Doyler, and that team, proved them all wrong, and it was thrilling to be part of it. Even though I only had three seasons under my belt, I was elevated to the role of senior player, becoming more involved in the management of the team and the decision-making process.

The Championship-winning teams of '82 and '85 were poles apart in terms of approach and make-up. When Doyle took over, he recognized a certain skill set within his group of players. We didn't have the biggest pack in the world, but we had some really athletic forwards. In the backs, Michael Kiernan and Brendan Mullin were both proven athletes – one sprinted for Ireland while the other ran the hurdles – as well as being excellent rugby players.

The most pressing problem was that the back line Doyle was anxious to put together didn't have a proven international place-kicker, and that was a major issue. Paul Dean fitted the bill perfectly when it came to moving the ball and playing an expansive game but, even going back to when we played on the Irish Schools side together, he was never a top-notch place-kicker. Doyler didn't view it as a major issue initially, however. It was only when we were playing a fundraiser for Pat Carroll, who had sustained a serious injury playing for Sunday's Well, that Michael Kiernan dropped out of the sky for us and showed real promise as a place-kicker.

Doyler built a philosophy of running rugby that was totally alien to anything we had done prior to that. He created a belief that we could run more and kick less, that we could score tries and play a continuity game that no Irish team had attempted before.

His first game in charge of us was against Australia in November 1984. That was the Wallaby team that was taking world rugby by storm with its flair, running and handling skills, and they had a huge influence on how Doyle wanted Ireland to play. As well as Brendan Mullin, he introduced other new players who fitted that mobile and athletic mould such as Michael Bradley at scrum-half and Willie Anderson alongside me in the second row, while Nigel Carr would soon follow. We lost 16-9 against the Aussies but we ran them the closest of any of the four countries in their Grand Slam of autumn internationals that year. Coming from where we were, with all those great names having retired, expectation levels were quite low and it gave us confidence in what we were being asked to do.

The other thing about that group is that there were a lot of guys who had grown up playing and winning together. I played on an Irish schoolboys team with Deano, Hugo MacNeill, Phillip Matthews and Brian McCall. Nigel Carr and David Irwin were also in the mix for that side. We'd all played Irish Universities together. We knew one another very well.

Doyle looked at the resources that we had, bringing in players like Anderson when Moss Keane retired. Willie had been playing No. 8 for Ulster for a number of years but Doyle appreciated what he could bring to the pack and converted him into a second row. It was all about mobility. I enjoyed playing with Willie and we developed a very good understanding and relationship as a second-row pairing. Doyle wanted players that could keep up with a fast game and retain possession with mobile, ball-playing forwards, and we were comfortable with that.

And to achieve that as a collective, our training changed completely. Everything was done in match situations with the ball in hand. Under Tommy or Willie John, half of our training sessions were taken up doing fitness sessions, running laps. It was a more physical type of training. But now, suddenly, everything was being done with the ball. You were expected to be fit when you showed up. Training was all about keeping the ball alive, running and supporting the ball carrier. In any event we ended up training at a far higher intensity and covering more mileage than we ever would have done running laps.

In 1985 we were due to play England in the opening game of the Five Nations. Doyle announced the team about three weeks beforehand, which was very unusual, with Brian Spillane and Nigel Carr selected for their first caps. It had been a long wait for Nigel as he couldn't get in ahead of Fergus Slattery. Nigel was my room-mate the night I got the call for my first cap in 1981, so it had been a long few years waiting for his opportunity to come along. I was particularly delighted for him.

With the team announced so far in advance we became more and more familiar with the approach Doyle wanted to introduce. It was drilled into us – 'We're going to keep the ball alive' – and the training was going fantastic. The guys were really excited. But it began to snow heavily on the week of the opening match, and on the Friday morning, the game was cancelled. That went down like a lead balloon but worked out in our favour in the long run.

There we were at midday on a Friday in Dublin being told of the decision in our meeting room. We stood around asking ourselves, 'Well, what are we going to do now?' We ended up going down to O'Donoghue's pub on Baggot Street and stayed there for five or six hours. We were locked in and had a great piss-up and a massive sing-song, which brought us even closer together. It was to prove the last piece of the jigsaw.

Mind you, we still hadn't played a match together. During the wait for that opening game we had Doyle continually telling us, 'We're going to keep the ball alive, we're going to run the ball.' After Dick Greenwood's 'brain transplant' comment, Doyler was constantly in our faces, reaffirming his beliefs. But we did have some self-doubt, no question about it. Phil Orr and I were looking at each other wondering, 'Jesus, is this going to work? What do you think?' At least now, with the game postponed, we had another two weeks to train this way.

Our opening game was now going to be on the road, away to Scotland in Murrayfield, and from the first minute we ran it from inside our own half and got close to the Scottish line. Hugo MacNeill gave a poor pass to Keith Crossan at the end of one long flowing movement when Crossan might have scored. Even though we didn't get the try it was almost like 'Jesus, lads, this could actually work'.

We went behind but then got two excellent tries from Trevor Ringland, with Deano working a brilliant loop play reminiscent of what Johnny Sexton would later do so effectively for Leinster under Joe Schmidt. Suddenly it was 'Christ, this really does work!'

Doyler, along with Ciaran Fitzgerald as captain, had driven us to this point. The front five were experienced with myself, Fitzy and Phil Orr still there from the '82 team, and Willie Anderson and his great friend from Dungannon Jimmy McCoy making a big impact. We had a very mobile footballing back row led by Phillip Matthews, who was an outstanding player. Nigel Carr proved that he was made for the international stage and was the best number 7 in the tournament that season. The continuity game was tailor-made for him and he was brilliant. At No. 8 we had Brian Spillane whom I knew well from our days playing together with UCC, and I just knew that he would thrive in this company. Spillane never lacked confidence but was able to back it up on the field. Then again, he is related to Kerry footballing legend Pat Spillane so it didn't take long to work out where he got that confidence from.

After all the talking and that unprecedented five-week build-up, to win that game in the manner we did with a great try out wide by Ringland at the end was an incredible boost. We knew the ingredients were there. Talking about it and doing it were still two entirely different things, but beating the reigning Grand Slam champions 18-15 on their own patch gave us huge momentum and, most importantly, belief in Doyler's philosophy.

We then played France in Dublin, which descended into the usual dockside brawl, a totally different kind of game to the Scotland one. We lost Matthews and Spillane to injury so we were down to the bare bones with my former Irish Schools second-row partner Brian McCall coming in to win his first cap. With only three forwards on the bench, Mick Fitzpatrick, our reserve prop, had to fill in in the back row. But we showed unbelievable courage and determination to hang in there. France scored the two tries but we got five kicks and drew 15-15.

Michael Kiernan's place-kicking proved invaluable to us on days like that. He'd only started kicking in that fundraising game down in Cork when he landed five out of five, but this was a different stage altogether. Now, suddenly, he was Ireland's place-kicker and was doing a brilliant job of it. That said, as with all good kickers, he applied himself and practised most days. Now we had someone who could put the ball over the bar, which was a major plus and allowed Paul Dean to do what he did best: run the back line. That was a huge bonus.

On the one hand, Doyler's philosophy and approach seemed crazy and illogical at times, but he exuded such confidence that it didn't matter. His original approach before Kiernan proved himself as an international-quality kicker had been, 'We don't need a place-kicker. We will get the tries and Kiernan will be fine.' He was invincible in his own mind – something that would inevitably come back to bite him at some stage.

There was a unity within the group, including the management, and winning games certainly helped to cement that. Mick Cuddy was chairman of the selectors, but he was also Doyle's right-hand man and he'd do anything for the players. He was one of the few in the IRFU who thought the players were more important than anybody else. A regime was installed in which everyone was made to feel ten foot tall.

Again, in fairness to Doyle, it was he who insisted that we were allowed to train and play those simulated matches in training on the main pitch in Lansdowne Road. Before that we'd always trained on the back pitch which was never in great shape. These were the small things that not only made you feel that little bit more important but which also got you used to playing on a wider pitch and a faster surface.

Then we had a captain in Ciaran Fitzgerald who was an outstanding leader and had this ability to bring people together. After the fall-out from the '83 Lions tour when he was heavily criticized after the whitewash in the Test series and then got dropped for the last two games of the 1984 Five Nations, Fitzy was out to prove the doubters wrong. When he got dropped for the game against England, the IRFU said he was injured and unavailable for selection as he'd got badly split playing against Wales and had to leave the field. Fitzy made his point when he played a friendly for his club St Mary's on the same day as Ireland were playing in Twickenham, just to show 'I was fit. I was available.' Fitzy being the strong character he was, when he came back in '85 he was a man on a mission.

One-on-one with people Fitzy is actually quite reserved, but he had the ability to sniff out and work on the leaders within the group. At team meetings before games he had this ability to make you feel invincible going out the door. And fellas believed in him. He was hugely respected and worked really well with Doyle. They were the perfect combination at the right time.

The captain in those days carried an awful lot of the responsibility because you didn't have an assistant coach and didn't have a scrum coach. Doyle was the only coach on the training pitch, though when our scrum was badly exposed in '86 he had the good sense to bring in Syd Millar to address the issues around that.

Doyler was very much in charge, but socially he tried to be one of the lads. When on tour, normally you'd be trying to sneak past the coach's room late at night. But in Japan in 1985 the biggest party was always taking place in his room. That was probably part of his downfall too.

His greatest moment, however, was about to come. Wales in Cardiff was the next game up in the 1985 Five Nations and it was going to be a major obstacle to our Championship hopes. It was also to prove the turning point.

6

Intimidate or Inspire

In 1982 and 1983, we were on the verge of two Grand Slams. The first we lost out on because of the month-long build-up to the France game in the aftermath of our historic Triple Crown win. The second Grand Slam got away because we lost a game in Cardiff that we should have won. You talk about the value of experience, but sometimes it can depend on whether that experience is a positive or negative one, and looking back, I think there was a residue of negative experiences for our senior players from that game in '83.

Fast forward to 1985 and there's a great photograph of the team standing for the Welsh anthem, all linking arms and thriving in the intimidating atmosphere. We had eight lads playing international rugby in Cardiff for the first time but they were all confident guys who couldn't wait to get out and do their stuff.

There's a blissful ignorance that works in your favour sometimes. We had that with those players, the vast majority of whom had no baggage from playing at the Arms Park, unlike many of their predecessors. They weren't consumed by a fear of losing there. I was to learn that lesson again in a management context in future years when Warren Gatland and I introduced Ronan O'Gara, Peter Stringer, John Hayes, Shane Horgan and Simon Easterby in one fell swoop against Scotland. Never underestimate the exuberance of youth.

We were sitting in the revamped dressing room in the bowels of Cardiff Arms Park and we could hear the Welsh fans in full voice before kick-off. They'd been there for hours beforehand, singing their hymns and their arias. The walls were reverberating, it was a din of noise, and you could see our fellows just soaking it up, wanting it, relishing it. That atmosphere can work in one of two ways: it can intimidate or inspire you. That day it certainly inspired us.

The volume of noise outside grew and grew and we just seemed to grow with it. Somebody in the dressing room turned round and said, 'You know what? I love the Welsh national anthem. Let's stand for it and sing along with it.' That was the attitude, and, of course, playing away from home at that time we had no anthem of our own to inspire us – a subject on which I'll have more to say later.

That photo captured the mood perfectly. The fifteen of us are linking arms, maybe not quite singing the Welsh national anthem, but taking it all in. Letting it be inspirational.

The Duggans, Keanes and Slatterys of this world would never have been intimidated but I think because they had played with a lot of those brilliant Welsh players of the seventies, they knew just how good Wales were. There had to be some explanation for why Ireland hadn't won in Cardiff for eighteen years.

That day, with the next generation on board, we won 21-9, with Keith Crossan and Trevor Ringland scoring two great tries. It was as if the hex had been broken and we'd crossed a threshold.

Things changed after that. Ireland hadn't won in Cardiff since 1967; after 1985, we didn't lose there again until 2005. In twenty years going there, Ireland delivered eight wins and a draw. That was some turnaround after so many years of failure. The mind-set of Irish players travelling to Wales changed dramatically after that win in '85. The mental block was finally gone.

We took Wales by surprise that day and we also enjoyed that bit of luck every successful side experiences. Their full-back and kicker Mark Wyatt missed three or four kicks on the day and we got over their line twice. The whole philosophy was about playing out of the tackle and keeping the ball alive. The tries Ireland scored that day in Cardiff have stood the test of time, especially Crossan's excellent effort. I appreciate that you didn't have the defensive blankets you have nowadays, but in terms of quality of passing, lines of running and putting people into space it was as good as anything you'll see.

That back line were all incredibly talented, Paul Dean being the perfect example. If he was playing darts he'd be hitting 180s. Snooker? He'd win that. Tennis? Yep, he'd win that too. Golf – he was playing off two. He just had it. Ironically he was never a great tactical kicker, certainly not in Campbell's or Ward's class, but he never saw it as a problem. He played at inside centre in '82 and '83 and was a very good defender despite being comparatively small. He also had mercurial hands. Would he have been playing at number 10 under any other Irish coach at that time? Perhaps not, but he was good enough to be selected by Ian McGeechan for the 1989 Lions tour to Australia.

Doyler also recognized the added value a player like Willie Anderson could bring to the cause. He was three years older than me and was getting his chance now at twenty-eight. He couldn't believe his luck even though he was out of position in the second row. So he thought the sun, moon and stars shone out of Doyle because he gave him an opportunity when he wouldn't have had it before.

I think Brian Spillane, too, was the type of player who would not have been picked by Willie John McBride, but Doyle saw the footballer and athlete in him. Plus, that cockiness fitted perfectly into the modus operandi of the team.

You hear people speculating about previous generations of Irish internationals now – 'Oh, he wouldn't have made it in the professional game' – but when you consider the vast majority of the players from that team, it's rubbish. Trevor Ringland was a supreme athlete. Keith Crossan was an outstanding player – the Shane Williams of the eighties game. Hugo MacNeill likewise was different class, while Mullin and Kiernan were international runners. Plus you had Dean and Michael Bradley who just hit it off together and formed a great half-back partnership. It was a team of players in perpetual motion. Beating Wales in Cardiff that day in March 1985 proved how far we had come.

In the final game of the Five Nations we faced England at home for the Triple Crown. From wooden spoon the year before to a potential Five Nations Championship, all in Doyle's first year in charge.

England had this massive pack that was going to be a big challenge for us, and on the morning of the game it was lashing rain. It was obvious we couldn't play the type of running game that we wanted to play. We had a meeting and said amongst ourselves, 'Look, we're going to have to roll with this here.' The conditions just weren't conducive to the way we'd been playing and it would have suited England, what with potential knock-ons and more scrums for their big, heavy pack. The last thing you wanted to do was play into their hands. It was going to be a different type of game.

I'd felt no pressure going into the Triple Crown decider against Scotland in '82 but there was definitely pressure going into this match. This team had come from nowhere and was playing fantastic rugby. There was almost an expectation that we were going to have to entertain now as well as win. But at Lansdowne Road that day we had to just get on with things instead.

Doyle had this ability to concentrate and accentuate the positives. He'd pick out all the best things you did. He also sold this concept to the rugby public in Ireland, that it was about having a go – 'Oh, we're just going to give it a lash' and all of that. People talk about the Jack Charlton years, Euro '88 and 'Give it a Lash Jack' – that all started with Mick Doyle and the rugby team.

Going over to Stephen's Green for our regular routine on the morning of the game, the thinking was 'We're going to have to knuckle down here'. We would have to rely more on our set-pieces and kicking game. That focused the minds of the forwards, and we delivered big time. It is the one game that stands out for me because the backs were getting all the glory up to then – and rightly so, given the kind of tries we were scoring. Against France, in that dogfight in Dublin, we stood up when it counted. But we were under pressure in the front five against Wales. Now we had no option but to perform against this big England pack, and we delivered when it mattered most.

It was a cauldron of an atmosphere, 55,000 fans screaming and roaring throughout. Our try resulted directly from a block-down by Brendan Mullin. England full-back Chris Martin was attempting to clear his lines when Mullin came racing in to close it down. It was a classic Gaelic football block.

England came back, and at 10-10, when Rob Andrew missed a vital penalty with time running out, other Irish teams might have thought that was enough. But the draw would have been the greatest disaster of all time, because we didn't win anything with a draw. The Triple Crown would have been gone, as well as the Championship.

There was the famous Ciaran Fitzgerald line that came out on television where he called on his players with the words, 'Where's your fucking pride?', even if I'm not too sure how many players on the pitch actually heard it. The confidence and strength in that group meant you played to the finish.

The manner in which it was won in the end, with the Kiernan drop-goal, was fitting for the group that was there. It was a drama team. There were a few fellas who loved the attention and thrived on it. Importantly, though, it showed the character of the group.

At 10-10 we were entering the closing phase of the game and under pressure. The weather conditions were foul and your body was aching, but that was the time when we knew we had to pick up the pace of the game. Fitzy decided that for any last few line-outs we had we'd get into the line straight away to keep the pressure on. Whoever was unmarked in that quick formation he was going to throw the ball at, and you just nodded if you wanted it. That's exactly what happened. We got a line-out around the English 22. We raced up, got there early, Fitzy looked up, Brian Spillane was the mark. He threw the ball to Spillane, who won it, but the referee wasn't happy that the line-out was formed properly. Opportunity gone, fine margins, was that our missed chance?

No. The next throw we do the exact same thing. Spillane is still available so Fitzy throws a quick ball to him. I had already carried a lot of ball that day and when Spillane won the line-out I ripped it out of his hands, peeled off, and all of a sudden this space opened up in front of me. I was leading the charge with three or four Irish players riding in my slipstream, supporting me. There's one stage where you can see the posts and you're building momentum and there's a part of you saying, 'Jesus, I can go for this.' But Rob Andrew managed to tackle me around the toenails and brought me to the ground.

What followed, though, was almost textbook play. I was on the deck placing the ball with two or three Irish forwards having cleaned out magnificently. There wasn't an English hand within a few metres of Michael Bradley. He passed to Kiernan, and it's now decision time. Kiernan, being the consummate footballer that he is, sees there's an overlap outside him, but instead he takes the responsibility himself, steps into the 10 channel and drops the goal.

And of course he read it right. Had he missed it, he would have been castigated because there was a clear overlap outside him. But he'd be the type of confident individual that it would never have entered into his head. If he was going for it, he was going to get it.

All this happened within seconds. The perfect catch from Spillane, a good drive, the perfect ball placement for Bradley to deliver the perfect pass for Kiernan to step up to the mark. It's amazing what goes through your head in those moments. I was on the deck, lying on the ground, but managed to turn around and was on my back looking up as the ball went sailing over my head. I had a perfect view of it, almost in line with the black spot in the middle of the crossbar. I watched it going over the bar as if in slow motion. I was looking straight at the terrace and could see all the Irish fans rising as one. If I'd been a snapper with a camera in that position it would have been the sports picture of the decade.

Even in that split second it registered that, not only were we going to win, but I had contributed to a significant moment in Irish sport. As I looked up at the ball sailing over me it dawned that this was something special. There are so many games and incidents that have faded from the memory over the years, but that moment, as soon as it happened, I knew.

The manner of the victory proved fitting for that team. Flamboyant. And it played right into Mick Doyle's script. All of a sudden we were feted and attracting attention from all over. With Doyler being a vet he was cultivating all the top brass in his field. We were even invited down to Coolmore Stud. We got the full tour, saw Sadler's Wells who was the champion horse of the time, and even played in a fundraiser in nearby Fethard. The Irish Triple Crown team playing Fethard, who were I think county football champions of Tipperary at the time. This was where the team had gone.

The following year, other teams had done their homework on us and targeted our scrum in particular. 'We'll dismantle them up front first.' But Doyler didn't adapt or change. His philosophy was still the same: 'The scrum is only a means to restart the game'. It worked for a year, but in '86 it wasn't going to work again. We needed to adapt and change but did neither.

From being within a whisker of a Grand Slam, we were whitewashed in the 1986 Five Nations Championship with a heavy defeat to France and the humiliation of our scrum being taken apart against England in Twickenham, as well as close defeats to Wales and Scotland in our final game. Phillip Matthews was a huge loss to us through injury that season and we just didn't have the strength in depth to cope with injuries to key players.

After the France defeat, Doyle dropped Phil Orr on his forty-ninth cap. Himself and Orr would have been very close when Phil was a huge part of that Leinster success under Doyle. Getting your fiftieth cap in those days was a significant milestone – the equivalent of getting a hundred caps now – and Phil was distraught. It seemed as if he was being made the scapegoat and Doyle was saying, 'I'm calling the shots here.'

Doyle had to eat humble pie, though, after what happened to us in Twickenham and Phil was brought back for the last game against Scotland. Ironically Michael Kiernan missed a very kickable penalty that would have won us the game. It was almost as if things had come full circle with Kiernan missing a kick he'd normally get with his eyes closed.

From the glory of the year before we were now at the bottom of the pile and things were starting to fall apart under Doyle. He had one more year to turn it around.

As predicted, the Lions tour to South Africa in 1986 didn't go ahead due to apartheid restrictions. But for those of us who had been selected, the IRB decided to celebrate its centenary with two games in Cardiff and London: one with the Lions facing a World XV made up of the best New Zealand, South Africa, Australia and France had to offer, at the Arms Park; the other, a Five Nations side taking on the same squad at Twickenham with the French contingent joining forces with us.

A Lions squad of twenty-three players was selected and I was starting in the second row with England's Wade Dooley. What grates a little is that game in Cardiff: despite being an official Lions match, and despite a specially commissioned 1986 Lions blazer being presented to every player, it is not deemed to be an official Test. The game against Argentina on the eve of the 2005 tour to New Zealand at the same venue is. The quality of opposition we faced in Cardiff that evening was far superior to that fielded by Argentina with several of their first-choice players not released to play.

The Lions game was played in a Cardiff downpour. The overcast weather set the tone for me, however. Rugby has been a huge part of my life but some of the milestones and successes have been tempered with personal sadness, the swinging from the emotional highs of sport to the heartbreak and sorrow that real-life scenarios can present. The match was played on 16 April, the first anniversary of the death of our little girl Sarah who had passed away after heart surgery at just eight and a half months old.

Just being there constituted a real crisis of conscience for me. I wanted to be with my wife Mary. I woke with a heavy heart on the morning of the match, thinking only of Sarah, and Mary back home. My Lions dream had gone up in smoke in 1983 and here I was again, three years down the track, wondering what I was doing. I wanted to play in a Lions Test match but, once again, it was complicated.

Des Fitzgerald was the tight-head prop for the Lions that evening and, in typically caring fashion, knew the significance of the day for me. He had other things to worry about at the time but his thoughts were with me. He approached me quietly after breakfast and said, 'If you want to go and say a prayer somewhere, we can do that together.'

So there I was, a year after my daughter's death and just hours away from playing for the Lions, kneeling in a church in Cardiff. Rugby was the last thing on my mind. I blessed myself and stood up knowing I'd have to play with a shadow hanging over me and a very heavy heart.

We lost the match 15-7 but it didn't really matter much to me. The following Saturday I was given the honour of captaining the Five Nations side against the World XV, but my heart wasn't in it. It had been a long week away from home and I wanted to be back in Cork with Mary.

Twenty-nine years later, on the day before Ireland played Argentina in Cardiff in the quarter-final of the World Cup, I went looking for the Church of St John the Baptist for the first time in almost three decades. I found it and once again said a prayer, not only for Sarah this time but also for Luke Fitzgerald who was on the bench for Ireland the following day and whose dad had been so thoughtful towards me on the day he would make his only appearance in a Lions jersey.

Ironically, the second row marking me that night at the Arms Park in 1986 was Springbok Schalk Burger. Twenty-three years later his son of the same name could well have been sent off in the opening minute of the second Test between South Africa and the Lions in Pretoria for gouging Luke Fitzgerald. Small world. And a cruel one at times.

Things were going to have to change in Doyle's third and final year in charge of Ireland, which was going to culminate in the first ever World Cup, in New Zealand and Australia. In

November 1986, we played Romania in Lansdowne Road and he dropped a bombshell when omitting our captain, Ciaran Fitzgerald. What's more, he appointed me as Fitzy's successor.

Following Fitzy as captain was always going to be difficult. We had spent five years playing together at international level and because he was the thrower, I had built a great rapport with him. I would go off and meet him at Cathal Brugha Barracks in Dublin, where we would work together to perfect the understanding between thrower and jumper. He was our leader, the fulcrum of the Irish pack, and we would have followed him anywhere. Fitzy was the type that inspired devotion in those around him.

Dropping him against Romania was the sure sign that Doyler was trying to shake things up, but to be fair, Fitzy's replacement, Leinster's Harry Harbison, was playing great rugby at the time and had acquitted himself well when replacing Fitzy in controversial circumstances back in '84.

In the mid-eighties Romania were actually a very decent side as in the Ceauşescu era the majority of their players were either in the police or the army. They were allowed to train like professional players. But the communist system was beginning to break down and at the dinner afterwards you could sense the change. The Romanian players were impoverished and devoured everything put in front of them.

We beat them 60-0, a world record win at the time. No team had ever won an international by 60 points. We played unbelievable stuff. I know it was Romania and all that, but we scored some stunning tries. As for my first game as Ireland captain, it couldn't have gone any better. Hopes were high for the 1987 Five Nations.

We played England in the opening game of the Championship

on a cold, wet February day in Dublin. We won 17-0 with tries from Michael Kiernan, Keith Crossan and Phillip Matthews, whose return from injury was a big bonus. My first two games as captain and we were 77-0 ahead on aggregate.

Next up we had Scotland in Murrayfield and, for whatever reason, Doyle gave us the Friday off with no team run, telling us, 'Ah lads, you're fine.' Some of us went into the gym and sauna in the hotel and did all the wrong things. We played like a bag of shite the following day and lost by 4 points. It was just one of those days. Michael Kiernan was over the line but couldn't ground the ball, and even though I scored my one and only international try that day, it didn't matter in the end. I was hugely disappointed.

Things were changing. We weren't even in the Shelbourne for training weekends any more, staying instead at the Royal Marine in Dún Laoghaire, away from the buzz of the city centre. The following Saturday night we had a team meeting to critique the loss to Scotland. Doyle stood up in front of the squad and said, 'I don't want to be remembered as the coach of a lucky Triple Crown team.'

In my opinion, that was the moment when the bond that had developed over the last two years began to break irretrievably. Fifteen words to shatter the previous two years' work. 'It's not about you,' I thought to myself. I wasn't the only one thinking the same thing. That was the turning point in the squad's relationship with Mick Doyle. In his mind, he had become bigger than the team. That was the moment.

The sad thing was, the potential in the team was still there. We could have and should have beaten Scotland. We played badly and lost narrowly. We played France next in Dublin. We were 8 points up and lost the game. That French team not only won the Grand Slam, but within a few months would make it to the first World Cup final, against New Zealand, after beating Australia in a classic semi-final.

At least we responded positively and beat Wales in Cardiff once again. Had we beaten Scotland it would have been another Triple Crown. As it was, we finished second on points difference.

After the Championship there was the World Cup to look forward to, but the relationship between Doyler and the players had fractured. In that team meeting, all he had been thinking about was his legacy, how he stood in the media's and the public's eye. I would still rate him as one of the best coaches I played under, though. The things that made him great were the things that also contributed to his downfall. We achieved something special under his watch and I will always be grateful for that. He inspired a bond between a special group of players that still exists today. For that I'd like to think we are all grateful.

Afterwards, when he was doing punditry with RTE and writing for the *Sunday Independent*, he attacked most of the players he had worked with. A lot of them couldn't stand him at that time. He loved the notoriety and would only laugh at you when you took him on. 'Doyle, you're a fucker!' It didn't bother him one bit.

You couldn't remain bitter with him, however, and there was no lingering animosity between the two of us. I appreciated what he did and thankfully was on very good terms with him when he died tragically in a car accident in May 2004. He appointed me captain of my country. I was fortunate to play with Ireland from 1981 to 1992, but that group under Doyle will always be special.

7

From 'The Sash' to 'The Fields Of Athenry'

'Lads, there's been a bomb blast outside Newry. David Irwin, Nigel Carr and Philip Rainey were caught up in it.'

It was a bright, sunny Saturday morning in April 1987 and we were gathered for a pre-World Cup training session at the Wanderers ground on Merrion Road in Dublin. Irwin, Carr and Rainey hadn't shown up. We'd had no idea where they were, and continued with our training.

Rugby's first ever World Cup was only a few weeks away and we were, belatedly, focused on getting ourselves ready. But thoughts of rugby disappeared when we were told the horrific news.

Three of your team-mates with whom you're preparing to go to a World Cup caught in the crossfire of a car bomb targeting Lord Justice Gibson who was passing by at the time. Bad timing and bad luck, but thankfully they weren't seriously injured. Tragically, Lord Gibson and his wife were killed instantly.

Later that day a few of us went to the Leinster Senior Cup final and it was there that Fergal Keane, the RTE news reporter (who had been in my class in primary school at St Patrick's in Cork though I hadn't seen him since those days), came over to me and filled me in with some more of the details. He asked for an interview and I agreed, even though talking about an IRA attack in the context of the Irish rugby team at a Leinster Senior Cup final was the last thing I'd been expecting. Preparing for our inaugural World Cup adventure was the only thing on my mind when I left Cork for training that morning.

For your team-mates, players you have played with and against down through the years, to be caught up in a bomb blast came as a massive shock. 'Chipper', as Philip was affectionately known by everyone in the squad, Davie and Nigel had all played together on a very good Queen's University team when there was a massive rivalry between them and UCC. We were rivals at college, club and provincial level, but we came together for Ireland as a thirty-two-county team. Despite differences of politics or religion, it was rugby, and playing together for Ireland that overcame all that.

The element of luck in these things – or bad luck, whichever way you want to look at it – is incredible. The lads were driving down from Belfast and the Gibsons were travelling in the opposite direction, and they passed each other as the bomb went off. Part of the blown-up vehicle landed on top of David Irwin's car. Two seconds earlier they wouldn't have been hit; two seconds later it could have been fatal. Such are the fine lines. How they weren't killed is a miracle. Davie was only slightly injured, Chipper was knocked unconscious but recovered, but Nigel suffered extensive injuries that meant he missed the World Cup and eventually had to retire aged just twenty-seven.

The mood was very sombre that day, and the days after. It definitely had an effect on us. From a playing point of view, Nigel was a massive loss. I know he tried everything to get back playing. A year later I invited him down for a CBC centenary game and it was the first time he had played since the incident, but he never made it back. I knew Nigel well and was a huge admirer of him, not only as a player but as a person. We played Schools rugby at the same time and eventually we both made our way on to the senior Irish team. And as I mentioned before, the night I was selected for my first cap, I was rooming with Nigel at the Shelbourne Hotel.

That was six years earlier. I had travelled to Dublin immediately after playing for Munster against Cardiff at the Arms Park. I knew it was a key game for me to make an impression as the Ireland team to play Australia in two weeks' time was being chosen that evening. Even though we lost to Cardiff, I played quite well.

Back in those days, picking an Irish team could take four or five hours, particularly for the first game of the season, because you were starting again from scratch. There was no word of the team when I went to bed that night. Then, at about one o'clock in the morning, the phone in the bedroom rang. I was in a deep sleep and barely conscious when I answered.

'Donal, congratulations.' It was Mick Molloy. 'You've been picked to play against Australia.'

It was the most important phone call of my career but I was so tired I just said, 'Thanks a million, Mick, that's great,' and fell back asleep. When I woke up the following morning, Nigel was in the other bed in the room and I remember thinking, 'Did I just get picked in the Irish team or did I dream it?' I'd liked to have said it to Nigel but I wasn't sure if he was in the team – he too was in the running for his first cap – so I said nothing.

I was fairly sure I had been picked, but I wasn't 100 per cent certain. I waited until I went down for breakfast, looked for Mick Molloy straight away and asked him, 'Did you ring me in the middle of the night?' He confirmed it hadn't been a dream and that was how I remember being told I was winning my first cap.

For guys like Irwin, Rainey and Carr, they sacrificed so much more to play for Ireland. We in the Republic could never truly grasp it, although we began to get some sense of it that day in 1987.

Of the Irish matchday squad that won the Five Nations Championship and Triple Crown in 1985, tight-head prop Jimmy McCoy was a police officer with the RUC, Nigel Carr was a forensic scientist whose job description required him to examine the aftermath of a bomb scene, and my former Irish Schools second-row colleague Brian McCall was now a high-ranking officer in the British Army. Someone once asked the dynamic Carr if he was ever frightened on a rugby field. He replied that when you spend your week examining a bomb scene wearing a high-vis jacket, knowing paramilitary snipers are in the vicinity, there isn't much to be worried about on a rugby pitch.

By virtue of their chosen professions they were seen as legitimate targets for nationalist paramilitaries, and the fact they played international rugby for Ireland not only gave them a profile but also unwanted attention.

Brian McCall grew up on a farm in Armagh playing for Queen's and Ulster before making the decision in his early twenties to join the British Army. When he made his Ireland debut in 1985 there were issues over his security flying in to Dublin from England but, he says, the British Army were nothing but supportive of him playing for Ireland.

We were rooming together for the match in Twickenham in 1986 when the phone rang in the bedroom. I answered, and a posh English voice on the other end asked, 'Hello, is Captain McCall there?' My first thought was 'Ciaran Fitzgerald is the captain of this team', but I just said, 'No, I'm sorry, he's out at the moment. Who's this?' 'Oh, this is Brigadier General so-and-so [some double-barrelled name I didn't quite catch]. I'm just ringing to tell Captain McCall that all the boys in the regiment are rooting for him. Can you tell him?' I said I would, of course, and remember putting down the phone, looking up at the ceiling and thinking, 'Jesus, what would my grandfather Jacko have made of this?'

I caught up with Brian during my research for this book. It was his first time back in Dublin since we played together against Scotland thirty years earlier.

'The British Army were very proud to have me playing for Ireland,' he told me. 'And they gave me every support to fulfil my rugby ambitions. The only issue was around security when I was in Dublin but then I'd have the lads from Special Branch with me and they enjoyed the craic just as much, I reckon! There would be security detailed for me even when I went back home to the family farm in Armagh, but you just lived with it and got used to it.'

Although from the Unionist tradition and fighting in the British Army, McCall is an Irishman who was proud to represent Ireland and stand for the tricolour and 'Amhrán na bhFiann'.

'I was conscious of the nationalist tradition absolutely,' says McCall. 'Although one day Des Fitzgerald had to put me right when it came to the issue of the swimming trunks I wore for rugby games. These were my lucky trunks that I had bought when I was eighteen and on holiday. The only thing was, they had the Union Jack on them, though it never occurred to me that it might ruffle a few feathers wearing them underneath my Ireland gear. One Sunday training session, however, Des Fitzgerald asked me, "Did you ever fucking think about those swimming trunks? You're playing for Ireland and you're wearing those?" I wouldn't mind but Dessie was entirely right in pointing out my flawed judgement and the next day I went out and bought a new pair of trunks.'

In the few days building up to an international, you had to contend with fully armed Special Branch from An Garda Síochána outside your door at night, guarding the players from the RUC and British Army in case of any threats. For the Special Branch lads it was the gig to have, being with the Irish rugby team on the weekend of an international. I remember a few of them, with guns in their holsters, coming up to me at about half one in the morning after one international, slightly panicked, asking, 'Have you seen McCoy or McCall anywhere?'

The Troubles were never far away, though. On the Sunday before the Wales game in '85 we had a squad session in Dublin and were told that Jimmy McCoy had the flu and wasn't training. We subsequently found out a threat had been made against him by the IRA. There was even a suggestion that had the game been scheduled for Dublin that Saturday he might not have been able to play.

How raw things were for some of our Ulster team-mates. Only two weeks earlier, on the Thursday night before playing France at Lansdowne Road, we came back from the cinema and had a sandwich and a cup of tea as usual before going to bed. I was rooming with Willie Anderson, and Jimmy McCoy came in looking devastated. The RUC barracks in Newry had been attacked. In the early evening, nine shells had been launched from a Mark 10 mortar bolted on to the back of a Ford lorry that had been hijacked in Crossmaglen. Eight of them overshot the RUC station in Corry Square, but one 50lb shell landed directly on a portable building containing a temporary canteen. Nine police officers were killed and thirty-seven people were injured including twenty-five civilian police employees. The death toll was the highest inflicted on the RUC in its history.

Word filtered through of the Newry atrocity. Trevor Ringland, whose father was a chief superintendent in the RUC, was also in our room and was visibly shaken. It was a long night.

I went to Mick Doyle the following morning. 'We're going to have to address this, Mick, the whole thing is a mess. We have been up half the night.'

In fairness to Doyle, he called a team meeting and expressed his sincere condolences to Jimmy, who had lost a number of his colleagues.

I always got on well with Jimmy. We had roomed together in Hilversum in Holland when we played on an Irish U23 side in 1979, when I was nineteen and studying in UCC. I got to know him well and respected him hugely.

A few years ago, in 2012, I caught up with Jimmy for the purposes of an *Irish Examiner* column to ask him about his work career v. rugby allegiances.

'I always thought my job was my career,' he told me. 'I went into the RUC straight out of school. I had great pride in playing for Ireland and had no problem whatsoever standing for "Amhrán na bhFiann". People in the police were proud that I was playing for Ireland. They knew that we got on well with everyone in the Irish squad, that there were no political issues between the players. I never met anyone who gave me grief or said that you shouldn't be doing that. I loved playing for Ireland.

'People knew me from both sides of the community. I would go into the nationalist estates and of course they wouldn't be long telling me I played shite for Ireland the last day. It was a bit of craic.

'It worked the other way in that people got to know you, but the week after that mortar attack in Newry, I'm not sure what would have happened, but a chap came in when I was on the beat and said, "Stay there." They came down and picked me up by car and I was told, "You're finished here," as there was an IRA threat.'

You could see the dilemma for those guys. When you lived through the Troubles and saw the effect of it, it made you appreciate even more what they had to do to come through it all. I never had an issue with the Ulster players not singing the national anthem, for example, as they would be castigated for doing so when they went home. It didn't stop thousands travelling down from the North's rugby communities to support their players.

We're hypocritical in many ways as we expected them to stand for 'Amhrán na bhFiann' in Dublin, to respect home jurisdiction, but when there was an international to be played in Belfast that was another matter. They had to stop playing international rugby in Ravenhill because of the southern players jogging on the spot during 'God Save The Queen' in the late 1940s. When Ireland returned to Belfast to play Italy before the 2007 World Cup in Ravenhill there was a massive furore because 'God Save The Queen' wasn't played. If you want to be a professional player now you accept everything that comes with it, but when you were an amateur you had to go home to your job and community and it was totally different.

There was an incredible bond amongst that group of players in the mid-1980s, built up through schools and university, so the North-South thing was never an issue for us. We respected their culture, they respected ours. We sang songs, including songs that were part of their culture – 'The Sash My Father Wore' being one of the main ones. I'll never forget the day in 1985 when it got a right airing as we celebrated beating England for the Triple Crown and the Championship.

Making our way back to the Shelbourne Hotel, the whole of Ireland it seemed was waiting for us, though ironically, coming around Stephen's Green, the song we were all singing on the team bus was 'The Sash'. I was sitting at a window seat and you could see the RTE cameras amongst the crowds waiting at the entrance of the hotel for us. I had this image of the main RTE news report showing the Irish team arriving back from the game singing 'The Sash', which I thought might ruffle a few feathers. I kept looking at the driver of the bus who seemed to be slowing down with the cadence of the song. He had the cop-on to wait until the song was finished before opening the door of the bus. There was a huge reception and all's well that ends well – but it might have been a different story!

We always had a sing-song in our team room. As I said, there was a great bond between us, and whether it was 'The Fields Of

Athenry' or 'The Sash', we all sang together as a team, which was a great unifier.

I used to sing 'The Fields Of Athenry', and pretty soon it was adopted by the squad as our team song, long before it was sung at sporting events anywhere else. It was a regular occurrence when, as captain, I was required to speak at the post-match dinner. The team would burst into the chorus before I could even utter a word.

Sing-songs were very much part of the dressing-room culture back then. We'd stay behind after matches on tour, have a few drinks and sing songs before heading out for the night. If we came together for a reunion and were asked to sing I have no doubt what would be sung, even if the gloss has gone off it a bit now after hearing it so many times over the last thirty years. Unfortunately, 'The Fields' has been flogged to death.

Every now and again, especially when drink was involved, things might flare up and the dynamics could change. Sometimes after singing 'The Sash' I might have countered it with 'Only Our Rivers Run Free', a song written by Michael McConnell about the constitutional issues in the North. I was a big fan of Planxty, and it was a great song on one of their albums. I just liked it. I recall giving it an airing in our team room while on tour in Japan in 1985 when Trevor Ringland took umbrage. Myself and Trevor go back a long way. We both won our first caps together on the same day, against Australia in '81, and that formed a special bond between us. But Trevor took the hump that night, ripped off his Irish tie and left the team room, which didn't sit well with some players, especially as we had all just participated in a rousing rendition of 'The Sash'.

It was just one of those things unfortunately. There was tension sometimes, but it was healthy tension and you moved on.

In later years Trevor made a massive contribution to the peace process and helped to foster and develop healthy relationships between the Catholic and Protestant communities in the North. Indeed he is still active on that front.

Then you had players like Des Fitzgerald, whose father was a Republican and fought in the War of Independence, who grew up in a strongly nationalist household in Dublin. 'There was a section of the island in Northern Ireland that was oppressed in terms of voting and civil rights and these were issues that I grew up with and was very much aware of,' he explained to me when I met him for this book. 'When I was picked to play for an Ireland B team against England in 1982 in Ravenhill and then realized that because of the protocols around home jurisdiction "God Save The Queen" was going to be played against the very team whose anthem it was too, I said to myself, "I'm not playing in that match." You have to remember, this was the Thatcher era – the Falklands War, not long after the civil rights marches, gerrymandering of votes, and we were also in the midst of the hunger strikes. It was a very heightened time for the North and I was going to have to stand for "God Save The Queen" and what it represented to Catholics in the North? Luckily I got injured and wasn't able to play anyway . . .

'Thankfully, as a country, and for me personally, we've come on a long journey from those days of the Troubles and there is now peace in the North and we can accept and understand both viewpoints on the island nowadays. When you've two distinct traditions you need to find the best of both, find the middle ground that we can both come together on.'

The Troubles were ever-present right through the 1970s and 1980s, though, and it's easy to forget how explosive the whole thing was, but we continued to play rugby in the North all the time. I played club rugby there, played for UCC against Queen's and against Instonians. Cork Constitution's oldest fixture in rugby was against NIFC, which was always respected. There was huge camaraderie between the two clubs.

There were never any threats made against us or anything like that. At least not as players. The only time I was exposed to issues of that nature stemmed from Ulster's landmark European Cup success in 1999, when they beat Colomiers on a memorable day at Lansdowne Road. It appeared as if the whole of Ulster decamped to Dublin that day. Ulster's successful run to that European final attracted a following from a wider community than normal. Everyone jumped on the bandwagon, while it also offered sections of the Loyalist community the opportunity to travel to Dublin – many for the first time.

After that success, Warren Gatland, Philip Danaher and I selected an Irish squad for the upcoming tour of Australia, and some north of the border felt aggrieved that it didn't, in their eyes, include a sufficient number of Ulster players to acknowledge their achievement on the European stage. Philip Browne, the IRFU's long-serving CEO, contacted me to say that a Loyalist paramilitary group had sent a threatening letter targeting Gatland, Danaher and myself. I didn't take any heed of it at first, but when Philip confirmed that the threat had been authenticated by the Garda Síochána, we had to sit up and take notice.

The problem was, I was due to travel to Cardiff on a three-day pre-World Cup conference and was reluctant to do so in the circumstances. In the end it was agreed that I would go on a shortened visit and that the local Garda would keep an eye on my house.

Gatland was a bit more concerned as he was comparatively inexperienced in terms of the Troubles and the North. It didn't help when I told him I was relatively unconcerned because, if they were coming, they would stop off in his home town of Galway first before heading on to Limerick for Danaher. By the time they hit Cork, we would know they were coming.

I never told my wife Mary about it, though, as I felt there was no need to worry her unduly. In any event nothing happened, but the letter was treated seriously enough by the authorities.

Going back to my playing days, you knew that for the Ulster players, the inter-pros were that bit bigger for them. Don't get me wrong, playing for Munster was a big thing, but the club rivalries in the province were such that we never really pulled together with the same level of intensity as those Ulster players did. For them it was different, but we understood that and respected them for it. All the more so when we got news that day in 1987 about Chipper Rainey, David Irwin and Nigel Carr being caught up in the bomb blast.

We still had a World Cup to prepare for, though, and little did I realize the storm I was about to walk into from Irish nationalists, and even my fellow Corkonians.

Above left: My grandfather Jacko (*fifth from left*), with the Listowel band at a Home Rule meeting held in Glin, County Kerry, in 1908.

Above right: My father Gerald was a big influence on my sporting career; he was Irish junior heavyweight boxing champion, as well as winning football medals with St Nick's and Cork.

Right: It was John B. Keane (*second left, between his son Billy and my dad*) who wrote about how close Jacko came to death at the hands of a British firing squad.

Below: Brother Philip O'Reilly (*centre*) was the man who saw the rugby potential in me. He is pictured here along with former CBC team-mates Gerry O'Donovan (*left*) and Barry Coleman (*right*) at a reunion of our 1977 Senior Cup-winning team.

Above: CBC U13s – the first rugby team I ever played for – pictured in 1971. I'm fourth from left, back row. Tragically ten years later when we were still playing together for UCC, Gus Barrett (*far right, front row*), suffered a horrific injury in a colours game against UCD and subsequently passed away in 1989.

Left: I enjoyed many a tussle against Shannon's international second row pairing of Mick Moylett and Mick Galwey playing for Cork Con, a club with which I am always proud to be associated.

Below: My Ireland debut came against Australia in November 1981, four days after helping Munster beat the tourists in a memorable game in Musgrave Park.

Above: Captaining Ireland was always a huge honour, especially leading this side to a memorable 17-0 victory over England at Lansdowne Road in 1987.

Right: Carrying out Mick Doyle's philosophy of attacking the opposition with ball in hand in the opening game of the 1985 Five Nations against Scotland at Murrayfield.

Below: Where else but O'Donoghue's on Baggot Street, celebrating with Moss Keane after Ireland won a Triple Crown for the first time in thirty-three years.

England games were always special occasions, whether getting the better of Maurice Colclough at Twickenham in 1984 (*top*) or when a Triple Crown was on the line as at Lansdowne Road in 1985 (*right*).

Left: Shaking hands with the President of Ireland, Patrick Hillery.

Below: My only try for Ireland came against Scotland at Murrayfield in 1987. It was little consolation for a narrow defeat that day.

Bottom: Brothers in Arms. Drawing strength from the singing of the Welsh national anthem in 1985 when Ireland recorded a first win in Cardiff since 1967.

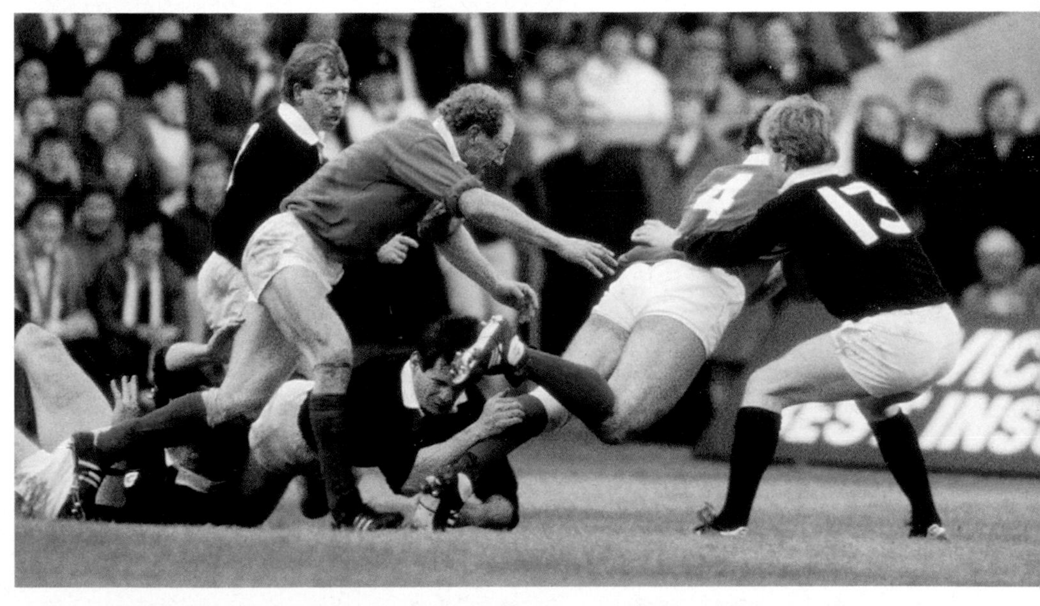

Above: Heading off to the inaugural World Cup in 1987 in good spirits, with (*from left*) manager Syd Millar, coach Mick Doyle and Michael Kiernan.

Left: Willie Anderson and I got our hands on the trophy, but the whole affair in New Zealand seemed at times more like a church fete than a major tournament.

Below: The IRFU also provided an extensive list of clothing regulations!

5. Dress

The official dress for the touring party will be Irish touring tie, grey trousers, white shirt, light grey so
Each member of the touring party will be supplied with

1 Tour Blazer
2 pairs grey trousers — 3 Touring ties
2 White shirts — 1 Green v-necke
2 Leisure shirts — 1 Green v-necke
1 Leisure suit — 1 Large hold-al
1 pair Leisure shoes — 1 Shoulder bag
1 Leisure jacke

It is recommended that each member should bring:-

1 overcoat or raincoat; a second blazer or jacket; 2 s
one which should be black; socks (including 2 light gr
underwear; handkerchiefs; bathing trunks and toilet re

6. Playing Kit

As the IRFU have entered into a contract with Three St
other manufacturers playing or training equipment, othe
worn on tour and such equipment should not be brought
The following will be supplied to each member of the p
International:-

2 Training suits — 1 kit bag for
1 pair boots — 1 pair white sh
1 pair training shoes
1 All weather suit

Below: Delivering line-out ball to Michael Bradley in our opening match against Wales, a game most remembered for the 'Rose Of Tralee' debacle. I have set the record straight in this book.

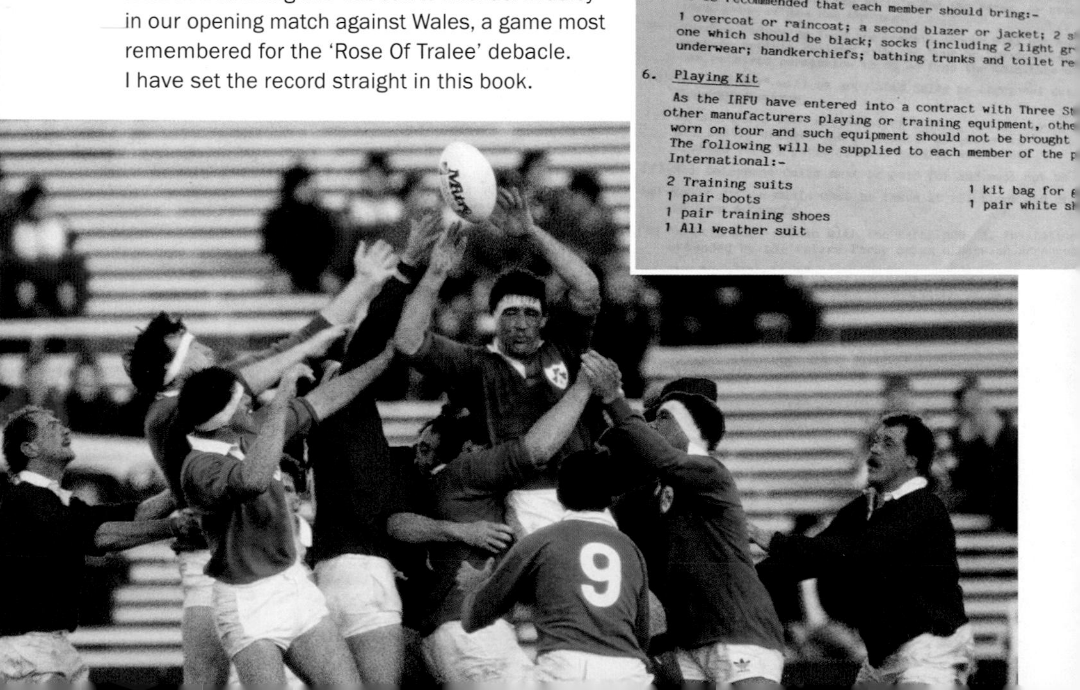

Above: The off-load was in vogue back in 1987 in our first ever quarter-final appearance. Unfortunately, Ireland still hasn't progressed beyond the last eight.

Right: Facing the press with Doyler following defeat to Australia in Sydney to end our first World Cup journey.

Below: Same opposition, same outcome. Losing out once again to Australia in the World Cup quarter-final at Lansdowne Road in 1991, albeit in different circumstances this time.

Above: Rugby has taken me to some incredible places, not least Namibia in this tiny two-seater Cessna.

Right: Image rights were a huge issue during the 1991 World Cup. I was sent this card, which shows how players were exploited back then and only once received their due reward.

Below: With Moss Keane after Munster beat Leicester at Welford Road in 2003. The proud tradition of Munster locks continued that day when Paul O'Connell and Donncha O'Callaghan delivered a masterful performance against Martin Johnson and Ben Kay.

8

Low Expectations and Poor Preparations

It was the inaugural rugby World Cup, and I was Ireland captain. As I lay on the bed in a New Zealand hotel room watching television, an ad came on which immediately caught my attention.

There was a young lad in his school uniform – short pants, socks, and with that old satchel-style school bag on his back. He goes two or three steps up to the front door of a house and knocks. He's calling for his granddad but nobody answers. Instead, the door opens slightly, and all of a sudden he's standing in the hallway. Again he calls out to his granddad but still there's no answer.

He thinks he hears someone upstairs so he goes up and into a bedroom. In the corner of the room his attention is drawn to an old photograph sitting on top of a tea chest. It's a picture of a New Zealand rugby team. He is drawn to it, and picks it up. As the camera focuses in on the detail of the photo, he recognizes the face of his grandfather in the back row.

He places the photo on the bed and opens the tea chest. Neatly folded inside sits a collection of rugby jerseys. The first one he picks up is an Irish international jersey. Suddenly an image appears of his granddad as a young man in an All Black jersey powering through a succession of Irish players. He blows them out of the way. He then picks up a French jersey and the exact same thing happens. A South African jersey – even bigger – and the focus shifts to a number of Springboks trailing in his granddad's wake.

Then down at the bottom of the tea chest he spots this old New Zealand jersey, and he picks it up. You can feel the sense of growing pride in this young fellow as he cradles the jersey in his hands. As he holds it up for a better view, the camera closes in on the New Zealand fern. Next thing, the silver fern starts glowing spectacularly. It's transformed into this massive, glowing light. Then arrives the punchline: 'You too can be an All Black'.

You knew you were in New Zealand, where every man, woman and child is besotted with rugby, follows the sport with a religious fanaticism from the moment they are born, is an expert in the nuances of the game, and wastes no time in telling you, regardless of whether you're from Ireland, England, Wales, South Africa or wherever, about what you do wrong in comparison to the All Blacks.

Despite the vast majority of the country's population already being infatuated with the game, here was this brilliant marketing campaign on TV. To this day it remains one of the most captivating promotions I've ever seen, selling a sport that everyone wanted to play anyway. For the New Zealand Rugby

Union to have the foresight, back in 1987, to sell the message that playing for the All Blacks is one of the biggest things you can achieve in life to an audience that didn't need any convincing was amazing. That ad had me jumping off the bed.

That campaign may have been geared towards the next generation of young players, but the current crop of All Blacks also enjoyed plenty of airtime themselves, even if it was in a format slightly different to what we were accustomed to. By that stage the NZRU appeared to have no issue with their players appearing in advertisements, or endorsing a range of products. Andy Dalton, the New Zealand captain, was a farmer at the time and there was a series of ads of him driving around his land promoting a specific brand of quad bike. These ads were in your face all the time.

As captain of Ireland, even if I had been approached to do something similar for financial gain, it would either have been blocked by the IRFU or I would have been banned, as it would have been in breach of my amateur status.

John Kirwan was the rising young star in New Zealand at that time and he was everywhere too. It was just totally different to our experience of rugby and how it was promoted, and it certainly opened a few eyes as we got ready for World Cup competition for the first time.

And it had all but come out of the blue. It wasn't as if there had been two or three years' notice – more like less than twelve months'. If someone had said in 1986 you would be playing in a World Cup in 1987 you wouldn't have believed them. There was little or no talk about the World Cup as such because you always had this doubt about it ever happening. There was supposed to be a Lions tour to South Africa in 1986 which never happened, so you kind of felt indifferent as to whether this competition went ahead or not.

It was certainly being pushed by the southern hemisphere countries, while the four home unions saw it (rightly so in hindsight) as the first step on the road to professionalism. With South Africa boycotted and Argentina not yet the power they would become, New Zealand and Australia had, in effect, apart from sporadic winter tours, only each other to play against. Rugby league was professional in Australia, so the Australian Rugby Union was coming under intense pressure to retain their best players. I just think they had more foresight in terms of appreciating the product they had. A World Cup tournament provided the perfect opportunity to grow and develop rugby union further and to a wider audience.

But rugby would never go professional. That we were agreed upon – especially in the northern hemisphere countries. You'd meet and chat to rugby officials at post-match dinners and you got a sense straight away of whether they were in favour of it or not.

I remember having a debate in New Zealand on the 1983 Lions tour with Eddie Butler, who was captain of Wales at the time, about the varying degrees of amateurism. In Wales there were suggestions in those days that players were getting a few bob for playing. I remember saying to him, 'Look, I play with Cork Constitution, one of the top clubs in Ireland, but we pay our own way. We pay towards our jerseys getting washed after the game, and you'd pay for your own strapping.' But the talk about payments in the game in Wales were just rumours. It never happened, certainly not in Ireland. I played international rugby from 1981 to 1992 and never got a penny off anyone, with the exception of the 1991 World Cup when the players signed an image rights deal and after the tournament each of us got a cheque for £1,500. That payment came directly from the IRFU on the basis of a collective player agreement.

During my playing days the only thing I got was a great choice of gear from Adidas if I committed to wearing their boots during internationals. We were in a privileged position as the main Adidas warehouse was based in Cork and you could just go in and pick whatever you wanted courtesy of the Irish franchise holder Michael O'Connell. The Cork contingent used to drive the other players mad when we'd arrive up to Dublin decked from head to toe in Adidas gear. That was the extent of my privileges, though. A penny never changed hands.

We were hugely enthused at the prospect of playing in a World Cup, especially as it was taking place in New Zealand and Australia – two countries for the price of one. But the reality was, the IRFU weren't behind the concept, and as a result our preparations were almost non-existent.

Places on the squad were tight, with trials being held in Dublin and Belfast for the twenty-six places up for grabs. If you had started in the Five Nations it was seen as a given that you were going, but for the players on the periphery it was a huge thing and they were giving it everything to make the cut. On the official side of things, however, the appetite just wasn't there, to such a degree that I remember organizing our own private training sessions in Dublin on a Wednesday night so the forwards could practise scrummaging against the Lansdowne club side. After the 1987 Five Nations we'd even received a letter from the IRFU saying we shouldn't play any rugby for the six weeks prior to the World Cup, which started at the end of May rather than in the autumn as it is now. I thought that was absolute madness. No rugby at all for six weeks before our opening game? Madness.

Obviously they were concerned about injuries or whatever, and it's the perennial debate even in the modern game: when do you play, and how much? It's a fine line, and it's very difficult to get the balance right.

But even the letter confirming your selection for the World Cup from the IRFU was so old-fashioned in terms of what you needed to bring, from leather shoes to your pyjamas. Essentially it was along the lines of what was sent out to a Lions party in the 1950s and 1960s when they were going away on tour for six months. It was the same mentality, just the name of the competition had changed.

It was even in the laws at the time that you couldn't assemble more than thirty-six hours before an international game; it was seen as approaching professionalism if you were getting together more often. Talk about a different world!

So we organized some additional sessions ourselves for the forwards – even Mick Doyle wouldn't be at them – and it wasn't too bad as only two or three of us had to travel. We had a very good set of forwards at the time and there was a feeling that we could do something at the World Cup and that we'd better take this on ourselves.

The travel arrangements were horrendous. It was obvious that the cheapest route to Auckland had been chosen for what proved to be the most exhausting of journeys. At least we weren't alone on that front.

We assembled somewhere in Gatwick airport and we had a session there. When we boarded the plane for Los Angeles there wasn't any suggestion of turning left for business class or anything like that. Even the exit rows would have been welcomed. To our horror, we were in good company in the cramped economy seats as the Welsh and Scottish World Cup squads were all down the back as well! Even some of the tournament referees were seated amongst us. As we struggled into our seats, there across the aisle were the Welsh players, our opponents in the opening game – and we were going to be stuck in each other's pockets for the next thirty-six hours? Hardly ideal.

It was uncomfortable, but I suppose we didn't know any better. We'd never had experience of travelling business class or anything like that in those days. Economy was just what you did. It was the same for everyone, but it was a horrific journey. Reading, eating, sleeping for hours in a very cramped environment with opponents we'd be gunning for in a few days sitting within touching distance. It was ridiculous.

After LA, the flight stopped off briefly in Hawaii before flying on again. Just as we were coming into Auckland there was fog. Knackered, hungry and restless, we were put in a holding pattern and flew around the skies for another two hours. Then the pilots realized they were running out of fuel so we had to fly down to Wellington and refuel on the ground. Another few hours sitting there before finally getting to our destination. It wasn't the best of starts.

Having finally arrived, we had a week until the opening game but the itinerary was a farce. We had to attend an opening dinner in Auckland despite the fact that our first game was in Wellington. We then had to travel to Dunedin three days later for our second game, against Canada. From there it was another 2,500km journey to Brisbane to play Tonga, this time four days later. You talk about player welfare . . . it was bizarre stuff. In total, we travelled over 5,000km in the tournament alone.

One of the benefits, I suppose, of sharing the flight to New Zealand with the other teams was that we got chatting to the Scottish players. I arranged with Scotland hooker Colin Deans to do some scrummaging sessions with them as part of our training for when we arrived. Syd Millar was the manager of the Irish squad and he thought it was a great idea. He had coached the victorious Lions in South Africa in '74, was a very good forwards coach, and that day he took us off to train against the Scottish pack. It was a great session. We were finally starting to get into gear.

Mick Doyle decided he was going to get fit over the course of the World Cup and started running with the backs, who trained separately to us as all the forwards had travelled over to Scotland's training base across the city. Problem was, you had the likes of Brendan Mullin and Michael Kiernan who saw Doyle trying to keep up with them, so they just started putting more and more pressure on, going faster and faster.

Later that evening we were getting ready to go to the opening dinner when Mick Molloy, the team doctor, came to me and said Doyler wasn't feeling well and wouldn't be going. I thought no more of it until word filtered through later that there had been some incident and he was being rushed to hospital. I visited him that night along with Syd and Mick and it was clear Doyler wasn't in any serious danger, despite having a whole series of wires attached to monitors hanging out of him. We were flying to Wellington the following morning for our opener against the Welsh, which meant he wasn't going to be involved with the squad for a couple of days.

With Doyler's profile in Ireland, his heart scare almost became a national incident back home. Even the Taoiseach, Charles Haughey, rang to wish him well. In the end, it was all fine. Doyle was way overweight at the time, his big belly doing nothing for his profile. I remember Brian Spillane enquiring, after he was rushed to hospital, if he'd had a boy or a girl. But that is typical of how players react in such situations. You just get on with it.

As far as the players are concerned – even in the professional game – coaches get sacked, and players are sorry to see them go, but within twelve hours they're re-focused. What's the new guy going to bring? Where do I sit with him? There was an element of that back then. Coaches changed all the time. That's the way it was.

We trained without Doyle for a couple of days and Syd took over the forwards while George Spotswood, an IRFU employee who was primarily in charge of logistics, got involved in training the backs. I had known George for years and had always sought his opinion after games as he had an excellent rugby brain. He had also been a very good coach.

So the lead-up to Ireland's first ever World Cup game was eventful to say the least. More controversy and headlines were to follow.

9

'Without an anthem, we have nothing'

We were marooned in Wellington, waiting for our game against Wales – the last of the opening round of pool matches – to finally arrive. New Zealand had played Italy in the opening match of the tournament and I was in downtown Wellington at the time. The whole place was deserted. Even going into a department store, the staff had little TVs strategically placed behind the counter. Everybody was watching the game.

Looking at all those first-round pool games, the one thing that stood out for me was the passion of the players during the various national anthems. Canada, Italy, Romania, Tonga – you saw the passion in their faces as the music played, and how much it meant to them.

If you were playing for Ireland in Lansdowne Road, 'Amhrán

na bhFiann' was always played, but when we were outside Ireland, you had nothing. You just got used to playing away from home and not having a national anthem, which I believe always gave an edge to the home side before kick-off. Not an ideal starting point, but it was never really an issue. Until now. We were going to be the only country at the first ever World Cup not to have a national anthem.

I was captain, so about two days before the Welsh encounter, off my own bat, I went to our manager Syd Millar, a fantastic rugby person and a highly respected figure in the game worldwide.

'Syd,' I said, 'I presume we'll be playing "Amhrán na bhFiann"?'

'Oh no,' he replied. 'Our policy is we'll have nothing.'

'But, this is a World Cup, Syd. We're on the world stage. We can't have that.'

'That's our policy, that's just the way it is,' he told me.

I went away, thought about it, and deliberately picked out the Ulster guys, Willie Anderson and Trevor Ringland in particular, to speak to them. It didn't feel right, I said, not to have an anthem on a world stage. To a man they said they had no problem standing for 'Amhrán na bhFiann'.

I then asked for a meeting with the management. In fairness, I always had a great relationship with the key people in the IRFU and never had an issue in terms of bringing up things that I felt would aid the performance of the national side. Whether as captain or not, I always felt I had the freedom to go and talk to them. Syd Millar and Tommy Kiernan were two of the most influential people in world rugby. People like Ronnie Dawson, Noel Murphy and Sir Ewart Bell were also well-regarded figures on the international stage and, at that time, key decision-makers in the IRFU. As I said, I never had an issue when meeting with them; they were always receptive and took what you had to say on board. They mightn't always agree with you, but at least they listened. This was slightly different in that we were isolated on the other side of the world, but it was an issue that was bothering me.

The meeting was arranged with Syd, Sir Ewart, who was in New Zealand as part of the World Cup organizing committee and who was also president of the IRFU, along with his immediate predecessor Des McKibben. Phil Orr, Willie Anderson and I represented the players.

'Look,' I began, 'I have spoken to the senior members in the squad, from North and South, and there are no issues in standing for "Amhrán na bhFiann".'

'No,' they said. 'This is our policy and it's not for changing.'

It was clear that this was going to be a long night. We went back and forth, getting nowhere. What was meant to be a short meeting turned into a very long, protracted discussion – this, mind you, was two nights before our opening game.

They explained that it was all about home jurisdiction, what you could do and couldn't do, etc. From the IRFU's perspective, 'Amhrán na bhFiann' was played in Dublin respecting home jurisdiction but it was a twenty-six-county anthem – it wasn't for the island of Ireland. That created a problem when Ireland played away from home.

'But we will be the only team without an anthem,' I said, trying to make my point as clear as possible. 'We have nothing.'

To make a long story short, the meeting went on and on and on. It ended up that Phil Orr had a cassette, *James Last In Concert*, with an instrumental version of 'The Rose Of Tralee' on it.

As a compromise, reached late into the night, that was the song chosen to be played. In hindsight, it was a disaster. We never even listened to the tape. I was the catalyst for what proved to be a bad call, even if it was motivated by and made for the right reasons. As it transpired the seeds were sown for 'Ireland's Call' that night as the IRFU at least took it on board that with a tournament like the World Cup, Ireland had to have some sort of anthem to play away from home.

One of the reasons I was persuaded to do this book was to clarify some of the mistruths, misperceptions and inaccuracies that are out there in relation to this issue, and I have read them all.

There was an interesting article in the *Irish Times* by Malachy Clerkin in January 2015, marking the twentieth anniversary of the launch of 'Ireland's Call', which caught my eye. Former Irish lock Neil Francis was interviewed and quite rightly confirmed what a disaster the playing of 'The Rose Of Tralee' proved to be. 'It was the worst compromise of all time,' said Neil. 'I'd say we had thirty seconds of discussion about it but it certainly wasn't the players who came up with it. It was a pretty crap version. It was embarrassingly bad. It was played before all four games and I just stood there totally unmoved each time. I didn't know the song, I hadn't ever heard it, I knew none of the words. None of us did. We just stood there in stony-faced silence and waited for the game to start.'

That pricked my attention as we were now delving into the realm of fantasy. The piece claimed Franno was one of only four people to have stood for three anthems for Ireland; in fact there were only three players who did that: Michael Bradley, Brendan Mullin and Terry Kingston. It was also inaccurate in other key aspects. Firstly, 'The Rose Of Tralee' was only ever played once at the 1987 World Cup, in that opening game against Wales – and Franno wasn't even playing. So if the recollections of a player who was part of the squad can be so off the mark, then it's time these things were put on the record and set straight.

That day when the tune started coming out over the crackly stadium speakers, it was a disaster. We were in our own huddle at the time and we were looking at each other thinking, 'What the fuck?' The thing is, we never did actually listen to the cassette. The first time I heard it was when it came out through that stadium sound system, and it did sound crap. The players are looking at each other, some wondering, 'Jesus, are we supposed to sing?' Others are saying, 'What the fuck is that?' It was a moment when we should have been pumping it up, bellowing out, really gearing ourselves up for the eighty minutes ahead of us with passion, but the music well and truly put paid to that. Did it have an impact on the outcome of the game? I don't think so. If anything, after the protracted build-up – the whole Doyle thing, losing Harry Harbison to injury, and then the anthem issue – we were nearly drained by the time we got to run out on to the pitch past the Webb Ellis trophy. We never hit the ground running. It was a sequence of events you certainly could have done without.

We had beaten Wales quite well in Cardiff a few months earlier and had no inhibitions about playing them. The game, however, was in Athletic Park in Wellington where the winds were often so strong and forceful that one of the stands used to visibly sway. In those days, understandably, a winning team was nearly always kept together and rarely tinkered with. Our only selection debate surrounded who to pick at out-half given the conditions that were expected to prevail. Tony Ward, who had been recalled to the squad for the tournament, had a better tactical kicking game than Paul Dean, but Deano had been outstanding for Ireland in the Five Nations and was key to the game favoured by the back line.

In the end, Deano got the nod.

It was a very tight game, but we lost 13-6, and that put us on the back foot straight away. It meant that should we win our remaining two pool games, against Canada and Tonga, we would end up playing Australia – the likely winners of Pool 1 after beating England in their opening game – in Sydney in the quarter-final.

We also had injuries to key personnel. We had lost Nigel Carr to the bomb incident. Harry Harbison, who had won his place ahead of Ciaran Fitzgerald – a massive call from Doyle a year earlier – and who had played really well throughout the '87 Five Nations, had injured his back and was ruled out of the tournament. Terry Kingston came in for his first cap and did well, but we'd lost two very experienced forwards at a vital time.

Despite all that, we still should have won the game. We also lost Phillip Matthews to injury during the match, but we were still competing well up front. With better preparation and a break on the injury front we would have won the game and topped the group.

I'll never forget being at a reception after the match for the ex-pat Irish community. Back in 1987, New Zealand seemed such a long way away, and when we turned up to a reception hosted by the Wellington Irish Association, the playing of 'The Rose Of Tralee' was the main topic of conversation. The disappointment amongst the exiles was plain to see. These local Irish had their kids dressed up in their Irish dancing uniforms and all the rest of it, and their Irish identity was a big deal so far from home. In my own mind it cemented my original motivation. We should have had our anthem, but, in the circumstances, having nothing would have been better. Would there have been a reaction from the Irish community in Wellington that evening if we had played nothing? Absolutely. I have no doubt about that. But the fact that we played 'The Rose Of Tralee' only served to highlight the matter, and annoy people.

There was a shit storm brewing back home in Ireland too. People were up in arms, and, in effect, I was the cause of it. The journalists covering the tour told us about the reaction back home, about the anger and disgust that were being vented.

That said, it was an issue that had to be addressed at some stage, and there was no more pressing a time, I felt, than the advent of a rugby World Cup. Perhaps others didn't feel as passionately about it as I did. When I saw the other teams in the tournament taking such pride in and giving such passion to their own anthems, I just felt we were missing out. I was motivated by the right reasons, even if the end result proved embarrassing – for which I must take responsibility.

It then started to become an issue at every World Cup. Because we played three of our four matches at the 1991 World Cup at Lansdowne Road it wasn't really a problem, even if, once again, we had nothing when we met Scotland in Murrayfield – my fiftieth cap, as it transpired. In fact that was the first time I stood for Scotland's new anthem, 'Flower Of Scotland' – an infinitely better solution for them than 'The Rose Of Tralee' had been for us. Perhaps that set the seed with the IRFU for a compromise effort for Irish rugby.

When 'Ireland's Call' was introduced to solve the problem of an anthem for the team at the 1995 World Cup in South Africa, an even bigger hullabaloo surrounded that. I have to say I wasn't a great fan but I understood and accepted the concept behind it.

Interestingly, the protocol attached to it has changed since then. It was penned to represent Ireland when playing abroad but has since crept into the home fixture also. When that happened I raised the question as to why 'Amhrán na bhFiann' wasn't played alongside it for internationals outside Ireland as well.

During the 1999 World Cup, the tricolour was replaced by the IRFU with the flag of the four provinces. I have noticed that Munster players in general tend not to be huge fans of 'Ireland's Call' and generally don't sing it. As I said, I am not a great fan of it either – maybe it's because Cork doesn't get a mention – but I do fully understand and accept the rationale behind it.

In any case, for our second World Cup game in 1987, against Canada in Dunedin, 'The Rose Of Tralee' was quickly dropped, and nobody within the squad complained. We won that game 46-19, a brace of Keith Crossan tries turning things in our favour after the Canadians had made life difficult for us for long periods. At long last our World Cup was up and running. Despite the long flight to Brisbane for the final pool game, we got a 32-9 win against Tonga to set up that first ever quarter-final against Australia in Sydney, just four days later.

The Aussies held no fear for us as we had a reasonably good record against them through the years and Ireland hadn't yet lost to them in their own backyard. It was a very good Wallaby side, however, with the likes of David Campese, Michael Lynagh and Nick Farr-Jones in the ranks. Playing at home, they outmatched and outplayed us from the start – despite Mick Doyle's ludicrous comment afterwards that we had won the second half. On the scoreboard maybe, but the truth is they had eased off by that stage and were looking to save themselves for the semi-final the following week. On another day we'd have fancied our chances but it just wasn't to be and we were soundly beaten 33-15.

I was back home in Cork by the time Wales were destroyed 49-6 by New Zealand in the semi-final. Somehow, the Welsh then bounced back and beat Australia in the third-place play-off.

So Wales finished third in the inaugural World Cup. With a different set of circumstances and better preparation, that could have been us. It wasn't as if they were a better team than us or had done anything hugely different to us. It was a momentum thing, as so often happens in tournaments.

Tournaments like a World Cup take on a life of their own. How can you equate France losing to Tonga in the 2011 event only to recover to push the hosts, New Zealand, all the way in a final the French could well have won?

Not being able to live up to the hype and expectation is certainly an accusation you can level against some of the Irish teams I was involved in. There was almost an acceptance of glorious failure. It was about being competitive, not getting hammered, doing way better than people thought we were capable of. This was very much an Irish thing. Sometimes it seemed like we needed to feel adversity before we could conquer it.

Over the last decade the Irish provinces, along with the national team, have succeeded in breaking that stereotype. The advent of professionalism has changed all of that with the foundations built on the glory years of multiple Heineken Cup successes.

There were no expectations on us going into the 1987 World Cup. It simply wasn't on most people's radar. The question was, did we see ourselves beating New Zealand or even Australia? What were the public expectations surrounding our participation? I'd say the man on the street barely knew we were involved in the tournament. Contrast that to the empty streets and roads of New Zealand when their team was playing.

The IRFU's mindset at the time certainly wasn't one of high hopes. In fact they didn't want us anywhere near a World Cup as they feared what it might lead to. It was almost as if we were there under sufferance. Also, as there had never been a World Cup before, nobody had any idea of what to expect from one. All the players had to go on was previous touring experiences where it was as much about getting the opportunity to travel and see the world as it was about winning.

At that time, rugby opened doors to travel the world. We would never have made it to far-off places like New Zealand and Australia had it not been for rugby. Even that has changed dramatically now, with so many young people taking time out to travel and broaden the mind. Thirty years ago, many who travelled down under had no intention of ever coming back.

After the Australia game, there were some supporters I knew who had emigrated only a year before and they were all standing behind me on the pitch while I was being interviewed by the great Fred Cogley from RTE, waving to their parents with banners and signs. That was the way you communicated. The world was a big place. This was an adventure, and the World Cup was only a part of it.

I do look back at the tournament with a nagging sense that we could and should have done far better. There were mitigating factors, including poor preparation and a horrendous amount of travel. The actual running of the tournament also left a lot to be desired. After it, I was asked to do a report for the World Cup organizers, giving my views on what was good and what was bad. I wrote, 'I do think the World Cup has a future, but . . .'

There was a sense that New Zealand and Australia were ahead of us, but from the minute the decision was made to host the World Cup final in their country, the All Blacks saw it as their destiny to win it. We certainly didn't see it as our destiny to win it.

Professionalism has changed the Irish mindset, but you have to ask why we have been so dismal in World Cup tournaments. That first World Cup was about different styles and different cultures. Southern hemisphere rugby was seen as being superior to ours at the time. France did beat Australia to make the final against New Zealand but appeared knackered by that stage and were blown away. We'd lost narrowly to France that year and knew all their players from competing against them over the years. Their magnificent semi-final victory over Australia opened up our eyes to the possibilities, and what we should be aspiring to.

So despite all the hardship, you began to appreciate that this World Cup thing had a future, and that Irish rugby badly needed to get on board and embrace it.

10

'Why don't you sing "The Rose Of Tralee"?'

Dear Donal,
I was delighted and relieved to meet you in person to apologize for my awful behaviour towards you on that night in 1987 in Mitchelstown. A couple of incidents that I observed first hand in the North in 1986 and 1987 caused me to be very annoyed with the IRFU at that time but that gave me no right to act like a dick . . .

After the disappointment of the World Cup, the summer of 1987 for me was about the GAA, the Munster and All Ireland Championships. Tipperary played Cork in Thurles in one of the greatest Munster hurling finals ever played, a scintillating 1-18 draw with Nicky English scoring Tipperary's goal, soccer-style, after losing his hurley.

A few of us would always travel to the matches together: myself, the late Trevor Barry, a club-mate in Cork Con and a fantastic character who we lost far too early to cancer in 2001, and Olann Kelleher from Dolphin, another great friend whose claim to fame was that he sat on the Munster bench on that famous day against New Zealand in 1978. We were usually joined for the journey home by the Cork team doctor Con Murphy.

We'd normally stop off for a few pints on the way back for the traditional post-match analysis. Con would always have the inside story and we weren't exactly short of opinions either. After that classic, we stopped for a pint and a chat in Walshe's pub in Mitchelstown.

We were minding our own business at one end of the bar when I became conscious of rumblings coming from the other end. Fellas were shouting stuff over at us. One guy was being particularly vocal, but it took a while in the busy pub for me to figure out what he was saying. Then it registered. 'Come on, why don't you sing "The Rose Of Tralee" for us?' He was being particularly antagonistic and I was getting really pissed off. Con Murphy recognized some of them. There was at least one known Republican sympathizer in the party.

The thing that annoyed me was that there was no way on earth they could actually know how and why the 'Rose Of Tralee' thing had come about. As I've explained, it was motivated by pride in where we came from, a pride in our having a national anthem.

It was a small bar and it was getting heated, but Con saw that Teddy McCarthy – Cork's famous dual All-Ireland winner from 1990 – was amongst the larger gathering. Con intervened because things were escalating and he knew that I was getting a bit too excited. Cheap shots were being directed at me and I wasn't going to stand there and take much more of this crap. Con had a word with Teddy to get these fellas to quieten down and it was decided it was best for all concerned to just drink up and move on. I knew Con recognized one of the main rabble-rousers and he was embarrassed over it as he felt it was as if the GAA were attacking me. He took that personally.

My intervention back in Wellington had been motivated by the right reasons, and to have it being questioned and thrown back at me really annoyed me. Some in the GAA community like to paint themselves as being more Irish than the rest of us – how is it that Joe Brolly refers to them, real Gaels? – and it's certainly the case where rugby players are concerned.

Incredibly, over twenty years later and completely out of the blue, I received a phone call one afternoon.

'My name is Liam Cusack,' he said. 'You probably don't remember me.'

'I know exactly who you are,' I told him matter-of-factly. Con had told me his name soon after the incident and it had stayed with me.

'Look, I'm ringing to apologize for that incident in Walshe's pub all those years ago. I was out of order.'

To be fair, I admired the man for having the balls to get in touch with me after so many years. Why ring me after all that time, though? I was always interested to find out why, and writing this book offered me the excuse.

I sourced his number and rang him to meet up. I just wanted to find out, face-to-face, what it was all about, and to be able to give the context and explanation as to my motives in the 'Rose Of Tralee' debacle.

Ironically, when we did agree to meet it was in a coffee shop just a few hundred metres down from the pub where all the hassle had erupted in the first place.

'That day of the hurling final there was a group of us, and one or two in the group would have been rabid Republicans,' Liam explained to me all those years later. 'We'd been drinking all day, from the morning of the match and then again afterwards. The playing of "The Rose Of Tralee" at the World Cup was a bone of contention at the time, of course, and would have incensed a lot of people.

'In fairness, I'd always support the Irish rugby because there were real Irishmen on the team – not like the soccer team that would have so many Englishmen on it. Then one of the fellas in our group pointed out, "There's your man from the Irish rugby team who had 'The Rose Of Tralee' as our anthem," and that, unfortunately, was how the remarks started being thrown your way and the trouble flared up.

'I knew afterwards that it wasn't right and I wanted to make up for it. Every so often it would come into my head and I'd try ringing before eventually, over twenty years later, I am able to apologize for my actions.'

For my part I was able to explain the reasons behind having an anthem played, and afterwards we shook hands, finally closing the matter, before going our separate ways.

Would the anthem issue ever have arisen if I wasn't captain at the time? Definitely not at the 1987 event, but as captain I felt I had to address the issue. I'd like to think that even if I wasn't captain I'd still have brought it up. With the advent of professionalism, the outspokenness is gone. It's the players' job to just get on with what they're paid to do.

From the context of that time, fast forward twenty years to when Ireland played England on that never-to-be-forgotten day at Croke Park in 2007 and 'God Save The Queen' was played. We have seen a remarkable transformation take place for the better in this country. The Troubles in the North have thankfully been consigned to history and the relationship between Ireland and England has never been better. The way the Queen was received and respected on her historic visit here a few years ago offered further evidence of that.

Two hours before that landmark game in Croke Park, I was being asked in an interview for Sky Sports News if 'God Save The Queen' would be respected. Did I think there would be booing, or trouble even? I told the reporter, 'I guarantee you that "God Save The Queen" will be respected and "Amhrán na bhFiann" will also be sung with gusto' – which is exactly what transpired.

The cameras missed a piece of class that day when England's Martin Corry, a great player and a smashing bloke, applauded the Croke Park crowd in appreciation of the respect that had been shown to his country's anthem.

The GAA deserve massive credit for the role they played in making that special Croke Park day happen. Former president Sean Kelly deserves huge kudos for his role in opening up Croke Park, but it disappointed me massively that my own county, Cork, was one of the few boards against opening up GAA headquarters when Lansdowne Road was being redeveloped. At the time I got a phone call from Jimmy Barry Murphy, a legendary figure in Cork GAA, to say he was embarrassed about the stance taken by the Cork County Board. He wasn't the only one. Several of the great Cork hurlers and footballers of my generation shared Jimmy's views.

I've a special photograph from 1990 when Cork held the Sam Maguire and Liam McCarthy cups, Cork Constitution won the inaugural All Ireland League, and Cork City were just pipped to the League of Ireland. All of these national titles for one county. For a city and a county that is so broad in terms of the number of sports played and followed, yet to be one of the few counties not in favour – in the special circumstances that prevailed during the redevelopment of Lansdowne Road – of allowing soccer or rugby in Croke Park was, as I said, disappointing.

Thankfully, time has moved on in the Rebel County also. The fact that a fully redeveloped Páirc Uí Chaoimh could yet host a rugby World Cup match, should the IRFU be successful in the bidding process for the 2023 event, would mark a proud day for me and hopefully all like-minded sports followers in the county.

Some people might argue that in an era of professionalism, issues such as identity and where you come from that underpinned the anthem row at the 1987 World Cup are not a priority for professional players. I don't believe that for a second. When Munster beat Ospreys in the semi-final of the Guinness Pro12 in May 2015 to mark Paul O'Connell's last game in Thomond Park, what were the last things he said to the players before leaving the dressing room? He talked about doing it for their families, themselves, and where they come from. That is the element for me that makes the collective bigger than anything else. O'Connell has that; it's the passion, the pride he brings on board in coming from Young Munster, from Limerick. Those old-school values are part and parcel of O'Connell's DNA. Does it still have a place in the professional era? Of course it does. Why did Brian O'Driscoll give up the money and the chance to go to Biarritz or Toulouse when those offers were on the table for him? Because he wanted to win a Heineken Cup with the team he was born and raised with. Conor Murray and Peter O'Mahony talk about it in a Munster context. They have it too.

Even in professional sport it has to mean more to win something from where you come from. It can't just be all about the money. Money talks, of that there is no doubt. Every year it seems the last round of Super Rugby down under is full of players getting standing ovations before setting off for club-land in Europe.

If we lose that sense of identity in Ireland, right across the four provinces, then you can forget about it. Having come back from New Zealand in 1987, where rugby is all-consuming, I remember thinking to myself on the occasion of that special hurling day in Thurles that if rugby was Ireland's number one sport and we could play the All Blacks here in Semple Stadium, we'd beat the crap out of them every time.

11
Triumph and Tragedy

With our World Cup adventure over, Mick Doyle's time in charge was also finished. It was now Jimmy Davidson's turn. Jimmy was very forward-thinking, and had done a brilliant job with Ulster. He saw that the way forward for rugby in Ireland was through the provincial route decades before anyone else, and he was 100 per cent right.

He had the Ulster players believing in his methods, but it proved a harder sell at international level and he struggled to get the Munster and Leinster contingents to buy into his methods and approach. It was just totally different to anything we had experienced before, and with nothing like the same number and quality of training sessions available to him that he would have enjoyed with Ulster – they trained together more often than a club side – it proved challenging for Jimmy.

But that is not to say he was wrong. He was very much into

a more athletics-based training, and using a lot more weights, which very few of us had been into. There wasn't the gym culture then that you have now.

Around 1980 a new gym was opened up in Cork by Billy Cogan, brother of the 1973 All Ireland winner Frank. I remember spending a whole summer in there with my great friend and incoming UCC rugby captain Finbar Dennehy. It was fantastic and revolutionary but it was never sustained. I was a student at the time, but if somebody had grabbed a hold of me and said these are the ways you can go and develop, I'd have jumped at it. The problem was, nobody was driving those standards. As a young player I should have built from that base but none of the more experienced players at Munster or Irish level were doing it.

I was on the Irish team from 1981 onwards but there was no real individual analysis. Half the time at international squad sessions was spent on fitness training as opposed to team coordination and tactics. As a senior player you were seen as one of the best on the team, but nobody was actually pointing out your faults or telling you how you could improve, what you could do better. Professionalism has changed all that, of course. Look at Paul O'Connell. He was a better player, in certain aspects of his game, at thirty-five than he was at thirty because he learned, he listened, and he sought the influence of other people. It's a totally different mentality.

Back in the late eighties, Davidson was introducing ideas from other sports into training as well but it proved a bit too much, too quickly. Unfortunately we weren't quite ready to embrace it. Looking back on it now, I regret that I didn't do the type of things he was promoting, because he was ahead of his time. We were all in full-time employment, of course, but the modern GAA player has had to learn to cope with those demands these days. I look back now and wonder how much better I could have been for those last two or three years of my career if I had invested properly in them. But at that stage other things in life had begun to take over and become more important.

Family issues also need their share of attention, and at times you realize that rugby is not the be-all and end-all in life. The modern-day professional acknowledges that he has to be selfish to succeed, and for long periods of my amateur career it was no different. As amateurs we had to be selfish to succeed. I am sure the modern-day GAA stars know that feeling well. You put yourself first even when it isn't the right thing to do. Everything is geared towards being ready for the next big game. It doesn't always fit in with family.

Each coach has his own 'vision' or way of doing things; some are better than others, and some are focused on methodologies while others are centred on personality. Mick Doyle was the complete opposite to Jimmy Davidson. Davidson was equally innovative but perhaps didn't sell his concept with the same charisma and clarity that Doyler did. Under Jimmy – Ulster were playing more games than the other provinces, seven or eight a season. He had them together from August to October and was in a better position to exert his influence. With the Irish team it was still just the four matches in the Five Nations with a November Test thrown in if we were lucky, so it was very difficult to initiate major changes in style and approach.

It's like cramming for an exam. You get together as a team late on a Saturday night because you've played for your club, you train early on Sunday morning, and you're gone by lunchtime. You're always cramming. You never had the time to properly instil drastically new practices.

The 1988 Five Nations Championship started promisingly enough under Davidson with a 22-18 win over Scotland in Lansdowne Road but things went quickly downhill from there, with defeats to France and Wales, and ended with the shambolic 35-3 loss to England in Twickenham when it was 3-3 at half-time. Once again we were bottom of the table. The English defeat hurt particularly hard because of the way we just crumbled in the second half. Those forty minutes also gave birth to 'Swing Low, Sweet Chariot' being sung by English fans for the first time after Chris Oti scored three second-half tries – a legacy all who played in green that day could do without.

That hammering by England in Twickenham was my all-time low point as Ireland captain. Walking off the field that day wasn't easy, and it spelled the end for a few quality players. That famous back line of Bradley, Dean, Kiernan, Mullin, Ringland, Crossan and MacNeill that had played together for so long would never do so again.

There was to be no bounce-back the next year. Jimmy D was under pressure. After sticking with me in his first year, for the 1989 season he wanted someone who knew and accepted his methods better and handed the captaincy to fellow Ulster man Phillip Matthews. That campaign saw another three defeats and a solitary win, once again against Wales in Cardiff.

I was glad to put the Five Nations behind me that year and begin looking forward to the Lions tour to Australia. I knew my days of experiencing a full tour were coming to an end. I hadn't yet turned thirty but in reality I wasn't going to be around for the next one in 1993 and was very conscious that this would be my last chance at Lions glory.

Plus, there was great excitement because there hadn't been a tour in six years. Competition for second-row slots was fierce but I was delighted to make the cut along with Bob Norster, Wade Dooley and Paul Ackford. It was a unique situation as well because out of the thirty players picked, only Bob and I had any Lions touring experience as we were the only survivors from the original 1983 party.

Once again we assembled in London. Just before conducting the medicals, our team doctor Ben Gilfeather announced to all and sundry that Donal Lenihan would not require a medical on this occasion. I thought it was a nice touch but I submitted myself for one anyway. I wasn't going to make the same mistake twice. Nevertheless, I knew from that moment forward that this was going to be a good tour.

It was also going to be the first ever Lions tour solely focused on Australia, and in comparison to playing in New Zealand, when we got there in mid-May it was like we had arrived in heaven. The sun was shining and there was even a golf course beside our hotel.

The Burswood in Perth was a palatial setting, built in the shape of a pyramid, and the facilities were just exceptional. Things had taken a step up since my last memories of being with the Lions – three to a room in some horrible motels in the middle of nowhere in New Zealand. Things were also changing in terms of the rugby. Preparation and training and the beginnings of professionalism were emerging all around us.

The opening game of the tour was against Western Australia, a team packed with South Africans and New Zealanders who tore into us from the outset. We settled down, however, and won convincingly 44-0, but my only memory of the game was getting stamped on the back of the head and being stitched up afterwards. David Sole, the great Scottish loose-head, had to get his ear stitched back also. Ben Gilfeather made an innocent comment after the game wondering how many stitches we were going to accumulate over the course of the tour. There was a declaration made after that. We said there and then that if there were stitches to be doled out, we would be the ones doing it. There would be no more shit on this tour.

The Test series subsequently turned into a bruising battle, with the second Test in Ballymore particularly violent. We lost the first Test in Sydney 30-12, having won all six games in the build-up, and in typical Australian fashion – just as they would do in 2001 – when you start beating them, they find ways to attack you in the media, going for you here, there and everywhere. You're isolated on the other side of the world and they're building a propaganda machine against you.

At the start of that second Test there was a massive fight and the Australians went ballistic, but we won through 19-12 and finally turned things around. It was us against the world, and Ian McGeechan as coach along with our manager, Clive Rowlands, really brought us all together as a group. The third Test, a closely fought contest that finished 19-18 in our favour, was decided by a calamitous mistake by David Campese which Ieuan Evans was perfectly placed to pounce on and score the decisive try of the series.

Winning the series was brilliant, but I hadn't made the Test side. Dooley and Ackford were there on merit, though, and the advent of the six-foot-seven-plus second row was upon us. Myself and Bob Norster, a magnificent player, a great adversary for years and a good friend to this day, ended up together on the midweek team.

The fact that I captained that unbeaten side was of little consolation, even if 'Donal's Doughnuts' appeared to capture the imagination for years afterwards. Everyone on a Lions tour wants to play in the Test series and while you have to put on a brave face and get on with things – which that group did spectacularly well – the Test side is the place to be. It was the first time in my career that I didn't make a team I had set my sights on, and that's why I don't really get overly excited about this 'Donal's Doughnuts' thing. I do acknowledge, however, that every player on that tour party played a significant role in achieving the end goal – winning the Test series – and for that we can all be proud.

I also remember the significance of the midweek game against ACT, or the Brumbies as they have become since, in the wake of the first Test defeat. At one stage we were 25-11 down and it looked like the entire Lions tour was unravelling before our eyes. We won a penalty, but I decided not to go for goal. We were getting the upper hand in the scrum and so I took that option, which resulted a few phases later in a crucial score. For the rest of the game we upped the tempo significantly and ran out 41-25 winners. All of the players who weren't involved in that game instinctively made their way to the sideline and applauded us off the pitch at the final whistle. There was a real sense of togetherness after that match, a sense that this was the moment when the defeat in the opening Test was put to bed and everyone could set their sights on preparing for the all-important second Test. It was the moment that just solidified the whole group.

The midweek side won every game on that tour and the myth of 'Donal's Doughnuts' seemed to just grow. Roger Uttley, our forwards coach and a member of the all-conquering 1974 Lions pack, called me 'doughnut' one day in training for messing or something, and the name just stuck. We got T-shirts printed and made it a badge of honour to get one, only handing them out to players who lined out on the midweek team. After turning things around against ACT, that was the moment when everything got back on track. There was a massive unity in the squad that was cemented that day and people appreciated that there was a bigger picture at play; it wasn't just about being selfish and getting on the Test team.

Yes, we played our part, but a series win just doesn't mean quite as much if you're not on the field when the final Test match whistle blows. That said, that Lions squad was special. There was a real coming together over the ten weeks we were in Australia; we were as one. The fact that there were only four Irish players in the squad – three after Paul Dean was injured in the opening game in Perth and replaced immediately by Rob Andrew – meant that hooker Steve Smith, midfield star Brendan Mullin and I had no choice but to mix in with everyone else. There was certainly no Irish clique on that tour. We didn't have enough players on board for that to happen.

With the English you had a special mix. From the West Country came hard nuts such as Dooley and Mike Teague. Then you had Gareth Chilcott, a brilliant character from Bath. They were like the Munstermen of English rugby. On the flip side were players like Rory Underwood, a pilot in the RAF at the time and a really nice fellow.

On tour you got to share with different players all the time. Our captain, Finlay Calder, a true leader of men, insisted from the outset that a forward and a back would always have to room together. Normally it was forwards with forwards and backs with backs. Getting the chemistry right between thirty such diverse characters from four countries can be difficult, but that proved a masterstroke by Calder.

I shared with Rory in London before we left and over the

course of the tour also shared with Robert Jones, Gavin Hastings, Ieuan Evans, Jerry Guscott, Gary Armstrong and Craig Chalmers. It was a small thing but it brought us closer together as a team. You knew the forwards pretty well from Five Nations encounters over the years but rooming with the fancy dans in the backs proved enlightening.

After that successful Lions tour, the biggest talking point for Irish rugby for the rest of the year was New Zealand's visit to Dublin in November. Buck Shelford had taken over the captaincy of New Zealand after the '87 World Cup and one of his first decisions as a proud Maori was for all the players to learn how to do the traditional haka properly. The team had always performed some version of it but it was Shelford who brought it up a notch by having them learn the 'Ka Mate' and attach more significance to its history and tradition.

On their tour of Britain and Ireland that autumn this more aggressive version of the haka was performed, and almost used as an intimidatory factor. Before the tourists' game against Newport, when the Welsh players decided to retreat to their in-goal area and ignore the spectacle, Shelford crossed the halfway line and had his players perform the haka on the opposition's goal-line where the Newport players were standing, looking for a response to their challenge.

Two weeks later Munster faced the All Blacks in Musgrave Park. We had no desire to make a spectacle of ourselves like the Newport players had and made the decision to link arms on the halfway line, face the haka and accept New Zealand's challenge as enthusiastically as all our predecessors in red. It was a great way to approach the haka, and I know from talking to Shelford after the game that they appreciated what we did.

The following Saturday Willie Anderson, who had taken over the Irish captaincy from Phillip Matthews, decided that we would do the exact same thing that Munster had done seven days earlier. So for the second Saturday in a row, this time in Lansdowne Road, I stood arm in arm as New Zealand got into position to start their Maori war cry. As Nick Popplewell was making his debut that day, I decided to stand beside him and link his arm in support. I was halfway down the line to the left of Willie, who was standing right in the middle with seven men either side of him, when suddenly, and without any warning to the rest of us, he started advancing on the New Zealand players. Along with everyone else, I was looking across the line wondering, 'What the fuck is going on here?' That's why you started to see this 'V' forming, with Willie as the arrowhead, leading the charge. It ended up with him practically in Shelford's face as the Lansdowne Road crowd went ballistic in response. To this day I'm not sure whether Willie had planned to do what he did or whether it just happened spontaneously.

The players and crowd were riled up after that, but the IRB decided they had to clamp down on this type of thing happening again. A rule was introduced stipulating that New Zealand had to remain on their 10-metre line during the haka and the same went for the opposition.

Other teams down through the years have tried different ways to face up to it, with the French particularly innovative at the 2007 and 2011 World Cups. Still, it didn't make much difference to the final result that autumn day back in '89. We lost 23-6 and we've still to beat them after all this time.

Jimmy Davidson's third and final Five Nations season was a repeat of his first two, with three defeats and a single win against

Wales in our final game. Willie Anderson remained Jimmy's choice as captain going into that 1990 Championship.

I couldn't take part in the opening game against England having broken my nose badly in a club game the previous weekend, and so missed an international for the first time since making my debut against Australia almost nine years earlier – a run of forty-three consecutive Tests. Ireland lost that game in Twickenham, but I was back in situ for the next one against Scotland, which we also lost.

I was surprised when Jimmy D dropped Willie from the side for the final two games and reinstated me as captain for the France game in Paris. Having not always seen eye to eye over the course of his three-year reign, it was a big gesture for Jimmy to turn back to me to try and rescue what had become a desperate situation. Having lost in Paris again, we needed to win our final game of the Championship against Wales in Lansdowne Road in order to avoid the wooden spoon, which we did with a 14-8 victory.

It was Jimmy's last game in charge; he resigned when the IRFU offered him no support for a squad get-together in Belfast at the end of the season. Having assembled a squad of over thirty players in spite of the IRFU, he informed us of his decision to resign at the outset. It was an inglorious end to a challenging period. I felt sorry for Jimmy as he deserved better and regret the fact he didn't always get the support his efforts and vision warranted.

Within a few weeks the IRFU announced that Ciaran Fitzgerald would be taking over. Fitzy may have been short on coaching experience but he was a great motivator and man manager. He also recognized his limitations and had no issue in bringing in expertise to aid the cause. Chief amongst those appointments was Eddie O'Sullivan on the fitness side. Former Irish international scrum-half Johnny Moloney was also brought in as a backs coach, with Fitzy assuming responsibility for the forwards.

The thing with Fitzy was he had a great way of making you feel like you were a crucial part of the set-up – even someone like me who had been around for so long. He had a great way of dealing with people and brought to the squad that army background of discipline, structure and organization.

Mick Doyle was flamboyant. Jimmy Davidson was very astute technically but had some daft ideas that would never take on. Fitzy would have been less complicated, more specific. However, I think that even he would probably accept now that he got that appointment a bit too soon and needed more coaching experience. The game was changing and the southern hemisphere sides had really ratcheted things up.

Yet, given that I had always had a pretty close relationship with him, I was delighted with his appointment. Even more so when he rang me over the summer of 1990 and said he wanted to have a chat with me.

We arranged to meet at the Cashel Palace Hotel, where we sat down and talked for a couple of hours. It was just about giving my views on the previous few years and on how long I intended to play for. I was in my early thirties, a time when most were beginning to think about when it might all finish. But with another World Cup on the horizon the following year and with some of those games being held in Ireland, I told him, 'Yeah, that's my ambition.'

Then we spoke about the captaincy. As I had been re-appointed by Jimmy Davidson for the last two games of his tenure earlier in the year, effectively I was in the hot seat when Fitzy took over. After that meeting in Tipperary, he announced that I would captain Ireland for the 1991 season, which had never happened before in Irish rugby. Prior to that, given the vagaries of the selection system, it had always been on a game-by-game basis with no guarantees. Little did I think after his declaration of faith in me that my playing career would look like being over before his reign as coach even took off.

That summer will always resonate with Irish people due to the hype surrounding the Italia '90 World Cup adventure when Jack Charlton's Irish soccer team brought the whole country on a magical rollercoaster ride. Mary and I will never forget it either, but for entirely different reasons.

John, our third child, was born healthy but arrived twelve weeks premature, in the middle of the madness attaching to Italia '90. Having lost Sarah when she was only eight and a half months old, it was hard to believe that another cruel tragedy could be about to unfold.

Twenty-four hours after he was born, John was transferred from the Bon Secours hospital in Cork to St Finbarr's, only a few minutes' drive from our home in Douglas, for more specialized treatment.

When Packie Bonner made that historic save against Romania from Daniel Timofte's penalty, it meant absolutely nothing to me. The World Cup was just about the last thing on my mind. With Mary in one city hospital and John in another, things were chaotic. It was difficult to grasp the reality of the situation.

Late that evening on my way to see John, the Douglas road was full of Irish supporters making their way home from the city centre after a full night of celebration, still waving Irish flags, still singing and savouring the moment. The contrast in emotions was so stark.

Within hours John had taken his last breath and our worst fears had been realized – again. After a private ceremony held in the hospital, John was united with Sarah. Our hearts were broken.

Early that morning while waiting in the hospital I'd thumbed through the pages of the *Cork Examiner*. The irony of the headline blazoned across the sports page has stayed with me to this day: 'Oh, What a Wonderful World'. Christ, you must be joking.

Every time I see a replay of that penalty shootout, I get transported back to that horrible day. A great moment for the country but a horrific time for Mary and me. In a strange twist, Packie Bonner, the hero of the day, was signed up for a series of promotions by my employers at the time, Irish Permanent. We ran a massive poster campaign depicting Packie's brilliant diving save – 'Save with the Irish Permanent' – and those posters were like gold dust. I covered a number of promotional events with Packie in the months that followed. The genial Donegal man was a sponsor's dream and an engaging personality but I never had the heart to reveal my circumstances during his moment of glory.

I have always been conscious that sports people have a life away from their chosen profession and as a commentator and analyst have often wondered what issues in their private lives are unknown to us, impacting on their performances on the field. Sports people are no different to anyone else and are not spared the cruel realities of life, as I know all too well.

12
Watching from the Sidelines

Ciaran Fitzgerald's first game in charge was against Argentina in November 1990 as part of their tour of the UK and Ireland. In the run-up to the game, however, I knew there was something wrong with my neck and arm. I was getting these pins and needles running up and down it and I was noticing a loss of power. I was captain of the team and you never want to let the side down so I didn't say anything.

As captain you had a room to yourself in the hotel, and the night before that game against Argentina I slept in a collar. Nobody knew anything about it. The next day we were fortunate to win a very tight encounter 20-18 but I knew I wasn't right. Argentina were a strong physical side and we just about got past them, but the pain was still there.

It was also the inaugural season of the All Ireland League and there was a huge hype around it. As a club, Cork

Constitution had always been very competitive in everything they had done over their ninety-nine-year history and we set out that season to become the first ever winners. There was a great buzz, with crowds swelling to new heights for the Munster club derbies in particular, and I wasn't going to bow out of those games either.

Playing against Lansdowne in Dublin, I cricked my neck again. This time I knew there was something seriously wrong. I was losing all power on my left side and struggling even with press-ups. I was getting stiffness in it all the time. I had tried acupuncture and was getting loads of physio but it was time for further investigation. I immediately got an appointment for an MRI scan, which confirmed that a disc in my neck was shattered. In some respects I was relieved as I knew there was something seriously wrong and this was the confirmation.

I had reached this point in my career without sustaining any serious injury but this was different, this was career-threatening. There were various medical opinions as to whether or not I should go for an operation or if I could ever play again. Some felt rest might be the best solution while others pushed surgery as the disc was shattered. After meeting Dr Sean O'Leary in Beaumont Hospital in Dublin, I leaned towards surgery, but there was concern right up to the last second whether I should go ahead with it.

My meeting with Dr O'Leary was refreshing because he knew nothing about rugby and didn't know me or my background at all. I mentioned that I was a keen sportsman, and asked, 'What are the chances?'

He just said, 'Yes, we can fix this,' and then followed it up with, 'You should be able to play sport again. There's no problem.'

'I'm talking about international rugby, doctor,' I said.

'Yes, that shouldn't be a problem,' was his simple reply.

All of a sudden, what looked like the end had turned into a window of opportunity opening for me once again. It was all I needed to hear. On the flip side, I continued to be advised by others that once you get surgery on your neck in your early thirties there's a point when you should be saying 'Enough is enough'. But that was not what I wanted to hear and the stubborn side of me just took over.

I had the surgery, and the minute I woke up I could feel this massive release from the pain I had endured for months. But I was handed a serious rehab programme that meant I was going to be out of rugby for a good few months.

Because of the operation, for the first time since making my debut for Ireland I missed a Five Nations campaign. I had to watch on television as Ireland lost to France, England and Scotland. The only respite came in mid-February 1991 when Fitzy's men drew with Wales in Cardiff. However, that was the last thing on my mind. All I was focused on was doing this rehab programme, pumping the weights with an emphasis on building up my neck and getting the chance to play again. That was enough for me.

While I missed the last few games of Cork Con's successful All Ireland League campaign, I made it back ahead of schedule for two Munster Senior Cup games at the end of the season. The effort had been worth it, and making the 1991 World Cup squad now became a bit of an obsession.

By this stage the rugby World Cup had begun to capture the imagination of the public. As it was being played across France, Britain and Ireland, it was definitely much more in the public consciousness. It was a far bigger tournament than the one in

New Zealand and Australia and was also run much better. In just four years the increase in television coverage was noticeable and everything had gone up another level.

The disappointment of the first World Cup four years earlier became a driving force for me, plus I was on the verge of winning my fiftieth cap. As I said earlier, winning fifty caps in those days was the equivalent of winning one hundred today. Only a small select band of Irish players had reached that milestone, and I was within touching distance. You're talking about the Jackie Kyles, Mike Gibsons and Willie John McBrides of this world, so it was an elite Irish group.

The problem for me was that Mick Galwey and new cap Brian Rigney, whom I knew quite well from his days with Highfield and Shannon, had acquitted themselves reasonably well in the Five Nations despite the fact that Ireland failed to win a match. In addition, Neil Francis had recovered from injury and was certain to make the World Cup squad. In those first few tournaments you were only allowed twenty-six players, as opposed to the thirty-one-man squads of today, which meant there was room for only three second rows.

The fact that the World Cup didn't start until October offered me more time to make my case for inclusion, but the Irish squad was due to travel to Namibia in July to start preparing for the tournament. That was another significant change from four years earlier, the IRFU having accepted that the genie had been let out of the bottle and that World Cups were here to stay and had to be prepared for properly.

Understandably, with little or no game time for so long, I wasn't included in the squad for the Namibian tour, but Fitzy asked me to join a wider panel of forty-five players for fitness testing in the impressive new facilities in UL in Limerick. As newly appointed fitness adviser to the squad, Eddie O'Sullivan's influence was beginning to bear fruit. The screening was designed to build position-specific fitness programmes for players during the summer, building towards the World Cup. This was the first time the IRFU had done such a thing but they could see it was an absolute necessity if we were to compete properly in the tournament.

I did all the tests, all the assessments, and Ciaran Fitzgerald called me aside afterwards. 'We're astonished with your fitness results and your physical conditioning,' he said.

'Fitzy,' I replied, 'I have been out there breaking my bollocks for the last four months. I have trained really hard in an effort to get back into contention.'

I knew that after the trip to Namibia, Ireland had three warm-up games pencilled in for August. If I could make an impression in those, maybe I could still make it to the World Cup. I said to him, 'If you give me an undertaking that I will get one of those warm-up games, I will continue the programme that I'm on throughout the summer with a view to fighting for my place.'

'OK, fine,' he said. 'I know we've picked the squad to go to Namibia but we're having two squad sessions in Dublin. Would you be prepared to come up and train as an extra?'

'Absolutely, no problem,' I replied, jumping at the chance.

After that chat, a strange thing happened which really pissed me off and gave me even more motivation. The regulations surrounding the commercial agreements for squads prior to the World Cup were being relaxed, but because I had been out of the system since the end of 1990 and hadn't been selected for the Namibian tour, I had no involvement with that.

A players' meeting was called while we were in UL but it was restricted to the twenty-six selected to travel to Namibia. Des Fitzgerald was the one charged with telling me, 'Unfortunately, you can't come into this meeting.'

Here I was, the most experienced player in the squad – I had been on the team for ten years and been selected as captain by Ciaran Fitzgerald – and for the first time in my career I was left on the outside looking in. I remember thinking, as I watched the likes of Galwey and Rigney file into that meeting, 'Fuck this.' If I was looking for any more motivation to get back into the fold, that was the moment when I promised myself I would be playing in that tournament in October. I attended those sessions in Dublin and wished the lads all the best as we headed off in different directions that summer.

Then, for no reason, and completely out of the blue, one man's misfortune becomes another's opportunity. When it does, you just have to grab it with both hands. Ireland, with Franno and Rigney manning the second row, lost the first Test against Namibia 15-6. It was incredible. Nobody had expected that. It was a terrible result, but if I'm honest, I was thrilled.

The Tall Ships had come to Cork and I was up in Camden in Crosshaven with Mary and our son David, watching these majestic old vessels take over Cork Harbour. It was a beautiful day, a magnificent setting, and a million miles from the turmoil and recrimination that I knew would be going on out in Namibia.

After taking in all the sailing and soaking up the colour of a wonderful day, I got into the car to head home with my family. I put on the radio and there was an item on RTE's Saturday sports programme saying that the Irish management were frantically looking to contact Donal Lenihan due to an injury to Brian Rigney.

When I got home there had been a call from Ralph Murphy,

Munster's popular team secretary: 'Donal, they're looking for you to go to Namibia. They need to know if you are available to travel out straight away.'

Bear in mind, this was Saturday evening. I had work commitments and everything else, but I made a couple of phone calls and rang Ralph back to say, 'Yep, I can leave straight away.'

I'd been around long enough to know what the Ireland management were thinking. To have any chance of playing the following weekend in the second Test I would have to play in the tour game on Tuesday, so I had to get there by Monday at the latest.

13
Out of Africa

The Irish team were heading for some godforsaken place called Keetmanshoop, a town in the middle of the desert in southern Namibia. I was leaving Cork on the Sunday morning and had to make it there by the following day. In fairness to the IRFU, a hectic travel schedule was hastily put together for me, and they acquiesced when I pleaded, 'Listen, I've been on these long-haul flights before and the coach will want me to play on my arrival. I have to get a business class seat.' And so, for the first time, I sampled such luxury, courtesy of the IRFU.

I flew from Cork to London and on to Frankfurt. From there I had an immediate transfer to a flight to Johannesburg, where I jumped on to a connecting flight to the Namibian capital Windhoek. From there the real adventure started when I boarded a Cessna for a journey across the desert. As there were only the two seats in the plane, I was occupying the co-pilot seat, and I could barely fit into the thing. My knees were touching my jaw. Business class seemed like a long time ago.

If I hadn't been at the end of all that travel, I could have appreciated the magnificent vista that spread out for miles below me. As we flew in low over the desert, with all these animals scattering below us, it was like that great scene from the film *Out of Africa*. That's the only part of that exhausting journey I would love to revisit again some day. Next time I might appreciate it more.

At last we reached Keetmanshoop, and I stepped off the plane after an epic twenty-four-hour haul. Ken Reid, the team manager, was waiting for me on the landing strip and I stood for a photo, if for no other reason than to prove that I really did land in the African desert on a two-seater Cessna plane in order to play for Ireland.

The minute I arrived at the team hotel, Fitzy came looking for me.

'How are you feeling?'

'Great, fantastic,' I said.

'You should train today,' he said.

'No problem.'

'How do you feel about playing tomorrow?'

I had prepared for this; I knew he was going to ask that question. In my own head, I also knew that if I had any chance to make the World Cup I had to play in the game even if I was exhausted after the journey I had just undertaken. Besides, I hadn't flown to Africa on a moment's notice *not* to play.

'Absolutely,' I said. 'Not a problem.'

After training that evening, the team was announced and Mick Galwey and I were picked in the second row. I knew there was a place up for grabs for Saturday's Test. Neil Francis wasn't playing, which meant he was definitely going to start at the weekend.

Galwey had played throughout the Five Nations Championship but had been left out of the side for the opening Test against Namibia in favour of Franno. With Rigney now having sustained a serious knee injury, there was going to be a battle for the second-row slot.

The match was against some second-string Namibian Select XV and was scheduled for an evening kick-off on Tuesday. I was happy about that as it meant I could rest up for the afternoon. The heat was phenomenal out there so at least it would be a little bit cooler come kick-off.

Then we were told that the Irish management weren't happy with the quality of the floodlights, that they weren't up to match standards. They were going to bring the game forward to the afternoon, when temperatures were expected to be in the high twenties. I was thinking, 'Jesus, are you off your game?' It posed the ultimate nightmare scenario for me.

On the day of the game it was boiling in the dressing room, and back then you didn't warm up on the pitch. I said to Terry Kingston, our captain on the day, 'Look, Terry, forget about me in the warm-up.'

'What do you mean?'

'I need to do my own warm-up.'

I told him it was something to do with my neck surgery. In any case he had no issue with it. I proceeded to sit on the toilet bowl for twenty minutes, taking in fluids and trying to keep cool and not overheat. I had only played two games, both at club level, in seven months and here I was in the Namibian desert about to play under a blazing African sun. I knew that somehow I had to preserve myself if I was going to make it through the match and make an impression for Saturday. So while the rest of the team were pumping the air out of themselves and sweating profusely before they even went down to the field, I stayed in the toilet doing my own stretches, trying to conserve as much energy as I could. Thankfully we had some new lightweight jerseys, which helped the cause somewhat.

We won the game reasonably well, 35-4, and I somehow managed to put in a decent shift myself. It felt good to be back. After showering and changing we were in this little reception area for the traditional post-match drinks when the Furey Brothers' rendition of the 'Red Rose Café' started playing in the background. Here we were in the African desert – who in their right mind agreed to this itinerary in the first place? – and the 'Red Rose Café' was blasting out over the speakers. Things couldn't get any more surreal.

Fitzy spoke to me after the game, said he was very happy with my performance. Incredibly, I got picked for the Test match on Saturday. My ridiculous, madcap dash had been worth it in the end. After a season out and against all the odds, I had forced my way back into the side.

Despite the fact that we lost again to Namibia in that final game of the tour – they were actually a decent team, far better than the picture painted of them back home – I knew I was now in with a very good chance of playing in the World Cup.

Arriving back home, though, I just hit the wall. I went training the following Tuesday and could barely walk. I was just feeling absolutely exhausted, drained of all energy. It was pure adrenalin that had got me through that Namibian trip. I'd never taken sleeping tablets before but I took some on that trip to give myself every chance. Then, when I came home, I was totally drained and felt flat for about three weeks.

I had led a charmed life as a rugby player. I was picked in the second row for Ireland at just twenty-two, which was very unusual in those days. I played forty-three consecutive internationals – forty-six if you include games that caps would be awarded for today, against Fiji and Japan twice – and was never seriously injured. I captained every team I played for and apart from being ruled out of the game against England in 1990 due to that badly broken nose, which required surgery, I never missed an international from my debut in November 1981 to that game against Argentina in 1990. The period of time between that match and the Namibia experience was my first time on the outside, looking in. That was hard, and it forced me to re-evaluate everything.

You took knocks on tour all the time, and playing through injuries was par for the course. It was inevitable that by the time you reached thirty years of age bits and pieces were starting to fall off. We didn't have the extensive rehab – or even prehab – that players have now, and that can help to prolong your career.

I found that I was now reaching the stage where once I got injured, the wheels were falling off. I had problems with my knees, I had problems with my hips. I was running out of petrol, to the extent that I decided that if I made it to the end of the World Cup season, that was definitely going to be it for me.

Juggling work and rugby was always a balancing act as well, and after my neck surgery I was out of work for a while. But I was lucky as I worked in the banking sector and my employers were always very accommodating. In the amateur days you were reliant on having the support of your employers, and not everybody had that.

About a week after coming back from Namibia I was feeling so flat that I rang Eddie O'Sullivan and met up with him.

'I'm completely shattered, Eddie,' I told him in despair. 'After all the work I've done, I don't know how I can push it any further.'

He analysed what I had done over the last few months and told me, 'An Olympic sprinter would be battered after that.' So he tailored my programme for the next few weeks, and it worked perfectly. I was back on track again.

The World Cup was fast approaching. There was a bit of pressure building from the outside but Fitzy was very good at bringing people together. There was a very good atmosphere within that group of players despite the poor results in Namibia. The side was struggling, though, at half-back, with Aussie import Brian Smith having jumped ship at the end of the Five Nations Championship to play rugby league back in Australia. Nicky Barry and Vinnie Cunningham, who was far more at home in midfield, were both tried at out-half in the Namibian Tests but without any great success. That opened the door finally for Ralph Keyes, who with just one cap after multiple appearances on the Irish bench had been badly treated. He too worked his way into the squad and offered stability. In addition he was a very reliable place-kicker.

Ralph was never the world's greatest trainer, but Eddie O'Sullivan pressed all the right buttons with him and designed a training programme that worked spectacularly well. It also helped that Ralph was put with the front five forwards for the 200-metre shuttles. I took great solace from that, and we used to take it in turns to push him all the way and not let him win them all – no great boast I admit! But it was great to have him on board. He deserved his chance.

Fitzy also knew when to let the leash off and let fellas enjoy themselves. I remember the day we assembled for the tournament, he brought us off on a bus trip and you're thinking, 'Jesus, where are we going?' Typical army, of course, we were dropped in the middle of the Wicklow Mountains and ended up walking miles and miles through forests, streams and fields, up and down, up and down. The last thing I needed with my dodgy knee was a trek over mountains and valleys, wading through water. The knee was feeling it now, and it got worse going downhill. I thought to myself, 'I can't let him see that I'm limping.' After a few hours we finally got back to civilization and regrouped in a pub somewhere for grub, a good sing-song and a few pints.

Despite the recent results, Fitzy had assembled a very talented squad. We were looking forward to the World Cup and felt confident going into it. Having most of our games in Dublin was a real bonus, and you could feel the excitement building.

Our opening match was on 6 October against Zimbabwe in Lansdowne Road – no anthem issues with that – and we hammered them 55-11. We had a good pack on show and destroyed them up front. Nick Popplewell, a future Lion, was at loose-head prop. Steve Smith, a Lion with me in '89, and Dessie Fitzgerald completed the front row. Dessie was around a long time and I had a great relationship with him. We understood each other. Neil Francis was a very talented athlete and, in my opinion, played his best rugby in that '91 World Cup campaign. Phillip Matthews and I were on the same Irish Schools side and knew each other extremely well.

The lads I probably wouldn't have known as well had come through the season before when I was out injured. Brian Robinson was a bundle of energy at No. 8, while Gordon Hamilton was an out-and-out openside.

Rob Saunders was at scrum-half, and Ralph had won the

battle for the key number 10 shirt having been superb for Cork Con in the successful AIL campaign. He finally got his opportunity in this World Cup and made a big difference to the overall efficiency of the side.

You also had the likes of Dave Curtis, Brendan Mullin, Simon Geoghegan, Jim Staples, Keith Crossan, Kenny Murphy, Jack Clarke and Philip Danaher who offered Fitzy plenty of options across the three-quarters. Curtis, Geoghegan and Staples were all playing regularly for London Irish in a higher-quality league than ours. Mullin was a class act, while Crossan was a very underrated player and a great team-mate. He'd won his first cap when Trevor Ringland was injured for the '82 Triple Crown game against Scotland and was a very effective performer.

Fitzy had a great way of bringing teams together and we were spending so much more time with each other now we were bound to get better. We had a great base out in Finnstown House in Lucan, you had Eddie doing all our fitness work on-site, and we had a fancy new scrummage machine that we used every day. Typical of Eddie, he never missed an opportunity to learn. Throughout that entire period he immersed himself with the forwards during scrum and line-out practice. He used to position himself on top of the scrummage machine, listening to the likes of Dessie Fitzgerald, Stevie Smith and myself talking about the nuances of the scrum. He never wasted an opportunity to learn. Then he would sit down at night when you were having your grub and ask, 'What were ye doing there on the right?' He was a sponge for information. He was developing into a handy backs coach in his own right, too, and by the time he coached Ireland over a decade later he had also been a Development Officer with the IRFU, which meant that he had run coaching courses at all levels.

A teacher by profession, he was very good at delivering and putting presentations together, and coupled with the experience he had accumulated as a backs coach, a strength and conditioning coach and subsequently as a forwards coach in his first stint with the USA – no doubt putting to good use there the foundations he'd learned out in Finnstown House – he had all the ingredients to make a top-class head coach. Years later he told me those two months together in 1991 was like undertaking a Masters in set-piece play. It stood to him as head coach in later years.

Next up in the pool stage was Japan – another comfortable win, 32-16. I watched that one from the sideline with Galwey and Francis manning the second row. Three days later we had the decider for top spot in the group, against Scotland in Edinburgh. This was a bit of a winner-takes-all scenario, with the victor going on into the quarter-finals to face Western Samoa, who had pulled off a massive upset against Wales in Cardiff, while the loser was set to face one of the strong favourites, Australia. Déjà vu . . .

It was also going to be a special occasion for me as I was set to win my fiftieth cap – a notable achievement in Irish rugby terms. The Irish rugby writers made a special presentation to me afterwards, which was a nice touch.

Scotland had a very good side and, with the game being played in Murrayfield, were favourites. They fielded the nucleus of the team that won the Grand Slam the season before including nine players I had toured Australia with two years earlier: David Sole, John Jeffrey, Derek White, Finlay Calder, Gary Armstrong, Craig Chalmers, Scott Hastings, Peter Dods and Gavin Hastings. We lost a close contest 24-15, with the game turning on a key moment when Calder flattened Jim Staples with a high tackle. Somehow it went unpunished – a TMO would certainly recommend a minimum of a yellow card today. Staples played on but wasn't right and dropped a subsequent garryowen that resulted in the crucial try for Scotland.

We were hugely disappointed as we were in a strong position to win until that incident with Staples which changed the course of things. There was a definite feeling that we had jeopardized a real chance of getting to a World Cup semi-final. The flip-side was we had Australia in Dublin, and as the days passed after that defeat in Edinburgh, the mood began to lift.

We flew from Edinburgh directly into Farranfore airport, heading straight for the Parknasilla Hotel, outside Kenmare, for three days. Fitzy knew he had to do something different, to take a step back from it all and had planned this retreat well in advance.

We had two days of rest and recuperation and did very little training. I knew Pat Spillane of Kerry football fame well, so I rang him and one evening we got the bus to bring us down to his pub in Templenoe. We had a few pints and a sing-song there, with Spillane an interested spectator.

Those few days in Kerry worked a treat and moulded us into an even tighter group, even more resilient and close-knit. After that it was back to Finnstown House where an ongoing issue between the IRFU and players over image rights had been building and had now reached a sticky impasse.

With the IRFU keeping the players in the dark about participation and commercial agreements, as a group we were now threatening to pull out of the Australian quarter-final in just a few days' time.

14

Whose Signatures Are They?

Four years on from the first World Cup in New Zealand, our eyes had been opened to the increasing commercialization of the game and the opportunities that existed for the players. From the time of that meeting in UL in Limerick during the summer when I was excluded from the players' get-together, I had been aware of ongoing issues being raised in relation to commercial agreements and image rights between the players and the IRFU. I wasn't involved in the negotiations because that group had been put together at the start of the 1991 Five Nations Championship, when I wasn't in camp, and, quite rightly, the negotiating team were kept together. I was happy anyway to stay on the periphery and concentrate on working my way back into the squad. When it came to the nitty-gritty of the whole thing, Des Fitzgerald would have filled me in on the background as he, Phillip Matthews and Brendan Mullin were the player representatives dealing with the IRFU on our behalf.

There was much more commercial interest creeping into the game on the back of the World Cup. For the players – in Ireland and in all the other participating countries – there were ongoing discussions between the union officials as to what rights the players, as a collective, had.

What really created friction within the Irish camp, however, was when the players found out only a few days before the opening game of the World Cup that a participation agreement existed that had been signed on their behalf and sent on to the IRB by the IRFU, all without the players' knowledge. The players told the IRFU in no uncertain terms that if they wanted the team to continue in the tournament they had better be shown the agreement that they were supposed to have signed. Finally, and reluctantly, it was handed over for the players to look through.

'The critical issue was our image rights,' explained Des Fitzgerald when I interviewed him for this book. Des had attended the meetings with the IRFU on behalf of the players and could give a first-hand account from the players' perspective. 'Professionalism was going to happen – maybe not in our playing careers, but it was happening around us. New Zealand players, for example, had "rugby player" as their official occupation; it was well known that French players were semi-professional; and Welsh players needed bigger boots for the cash stuffed into them. It just wasn't a level playing field at the time.

'For us, as players, it was about establishing precedence for future generations and standing up for what we believed in. The days of two sessions a week playing for your country were gone, and with the advent of the World Cup you were seeing the gaps between the northern and southern hemisphere countries expand further. The demands on time and commitment were increasing for the players, as were the commercial opportunities, and the players wanted their fair share.

'What made it difficult in Irish rugby terms was that the traditional ethos of officialdom came from an amateur era, where it was about community spirit and giving your all for the union and your country. The development of the game into areas of image rights, commercial deals and contracts was a new departure for them that they found difficult to accept.'

An agreement with the IRFU over the use of the players' image rights wasn't reached until the eleventh hour, just before the Zimbabwe game, when amendments as requested by the players were accepted by the IRFU.

Strangely, this didn't seem to create the type of distraction that, looking back now, you'd expect it might. I think it was actually a unifying force for the group. I imagine some of the younger players were shitting themselves at the prospect of not playing, but there was a resilience there throughout. Ralph Keyes, who had been on the periphery of the Irish team for so long, did speak to me about it, though. His father Michael was a great rugby man, well known to me as a former president, coach and selector of Cork Con, and Ralph was saying to me, 'Jesus, can you imagine ringing my old man and telling him we're not playing in the World Cup?' Everybody stuck to the task at hand, however, and put it up to the IRFU.

It wasn't an ideal scenario, and I don't think Fitzy was too happy with it either. When he first took over as coach he had recommended a third party to the players who could help them with commercial deals. He appreciated that the game was changing and that the players needed someone with commercial nous to guide them through it.

But that wasn't to be the end of the matter. Days before our World Cup quarter-final against Australia it turned out there was another agreement that the IRFU hadn't made us aware of. In addition to the participation agreement, there was a commercial agreement that the players were also supposed to sign but the IRFU hadn't told us about this one either. When the players found out about it the IRFU again dragged their heels on the issue, even though there was nothing contentious in this second document and the IRFU had no reason to be hiding it from us. It showed up the pervading culture at the time whereby rugby officials were reluctant to cede any kind of influence or power to the players when it came to commercial matters.

There had been some talk of the possibility of the game going professional in the early nineties; in fact it first raised its head as far back as 1983 on my first Lions tour. I could never see it happening, though, unless it was under the auspices of the respective rugby unions. When a rival professional set-up appeared to be in the offing in '95 I was getting phone calls from Irish players who were being approached to sign up. 'What do you think?' they asked me. I was out of the game then but told them, 'Lads, I can't see how this will sustain itself if it doesn't have the backing of the various unions. Where are you going to play? What happens when you're gone out of the system? Ireland and England will continue to play international rugby without you. The quality mightn't be great for two years but they will sustain it, and you're out there on a limb. If you're going to do it, it has to be under the control of the IRB and the various unions.'

Back in 1991, as the heel-dragging continued over the second agreement, there were more threats from the squad just days before the biggest game of our lives. Had I been in Ciaran Fitzgerald's situation then I wouldn't have been too happy with how things were dragging on so close to our quarter-final, but to be fair, he let it run its course. He trusted the people who were involved, and I think deep down he accepted where the players were coming from. He saw it as a managerial issue, not one for the coach.

Had our threatened walk-out been leaked to the media there was a danger of 'Who do they think they are, looking for money?' Out in the public domain there were rumblings, but people didn't know the full extent of it until the World Cup was over. The IRFU were in no position to leak the details either as they were in a very exposed place.

The bottom line was we played the game and each of us got a cheque for £1,500 from the IRFU about four weeks after the tournament was over – the one and only time in my entire playing career that I got money for playing. We had won a key battle, and £1,500 wasn't too bad either in 1991.

On the pitch, preparing for our quarter-final, we knew we were facing one of the best teams in the world with David Campese, Michael Lynagh, John Eales, Tim Horan and Nick Farr-Jones on board. We knew we had our work cut out to compete with them. But at the same time, Australia never held any fear for Irish teams. I always fancied my chances against them. Every time we'd played them, apart from that '87 World Cup quarter-final in Sydney, there had never been much more than a score in it. The first time I played against them was with Munster and we beat them. My first cap for Ireland was against them and we lost by 4 points. No, I never had any inhibitions about playing Australia.

And we were going to be playing them now in Lansdowne Road – a different world to what we faced in the Concord Oval in 1987, in front of a packed house where the old stands would rock if we were able to give the supporters something to shout about.

One of Australia's key strengths was their line-out. John Eales was probably the leading second row in the world and Rod McCall, their other second row, was also a very good operator. When they announced their team, however, they picked Willie Ofahengaue, a very powerful ball carrier who was only about six foot one in his boots, alongside a groundhog in openside flanker Jeff Miller. We now carried a distinct line-out advantage in our back row and had to use it to nullify their strength.

I had an idea, so I went to Fitzy.

'I see a way that we can take on their line-out,' I told him.

We had two outstanding line-out forwards in Phillip Matthews and Brian Robinson in the back row. Neil Francis was playing really well, had surpassed me at that stage as our principal ball winner, and was going to pick up John Eales. On our throw, if Franno moved position, Eales was going to follow him while McCall had to pick me up.

I said to Fitzy, 'For a lot of our ball, put Franno on the tail of the line-out, or one from the back. Eales will follow him. I'll be at the front and McCall will definitely follow me. Now you've got a complete mismatch with Matthews and Robinson against Jeff Miller and Willie Ofahengaue, who's not a leaper.' Bear in mind that there was no lifting allowed back then.

In fairness to Fitzy, he saw merit in what I was proposing and we started to piece it together.

There are a couple of other things that stand out about that game. It was the first of two quarter-finals that day and had a one p.m. kick-off. As everybody expected us to be beaten, that meant that you were going to be heading straight home the next morning. The IRFU, in their wisdom, got us to move out of our hotel in Finnstown House on the morning of the game – so, just a few hours before the biggest game of our lives, when we should have been focusing on that, we were instead packing our bags to check out.

Then our coach journey from Lucan to Lansdowne Road ran into problems. We got stuck in traffic as nobody was used to such an early kick-off time for a rugby international. At one stage the bus driver had to go the wrong way down a one-way street because we were running completely behind time. It even got to the stage where we were putting on our strapping in the bus. We only arrived in Lansdowne Road about thirty minutes before the match, which had never happened before or since.

Before we knew it, we were on the pitch about to play in a World Cup quarter-final. The timing was all over the place. In some respects, the game was nearly on us before we knew it and there wasn't much time for nerves or anxiety to set in.

There was a bit of a punch-up right from the kick-off and that kind of settled things down. Then Nick Farr-Jones got hit and, for the second quarter-final in a row against Ireland, was taken off injured. Ironically he was replaced by Brian Smith that day in 1987, and had Smith not jumped ship for the money in rugby league, he could well have been playing for us in 1991. That said, I was far happier with Ralph Keyes on board.

The loss of Farr-Jones, their talisman and captain, upset Australia. We never allowed them to get into their rhythm. They were out of their comfort zone, and we were getting stuck in and were competing. They were never getting away from us and we were always in the game.

It was 6-6 at half-time, and deep into the second half we

were still within a score. When Gordon Hamilton got that famous breakaway try with five minutes to go, Lansdowne Road went ballistic. In all my years playing there, I had never witnessed anything like it. That's what made the place so special when it was full.

To this day I can still recall trotting back to the halfway line to receive the kick-off after Ralph had spectacularly converted Hamilton's try from the touchline, trying to calm fellas down, 'Lads, concentrate. We have to win the kick-off.'

We did that bit, but unfortunately Rob Saunders went for too much distance with his kick and missed touch. If he had only found touch, we'd have composed ourselves and competed in the line-out. At worst we would have created bad ball for them. They kicked back immediately and the ball was knocked on. The net result was an attacking scrum to Australia.

Problem was, we had a chink in our armour, in our defensive alignment, in that we were conceding space on the outside channel due to the winger standing deep to cover the kick. It meant that we were encouraging teams to attack that channel all the time. This had been a bone of contention with some of the back line throughout the tournament and was always being brought up in team discussions. Michael Lynagh picked up on this vulnerability in our defensive system too and had the balls to call it behind the Wallaby posts while Ralph was converting Gordon's try. Not only did he go on to score a try, he converted it, and the Aussies won 19-18.

It was sickening. We'd been within touching distance of a home semi-final against New Zealand. But we blew it. It was a collective failure in that we missed touch after scoring the try, knocked on subsequently, and our defensive organization, which had a question mark hanging over it, didn't come through in the end. The bottom line is we should have been competing in their half of the field in the closing stages.

I was never so gutted after losing a game. What made it worse was the fact that I knew my days at this level were coming to an end and we'd been within a whisker of making history. I'll never forget going into the dressing room afterwards to sheer and utter devastation.

In the old Lansdowne Road dressing rooms, the forwards were always on the left-hand side when you came in the door with the backs on the right. I sat in the same place for eleven years – told where to sit by Brendan Foley originally, when I started off all those years ago. That was the second row's corner. I remember coming in after that quarter-final, absolutely shattered, and sitting next to Des Fitzgerald. Rob Saunders was a bit too excited for my liking. All he wanted was an Australian jersey. I was about to let him have it. An Australian jersey was the last thing on my mind at that stage. Luckily Ciaran Fitzgerald spotted me. He could see exactly what was unfolding. He just grabbed me and said, 'Sit down.'

My anger wasn't so much geared at Saunders; but the younger fellas just didn't appreciate that we'd been within an inch of making history. Instead they were happy that we had pushed Australia all the way. This was the Irish mentality. Here we were, once again, gallant losers. But I knew this was different. We'd blown it.

Those last five minutes, we had them. We knew we should have won. Showered and changed, it was a sombre atmosphere as we headed back to the hotel for a meal with the Aussies. They were a bit shell-shocked themselves because they knew just how close they had come to being on the first plane home.

It had almost been a case of history repeating itself when they blew the semi-final of the 1987 World Cup on home soil against France with a sizeable proportion of the same players on board – Lynagh, Campese, Farr-Jones. Four years on they'd learned their lesson and held their composure.

With typical Aussie arrogance, a lot of the wives and girlfriends of the players had only arrived in Dublin that weekend, looking to follow them for the last two weeks of the tournament from the quarter-final onwards.

Tim Horan was at my table at the post-match dinner. He was one of their rising young stars, having only come on to the team a year or two previously, and we got chatting.

'It's amazing what goes through your head in the middle of a match,' he said to me. 'All I could think of when Hamilton got the try was that I'd put all my clothes into the hotel laundry on the morning of the match and they wouldn't be back in time. We'd all be going home the following morning and my laundry wouldn't be ready.'

He'd thought it was all over when Hamilton scored, but Lynagh of course had other ideas.

Have we moved on from gallant defeats and near-misses? Would modern-day Ireland under Joe Schmidt blow an opportunity like that? I'd like to think not. They too blew a similar opportunity against New Zealand in 2013 but have moved on since then.

We were within a whisker of beating Australia that day and would have been in a World Cup semi-final on home ground. Instead, a quarter of a century later Irish rugby is still waiting for that to happen.

15
End of the Line

I only played once more for Ireland after that defeat to Australia. The 1992 Five Nations Championship came around quickly enough after the World Cup and we were soon preparing for the opener at home to Wales on 18 January. We'd had a review of the World Cup campaign at Christmas and, again, the focus was on the vulnerability of our defensive system because of that gut-wrenching Lynagh try at the death.

There were a couple of changes to the side with Richard Wallace – the first of three brothers to make their mark with Ireland and the Lions – and Mick Fitzgibbon both winning their first caps, on the wing and in the back row respectively.

Fitzgibbon, a bone-crunching tackler from Shannon, provided the perfect symmetry with a link to my first cap over a decade earlier. Photographers are nothing if not predictable and love pairing the old with the new. Prior to my debut against Australia in 1981, I was asked to pose with my second-row partner Brendan Foley – youth and experience coming together; Shannon and UCC, great rivals at the time, united as one. That was Brendan's last cap for Ireland. Little did I know that history was about to repeat itself when I was asked to pose in similar fashion with Shannon's most recent recruit to the international stage.

The photographer wanted me to go down on my haunches but my knee was inflamed at the time after a week's training and I couldn't actually crouch down fully.

'No,' I said. 'I'm not squatting down.'

By that stage I had spent over fourteen years immersed in the great Munster club rivalry between UCC, Cork Constitution and Shannon. That photo with Brendan and the great journey I had travelled in the intervening years flashed through my mind.

'Jesus,' I thought. 'I've come full circle here.'

We lost narrowly to Wales, 15-16, and I was subsequently dropped for the one and only time in my career. I knew I was in trouble even before I got back to the team's new base at the Westbury Hotel in the city centre.

Stepping off the team coach at the top of Grafton Street, one of the selectors, Ulster's Harry McKibbin, said to me, 'You have been a fantastic servant to Irish rugby.' I turned to Ralph Keyes on our way towards the hotel and just said, 'I'm dropped already.'

After the previous year's exertions with my neck operation, getting myself fit again, getting called out to Namibia, forcing my way back into contention for the team, and then the World Cup itself, the effort had taken its toll, but I was keen to keep ticking over and to play for Munster in the inter-provincial championship immediately following the World Cup. The thing is, it was also Cork Constitution's centenary year and I was captain – a singular honour in a very special year for a special club. Many of the players who partook in the World Cup were allowed to pull out of the inter-pros. I wanted to play, but I'd missed a lot of game time with the club in such a big year and I committed to them instead.

Losing to Wales in the opening game seemed to let the air out of the tyres, and any positive benefits from a decent World Cup campaign quickly fizzled away. Ireland had England next up in Twickenham but I got the dreaded call from Ciaran Fitzgerald. He told me that I was being left out of the team and they were going with Mick Galwey in the second row.

I wasn't overly surprised. Was I annoyed? Yes, I was, but I never had an issue with Fitzy about it. I was having major issues with my knee and I knew my international career was coming to an end pretty soon. I had already made my mind up to call time at the end of the season and would have preferred to be able to call time on my international career at my own discretion. Unfortunately, that rarely happens.

Was I as effective as I had been? No question, I wasn't. I'd trained so much to get into that World Cup squad that the same level of hunger just wasn't there afterwards.

I think it was a case that the selectors couldn't make wholesale changes to the side that had run Australia so close only a few months earlier and it was easier to start with the older brigade. By the end of the season, practically the entire pack that had performed so well against the Aussies was gone, for one reason or another.

I had fought back against the odds after serious neck surgery to regain my place and felt I had no more to prove. That was the last piece of the jigsaw, and although I was annoyed and disappointed, I could take it coming from Fitzy. It also helped that it was Mick Galwey taking my place.

There was a certain symmetry here with me having experienced so many good times at the outset of my career alongside Moss Keane, a proud Kerry man. Now here I was handing over my jersey to another Kerry man. Moss had been a great help to me and I'd like to think that I had assisted Gaillimh along the way since he joined me in the Munster second row a few years earlier.

Ireland got hammered 38-9 in Twickenham after I was dropped which, if I'm honest, made things a little easier. The next game was at home to Scotland. That was the day the crowd turned on Ralph Keyes. He was kicking away a bit too much possession and the fans started booing him. It was the first time I ever saw a player getting booed in Lansdowne Road. There were a few so-called supporters around me jeering him also. I couldn't keep my cool any longer and just got stuck into this gobshite behind me.

I shouldn't have, of course, but it's hard to take when you've been in the trenches with your team-mates. When I think of the fall-out from the time Ian Keatley received a watered-down version of that when substituted against Leicester in the Champions Cup in Thomond Park in 2015, it makes you wonder.

I don't remember the IRFU issuing any diktats about RESPECT after the treatment directed towards Ralph that day on what turned out to be another poor defeat to Scotland. The final game of the campaign proved even worse – a 44-12 trouncing in Paris.

That same weekend I had been invited over to play in a golf tournament organized by Robert Paparemborde, the great French prop against whom I had soldiered in the early 1980s. The French brought together a collection of former players from all the five nations. I was reunited with my eighties team-mates Hugo MacNeill and Michael Kiernan representing

Ireland, but not in the fashion I had hoped for at the outset of the Championship. In fact I was the only one there who had played in that season's Five Nations. It finally cemented my status as an ex-international. From that moment on I was always referred to as a 'former' something – former international, former Irish captain, former Lion. Life as I had known it was about to change.

Defeat that day at the Parc des Princes meant that Ireland finished up with the wooden spoon, just five months after being on the brink of a World Cup semi-final. That also made it a bit easier to accept that my time was up on the international stage.

Little did I realize that my playing days at any level were also going to be brought to an abrupt end fairly quickly. Cork Con were struggling in the AIL having won the inaugural league the season before and were now battling against relegation. In March 1992 we had to beat St Mary's in Dublin to avoid that fate and introduced a young kid straight out of my old alma mater CBC into the back row for his senior debut. David Corkery had a blinder that day, underlining his potential as a future international.

But with about twenty minutes to go, I injured my neck again. I was treated on the field for a protracted period, and somehow my father made his way on to the pitch and was standing over me with a worried look on his face. I knew that was it. I had made a promise to Mary, who wasn't overly keen on my playing again after my initial neck surgery, that if I had any recurrence I would retire. I never played another competitive game. I was literally finished from all rugby within two months of being dropped from the international team.

Leading Cork Constitution in my final competitive outing seemed fitting, especially as we won. Despite all the changes that have served to dilute the importance of the club game in this country – a factor that has done nothing to help the

Munster cause in the professional game – Cork Constitution remain an outstanding rugby club and a model for the club game in this country.

Con created so many great memories for me down through the years. Great men like Tom Kiernan, Noel Murphy and Jerry Murray, to mention but a few, set the ground rules for what was expected of you when you donned the famous Con jersey, and I was happy to have contributed to that legacy.

I certainly didn't intend finishing my career in that way, however. In an ideal world I'd have finished my playing days with Ireland on that summer's tour to New Zealand, but that wasn't going to happen.

As part of Constitution's centenary celebrations, I ended up instead going on a far more relaxing and enjoyable tour to California, but never played a game. I decided that it just wasn't worth it. In the final match of that tour I was togged out and came within a whisker of coming on for one last twenty minutes of rugby. But it dawned on me that if I finished up that year on the field, I would only try to play the following year again at club level. It proved a good decision to stay on the sideline.

The frustrating thing was, I had experienced the opening two years of the All Ireland League and it was fantastic. It had provided a fresh buzz for me after thirteen years of club rugby with UCC and Cork Con when the Munster Cup was the only highlight. The AIL was something new and shiny. I felt disappointed that it hadn't been introduced earlier in my career as it had been mooted for some time, but grateful at the same time that I got to experience it at all, and even pocketed an AIL medal at the first time of asking. Con's first ever game in the AIL had been against St Mary's at Temple Hill the previous season. We'd got off to a winning start, and I'd even had the privilege of registering Con's first ever try in the AIL on the road to victory that day.

I would have loved to experience another year, just as an ordinary club player. For vast periods of my career, after playing a club match on a Saturday it was straight into a car for the long drive to Dublin for a national squad session the following day before getting back into the car for the long journey home. The Munster and Ulster contingents envied the Leinster lads, who were sitting at home on a Sunday afternoon, before we reached Newlands Cross. Stopping off in Morrissey's famous hostelry in Abbeyleix on the journey didn't exactly aid our cause either. You were always rushing off somewhere else after a club game, to attend Munster or Irish squad sessions, and the prospect of having a year or two at club level with nothing else to focus on, especially with the All Ireland League becoming even bigger than the inter-pros, would have been enough to sustain and energize me.

In the end, though, it just wasn't feasible. The body said no. My knees were shot, and with one disc removed from my neck already, it just wasn't worth it. That was it. My playing career was over. It was hard to accept, but then again, eighteen months earlier I'd been told I'd never play again, so having beaten the odds and made it back for a second World Cup was a bonus.

For me, playing for Ireland was always a privilege. Captaining my country on seventeen occasions was something I'd never have even considered growing up. I wasn't from a rugby background. I didn't grow up wanting to play for Ireland, never mind lead the side.

In my first season as an Irish international we won a Triple Crown and the Five Nations Championship. You just think, 'This is great,' and almost take it for granted, despite the fact that several of that side had soldiered for years without ever winning a Championship.

I remember after the final whistle in Namibia, my opposite number was looking to swap jerseys but I had to say no. 'Sorry, but I want this one.' It meant so much to me to play for Ireland again when my career was supposed to be over due to injury.

I brought that jersey home and gave it to my son David, who was four at the time. That was extra special, given that I had been on the brink of never playing again. David then made it to Lansdowne Road for the opening game of the World Cup against Zimbabwe. Bringing him into the dressing room after that match meant a lot to me. An eight-year-old Anthony Foley flashed into my mind as David sat there with his Irish flag in his hand.

The bottom line was, my time was up. I'd had a good innings. I had sampled the good times and the not so good – Triple Crowns and Five Nations Championship successes with a few wooden spoons thrown in for good measure. It would have been nice to finish the season on my own terms and never to have been dropped from the Ireland side, but that wasn't to be, and I have no regrets, apart from leaving a Grand Slam behind us in 1982 and losing that quarter-final to Australia in 1991.

Captaining my country was a singular honour, and leading the side to that 17-0 victory over England at Lansdowne Road in February 1987 was a special day for me – especially as the man who introduced me to the game and who played such a massive part in my formative years in Schools rugby, Brother Phil O'Reilly, was a special guest of the IRFU at the game and the post-match function. That seemed entirely fitting.

16

The Wild West

Once my playing days were over, I always knew I was going to get involved in the management or coaching side of the game. The All Ireland League was huge at the time and Cork Con was in my blood, so I was definitely going to be involved with the club. It was in my nature to have a say.

Within a year of retirement I had been invited by the IRFU to chair a group tasked with examining a wide range of issues affecting the club and international game. I wasn't afraid to express my opinion, but at the same time I enjoyed a good relationship with key figures in the IRFU such as Ronnie Dawson, Tom Kiernan, Syd Millar, Noel Murphy, Sir Ewart Bell and Billy Lavery, to name but a few of some of the very hard-working and dedicated people in Irish rugby.

It was happenstance in the end as to which direction I would take. Having coached Cork Con at U20 level for a year after retiring, I was coaching the senior forwards the following season when I was asked to become a Munster selector. Before long I was combining that role with the one of manager to the Ireland A side, which had a full programme of games running parallel to the Five Nations Championship. Ulster's Harry Williams was coach and I found him very organized and easy to work with. The role also put me in direct contact with the management of the full Irish side. That set me on a particular path.

You're often led down a road and it just happens without any specific process or pre-determined thinking. If I had my time again I'd probably be more interested in going down the coaching route, but that's all water under the bridge now. Coaching wasn't exactly a career option then and I couldn't see how the specialization in coaching was going to develop. I still had my own career in finance, which was going well, though in the back of my mind I had this drive to work for myself. I didn't really want to put myself into a scenario where I was dependent on what might happen as professional rugby developed.

When I started out, the role of the manager was key in that he was the reporting line to the IRFU. From their point of view, it was your head that was on the block, even more so than the coach's. I saw my role as manager as being to support the coach in every way possible. You were his back. You took all the pressure off when it needed to be taken off. You acted as a buffer between him and the machinations of the IRFU committee.

In my years in Irish rugby I got to learn what crisis management was all about. There were just so many different things going on during this difficult transitional period that it was all about taking the pressure off the coach. I actually quite enjoyed that type of thing.

When Warren Gatland came into the Ireland job in 1998, he

was a young coach and could be volatile at times so you had to smooth over issues, like the times when he wouldn't talk to the press. You were the buffer, responsible for ensuring that it remained a working relationship. It was about leading the dynamic of the team, and in my view it was a hugely important role. Then the IRFU sought to downgrade that role to one that was more administrative.

Before the 2007 World Cup, after a conversation with Eddie O'Sullivan in Cork, there was a suggestion that I might get back on board again, seven years after my first stint as Ireland manager had ended. Eddie was now the national coach and we spoke briefly about it, but the IRFU weren't keen. I had already been told by one member of the committee that there were a few figures in the IRFU who saw me as a threat and weren't exactly jumping up and down about the prospect of me resuming my old role.

I probably hadn't helped myself as in my previous regime I'd had a habit of doing things that I thought were best for the team and telling those in authority after the event. That didn't always go down well, and with the benefit of hindsight I can see that perhaps I was a bit impetuous at times. That said, in most instances I knew that if I had to go through the regular channels things would take too long, or might not get done at all.

In any case, I wasn't in favour of the way the manager's role had been downgraded, and I think I was proved right the way things unfolded at the 2007 World Cup. I could see the danger with Eddie, who had this all-encompassing role where he was doing everything. Ultimately he took on too much, in my view. There was nobody in his management team shouting 'stop', or questioning things the way they should be questioned. Eddie was an outstanding coach and at the time the IRFU wanted the manager in a purely logistical role, whereas I would say you needed somebody there to play devil's advocate. You need someone to say, 'Why are you doing this? And why are you doing that?' You need to get the other coaches to question things too. If you get to the stage where the assistant coaches don't challenge the head coach, you're in trouble. Unfortunately, I think it got to that stage in the run-up to the 2007 World Cup.

But I'm getting ahead of myself here.

When I was appointed manager of the Ireland A team for the 1993/94 season I had access to the senior Irish management system and was getting to see how it all worked from the 'inside'. Gerry Murphy was the coach, having succeeded Ciaran Fitzgerald, with Noel Murphy as the manager. I was invited in for meetings and we would discuss the make-up of the A team as we played matches on the Friday night before the full internationals, but the side itself, quite rightly, was picked by the senior selectors.

Following on from my two-year stint with the A side, which also corresponded with my time as a Munster selector, I was appointed a full Irish selector for the 1995/96 season, just when rugby was turned on its head and went professional.

But if you look at this whole period, things were a bit shambolic as everyone, including players and officials, was coming to terms with what the change to professionalism actually meant in practical terms.

Murray Kidd was appointed Irish coach, but after less than two years in charge, he was gone, a home defeat to Samoa in November 1996 the final straw. Brian Ashton came in from England and signed this glorified six-year contract, but he too was gone twelve months later, Warren Gatland then taking over. That made it three coaches in a tumultuous period from 1995 to 1998.

Irish rugby had been going through a traumatic time since that point in the 1980s when we won three Championships in the space of five years, losing a lot of games and being hammered on a regular basis. It wasn't a nice time to be involved with the team.

To give an example of how bad it got, in January 1995 Michael Bradley was captain of the side and doing an excellent job but had to step aside due to family circumstances. Ireland were playing England in the Five Nations and the captaincy was offered to Philip Danaher for that game, but he declined to take it.

I was involved with the A team at the time and had no input as to what was happening with the senior side. I was dismayed that someone of Danaher's calibre, who had captained the side with distinction in the past, would turn it down now.

Next they asked Nick Popplewell to step into the breach. He too declined, but did captain Ireland subsequently. Finally, almost by a process of elimination, Brendan Mullin took it on, for the one and only time.

I didn't think this prestigious appointment should be viewed this way, yet at that time, with Ireland on the receiving end more often than not, the captain bore the brunt of the abuse in the media. What should have been viewed as an honour was seen by the mid-nineties as an unwelcome chore.

You also had the fact that after Euro '88 and Italia '90, and through into USA '94 and beyond, the Republic of Ireland soccer side had won the hearts and minds of the Irish sporting public. Walking around the streets you saw Irish flags and bunting everywhere, and I remember thinking to myself, 'Rugby is starting to be swallowed up here.' I wondered if we would ever get to the stage in Ireland where we had this level of support for the rugby team. It was almost a perfect storm in that those successful Jack Charlton years came when the performance and results for the national rugby side were going steadily downhill.

Then the game turned professional and, as in soccer, the players were heading off to England to earn their corn. You had fellows who had run club rugby here for years seeing what they wrongly interpreted as their players – players from the likes of Cork Con, Garryowen, St Mary's and Lansdowne, to name but a few – leaving to go to clubs in England. These club guys were saying, 'Fuck them, we can do without them.' That was the type of environment the players found themselves in.

The amateur AIL was still the dominant force in the game at the time and I would say that even the key people within the IRFU never thought for one minute that the game would actually turn professional. But I was in South Africa for the 1995 World Cup and, speaking to players from the southern hemisphere countries, I knew there was something happening. The IRFU just didn't see it coming.

Around this time, the southern hemisphere unions had their own issues to deal with. They knew their players were coming under serious pressure to switch codes to lucrative contracts in Australian rugby league. They also had to contend with the fall-out from an impending battle for TV rights which would transform rugby union.

Because of the 1995 World Cup – South Africa, Mandela, the end of apartheid and all of that – rugby had captured the imaginations of people around the world. I sat in Ellis Park that day when South Africa won the tournament in extra time against New Zealand. It's hard to convey just how emotional that game, the entire occasion, was. People talk about Munster winning the Heineken Cup for the first time in Cardiff, but even that was nothing compared to what happened in Johannesburg on 24 June 1995. The place literally shook. I've never experienced anything like it before. This jumbo jet came flying over within touching distance of the stands and it was like an earthquake happening around us.

When Nelson Mandela came out to meet the teams, the effect he had on the people was incredible. Everyone was getting caught up in a wave of emotion because, after so much pain and so many false dawns through the years, you could see the signs of unification taking place. You just sensed that something different was happening. Rugby was on the world map after that and the profile of the sport was never higher.

The television moguls Kerry Packer and Rupert Murdoch had the vision. They understood the market and knew that if they controlled the television rights to games then they could control access to viewers, which would drive subscriptions. In comparison, rugby officials in Europe were used to sitting down every few years to negotiate with the BBC and RTE for comparatively small money for the product on offer – the Five Nations. They were thrilled because the money coming in from TV was more than sufficient to run the administration of the game and pay for the national team's hotels and training. Nobody was paying the players.

In the southern hemisphere a 'rebel' organization called World Rugby Corporation (WRC) had emerged as a real threat. It was formed in Australia by lawyer Geoff Levy and former Wallaby Ross Turnbull who wanted a worldwide professional rugby union competition that was going to be funded and broadcast by Packer. At the same time, Murdoch was negotiating with the Australian, New Zealand and South

African unions with a ten-year Aus$550 million deal on the table for what would become the Tri-Nations and Super Rugby competitions at international and club level respectively.

At one point WRC had a majority of the All Black and Wallaby players signed up to their competition. It was almost as if the players were selling their souls for a quick buck. Then again, they were only looking for commercial and market value for what they were worth in a short-term career. After you had leading All Blacks go on the Cavaliers tour to South Africa for money in 1986, which effectively ended their participation in the World Cup the following year, it was no surprise that their players in 1995 were willing to pursue the professional route with or without their union. They knew their true worth.

Ultimately the unions won out when the South African players blinked first and signed with their existing union, and soon the Australian and New Zealand players rowed in with them, ditching the WRC.

The northern hemisphere countries were all caught on the hop. Suddenly, overnight, the game went from being an amateur one to being a professional sport with contracts, wages and negotiations. As Paul Rees, the *Guardian*'s rugby writer, memorably described it, 'The end of amateurism was like the fall of communism in eastern Europe: one day it was there and the next it had gone.'

While SANZAR were immediately able to contract their leading players because of the Murdoch money, there was no such deal in Europe. Although Sky came into the UK market, costs for clubs were spiralling by 300 per cent plus and debts in their millions were mounting around the game.

I was just after coming into the senior Irish set-up as a national selector and we were being asked to rank players into three different categories – A for top of the pile, B and C – but there were no criteria for them. Then you had this ridiculous scenario where the provinces were given four full-time professional contracts each, but because the vast majority of players were still working, the squads were training at seven in the morning or at five in the evening. It made no sense whatsoever.

Within a year all the best players were off to England. The worst of it was when Ireland held squad sessions in the Aer Lingus social club out beside Dublin airport. The players would fly in, go through their paces, then rush to get back to their clubs in England.

It was becoming a complete waste of time with sessions always compromised and the management having little real control. Travelling home to play for Ireland was becoming a chore, and that was what worried me the most. Things were going downhill pretty rapidly. It was real finger-in-the-dyke stuff.

You even had the crazy situation where players based and contracted to English clubs were coming home to play for Munster and Leinster in the Heineken Cup. 'It was like the Wild West when the game went professional,' recalled Rob Andrew in an interview about the game in England at the time. 'No player had a contract and everyone was running around trying to sign us up. No one had a clue what we were worth. I was a chartered surveyor then working in London but within a few weeks I was on my way to Newcastle in what was a big leap into the unknown.'

There was poor control in England because the coaches weren't full time and the players were being left to their own devices, to do what they wanted. The Irish lads based with London Irish were having a ball. They did a bit of training but then might go out for a few pints two or three nights a week, and they really couldn't believe their luck. They were in London and being paid to play rugby. What a great time.

The game was struggling to adapt and change. The first thing to go was the archaic five-man Irish-selection committee, which was not before time. But how we actually found out about its demise was still reminiscent of the old way of doing things.

Brian Ashton was in charge and we were flying out of Dublin airport on the Thursday, playing Scotland in Edinburgh. Pat Whelan (Pa to his friends) was manager and chairman of selectors, Ashton was the coach, and Joey Miles, Frank Sowman and I were the other selectors. Joey, Frank and I were waiting in the departures lounge while, unknown to us, there was a press conference going on upstairs with Brian and Pa at the top table confirming, amongst other things, that the five-man selection committee was being disbanded after the 1997 Five Nations. Incredibly, nobody bothered to tell us, and there we were sitting around waiting to fly out with the team for the game. It was embarrassing.

I saw perfect logic in the rationale behind it and would actually have supported the decision, but we were raging at the fact that it was announced publicly before telling us. The first we got to hear about it was when someone on the IRFU committee came up to us and said, 'You're all shafted now anyway.'

'What do you mean?' we asked, and of course it was then that we found out that our involvement was about to come to an end. At least we were spared any part in what proved a shambolic tour to New Zealand that summer which saw an Ireland Development squad lose seven of their eight games.

After that debacle it was obvious that strains had emerged on the tour between Brian Ashton and Pat Whelan as manager. Ashton had come from a very professional club in Bath and now he found himself in the middle of an Irish rugby set-up that was in a state of flux. It was inevitable there was going to be conflict. It didn't matter who was there at the time.

The game in Ireland just wasn't ready for someone like Ashton. In fairness to the man, he was a visionary in that his modus operandi was geared towards a very expansive style, but unfortunately our skill levels were nowhere near good enough. We didn't have the players capable of playing that type of game.

Ashton was too much, too soon. The guy was a brilliant footballing coach. But to put him in charge of the structure of Irish rugby at that time was just the wrong fit. His head was in England. As the majority of our players were also based in England he actually suggested that we should train there. Our reaction to that was, 'Under no circumstances. We're an Irish team and that's where we will train.'

In the midst of all of this, there was ongoing conflict between the provinces, who were struggling for control with the domestic clubs. Ashton, though, had no time at all for the AIL and wouldn't even go to the games, no matter how many times Whelan suggested to him that he should.

Alongside Ashton, Connacht's interesting new young coach Warren Gatland and Leinster's Mike Ruddock had been brought in by Pa for specific hands-on work with the forwards. Ashton was a visionary backs coach, and he was brilliant at that, but I think when he saw where we were at in terms of quality and skill level, well, I'd say he was pretty deflated by it.

The stress of it all became too much for him in the end and he was gone after our opening Five Nations defeat to Scotland in February 1998.

17

Thrown in the Deep End

In the wake of Brian Ashton's resignation a storm of public criticism broke upon the IRFU, and Irish rugby was at its lowest ebb. But we weren't the only ones. Scotland and Wales, too, were struggling to cope in the early years of professionalism. A fortnight after Ireland's loss to the Scots at Lansdowne Road, Wales, which had given us that swashbuckling team of the 1970s that was revered right around the world, were put to the sword 60-26 by England – a record total in the history of the Five Nations up to then. The same day, Scotland conceded 51 points at home to France.

It was obvious that in the face of the bigger, more powerful French and English rugby nations who had the financial clout of the clubs to back them up, the smaller Celtic nations were struggling to play catch-up.

Small wonder, then, that the Irish players wanted to take

their chances with English clubs where the pay and benefits being offered were significantly better and where, professionally speaking at least, the chance to play at a higher level could be attained in the English Premiership. In a short space of time, Irish rugby had become like its soccer counterpart, with the best players playing abroad and with little connection to Ireland.

Crucially, we recognized that if we were ever to have anything of any substance for the long term in Ireland, we had to get the players back playing in their own country.

At the time, the players had three masters: the clubs, the provinces, and Ireland. You had guys who were semi-professional with their provinces but were also working along with college students who were willing to train at night. The provinces were playing irregularly, maybe eight or nine games altogether between the inter-pro series along with three or four matches in Europe. And then, outside that mix, you had a number who were playing in England.

When Warren Gatland was asked to step in, on a temporary basis, after Ashton had gone down with shingles before the game against France in Paris in early March 1998, he proved the perfect fit for where we were at. From his time playing with Galwegians and coaching Connacht, he had a fair handle on Irish rugby and was able to bring it back to basics, play to our strengths and get everybody on board again.

I remember earlier that season travelling to France to watch Connacht take on Agen in the quarter-final of the Challenge Cup. It was a real bear pit of an atmosphere with these high-wire fences around the ground to keep the fans out, but Connacht just took it in their stride, before losing out 40-27 in the end. I walked into the dressing room soon after the final whistle and ended up standing in a circle with their players and management as they sang a pumped-up rendition of 'Red Is The Rose'. 'These guys have something going for them,' I thought to myself. They were a team, and Gatland was the one who had brought it out of them.

Going into that Five Nations game against France there was a real fear that they could put a cricket score on us. But Gatland got the public to send all these messages of support to the team and they ended up plastered over the walls of our team room. The players were surrounded with best wishes and good luck charms and suddenly they went from being a group who'd been ridiculed and were feeling unloved to knowing that people did actually care and it wasn't all negative. It definitely hit a chord, and by the Friday we felt we had a chance.

We battled and battled, and in the end France sneaked it by a couple of points. I remember Victor Costello made a huge break down the field with a couple of minutes to go and tried to put a floated pass over one of the French players' heads into Richard Wallace, who would have scored if he'd gotten it, but the pass didn't stick.

We had lost a one-score game but we had shown belief in ourselves again, and Gatland contributed massively to that. I found him very easy to get on with. It helped that we shared a lot of views on how things should be run. Pat Whelan also brought in Philip Danaher to work with the backs, and communication within the management group was far better. I think the players sensed a more relaxed and less tense atmosphere.

We weren't a brilliant team but we were becoming competitive. We were aggressive and hard to play against. That was the starting point. Although we lost 21-30 at home to Wales in our next game, there was a feeling that we had something to work on.

We needed to put the Irish team back on top of the tree. Not below English clubs, and not below the provinces.

After the 1998 Five Nations, we were getting ready to go on a demanding tour to South Africa. In the run-up, there was an AIL semi-finals weekend in Limerick. Pat Whelan, Warren Gatland and I had a meeting at Pa's house in Limerick. It was about the itinerary, when and where we should assemble for a pre-tour camp, the type of training, that sort of thing. At that stage I was billed to travel as assistant manager to Pa and was delighted with that.

It was a very positive meeting, Warren came out of it really happy, and we all went to watch Garryowen play Blackrock at Dooradoyle. I drove back to Cork immediately after the game but was back up again the next day for the second semi-final between Shannon and St Mary's. I had a quick chat with Pa and Warren after that match then headed home once again.

The next morning, I got a phone call from Noel Murphy.

'I need to meet you,' he said.

He pulled up outside my office and we headed off in his car. Out of the blue, he said, 'We want you to manage the Ireland tour to South Africa.'

I was looking at him as if he had two heads.

'What do you mean?'

'Pat Whelan has decided to step down for business reasons.'

That just didn't sit with the meetings we'd had over the weekend. I knew there must be more to this. In any event, I told Noel I'd have to talk to my employers, because now, all of a sudden, this was a different agenda.

It helped that Irish Permanent were also the sponsors of the Irish rugby team at the time and in fairness they had been very helpful and supportive of my role within the management team up to this point.

I was about to pick up the phone to Pa to see what was going on and what had changed since our productive meetings over the weekend when my phone rang again. Philip Danaher's name popped up on my screen. He told me of some alleged incident between Pa and a journalist late on Sunday night, and the reason why I was being parachuted into the hot seat for the tour overnight started to make sense.

Warren was thirty-four. Danaher was the assistant coach and only a year older. I was the manager and still just thirty-eight. It was a big risk sending out such an inexperienced management team to the world champions on their home turf. We were finding it hard to compete against England; this was a different planet altogether. It was going to be a steep learning curve for all of us. We would be swimming in the deep end, starting from scratch, but it was a great opportunity because we had nothing to lose.

The one thing that myself and Warren felt from the outset was we had to get the players on board. We had to get the sense of enjoyment back for a start. The chances of us going to South Africa and winning a Test were slim to none, but we had to regain our identity. We had to get the players to a stage where they craved to be part of the set-up. We put things like tour committees in place, with fellows in charge of music, social activities, all that sort of thing. Every single player had a role on that tour.

Even the players who weren't involved in the matchday

squad, we would take them out the night before for a meal, and we'd have a few pints with them. These were the fellas who weren't playing in the Tests, but you could see they were still feeling a part of things. Now, I'm quite sure they headed off after we went back to the team hotel and did their own thing, but at least we had them under some control.

They were a great group. Young fellas like David Wallace got a taste for it, along with his two brothers Paul and Richie; we re-introduced Anthony Foley, who had been out of the scene for a while; Peter Clohessy, Victor Costello, Reggie Corrigan – all good guys. It was important to make them feel that they had an input.

There were a number of players in the squad I would have played with, and I suppose that made it easier for me to get the senior players like Paddy Johns, Mick Galwey and the Claw on board. We had an immediate rapport with the key personnel in the group.

The one thing I felt was vital, coming back into an Irish environment, was to make the players feel they were special. I often ran into trouble with the IRFU because I went away and would get the best gear, negotiating deals or sponsorship for leather coats, sunglasses, Raymond Weil watches, the best of everything. There must have been times when Philip Browne in the union said, 'Jesus, what's he after doing now?' But for me, the priority was the players.

As anticipated, South Africa proved a tough place to tour. It was a year after the Lions visited, when they won the series 2-1 against all the odds, but it was clear from the moment we arrived that we were being treated like second-class citizens. Everywhere we went there was always a bolt or a set of elastic bands missing from the scrummage machine. There was always something not quite right. I learned afterwards that it was the same for every team that went out there. New Zealand even had three of their own scrummage machines planted out there for their Super XV sides – you had to be self-sufficient. Ian McGeechan learned that from the New Zealand management in advance of the '97 Lions tour, but we didn't have the time or resources to be similarly independent.

Three years on from hosting that incredible World Cup tournament there was genuine change going on in South Africa – you could see it happening around you. We were coming up against a lot more black players in matches. The only place that hadn't seemed to change and where the crowd were obnoxious to us going into the stadium was in Bloemfontein.

Bloemfontein was a mad place. After Ireland's game against Japan there in the 1995 World Cup I was with a tour party that included my close friends Trevor Barry and Olann Kelleher, both survivors of that 'Rose Of Tralee' night in Mitchelstown eight years earlier. After the game Olann heard some music coming from a nearby bar. It turned out it was a sportsman's club and we decided to pop in for a look. Twelve of us went upstairs and the first thing you saw going into the club was the rack where the locals put their guns for safekeeping.

In we go, and a silence descends on the place. Everybody is staring at us. This big Afrikaner with trademark bushy beard comes up to me speaking Afrikaans – and put it this way, I don't think he was welcoming us with open arms. It was a dodgy place, so I said we'd have one drink and I dispatched Trevor to organize three taxis and get the hell out.

Trevor came back up from getting the taxis looking a little flustered. 'Jesus,' he said. 'The taxis are organized but I nearly got killed. There are fellas out there playing chicken in their cars, trying to blow you off the footpath.'

Welcome to Bloemfontein in 1995. Three years later it hadn't changed a lot.

Though the rest of South Africa was definitely improving, it was still a dangerous place. When we stayed in the Waterfront in Cape Town we had to explain to the lads that you couldn't walk 500 yards down the street, you'd have to get a taxi. You got a taxi everywhere. It just wasn't safe to go on foot.

We had a solid core of players in the group on which we could build, including the likes of Jeremy Davidson, Eric Miller and Paul Wallace who had been there with the Lions the year before. Injuries to key players always complicate things, however, and with hookers especially we were suffering. Keith Wood had decided to take a break at the end of the season and, by arrangement with Pa, wasn't going on the tour originally, but we approached him with a proposition telling him we needed him for the Test series. So he went off on a holiday to America, then came back out to South Africa and joined up with us two games into the tour.

I had great time for Woody. I admired the fact that when he damaged his shoulder badly in the 1995 World Cup and as a result would be out of the game for some time, it never dampened his ambition or belief in himself. He was a rare breed in Irish rugby at that stage because he backed himself, and, despite his injury, he signed for Harlequins. As a home-grown Irish player, he was ahead of his time in terms of foresight, attitude and professionalism.

His father Gordon was a Lion and a famous Ireland international but died suddenly when Woody was only ten. It's difficult to lose your father at such a young age and Woody didn't get sucked into the rugby culture. He was more involved with other sports. It wasn't until his latter years in school that he got back into it.

He always stood out for me as being a little different. Different to the rest, not just following the pack. He interested me as a person and character and I would always look out to see what he was up to.

Along with Woody, the other key guys based in the UK were Davidson with London Irish, Miller with Leicester and Wallace with Saracens. These were key players whose profile had shot up after that Lions tour. We needed to get them back playing at home if we were serious about progressing things in Ireland.

The money they were getting in England was better but we had a more attractive package to offer in some respects. Plus, some of the clubs in England were starting to lose their backers; there was no proper structure in place. Some clubs with Irish players on board, like Richmond and Bedford, were starting to go to the wall. There were loads of times when fellows wouldn't be paid. At least with the IRFU you knew there was a solid financial structure there. If you signed a contract with them, you were going to be paid. That became quite a selling point, and our discussions trying to get the players to consider coming back home would have started when we went on that South African tour.

Although we only won two of the seven games, I see that tour as a success in many ways. We won the first game against Boland Cavaliers 48-35, and despite being thrown in at the deep end, managing a tour of this magnitude without any previous experience (apart from my playing days), I thought things were going smoothly. I should have known better.

The second tour game was against South West Districts, a

game we should have won but lost 27-20. In the dressing room afterwards, Trevor Brennan approached me for a quiet word. This was his first time playing for Ireland at senior level and he acquitted himself superbly, winning the man of the match award.

'Can I have a word with you?'

'Yeah, no problem,' I said. 'What's wrong, Trev?'

'I'm after clocking some Afrikaner out on the pitch.'

'You what?'

We had all gone in after the final whistle while Trevor was being presented with his award. Some of the locals started abusing him, so Trevor being Trevor, he hit one of them a dig.

'I'm terribly sorry,' he said.

'Where did it happen?' I asked him.

'Ah, it wasn't too bad. It was in behind the stand.'

Great!

A sizeable representation of the Irish media were also at the game so I said to Warren, 'Brace yourself, we could be asked questions. There was some incident and I haven't really looked into it yet.' This was just a few minutes before we were to go into the press conference.

We sat down in front of the media and I'm waiting and waiting. But no question about Trevor came up – at least none relating to the incident he had just informed me about – and we heard no more about it.

Two months later, though, Leinster went on a pre-season tour in England and their game was abandoned. Trevor was involved in some other incident and the *Sunday Times* rugby writer Peter O'Reilly rang me saying, 'Trevor's been involved in an incident – was there something in South Africa over the summer as well?'

'Peter,' I said, 'you were in South Africa, do you recall anything happening?'

'No, nothing,' he replied, and that was the end of that. I blew Trevor out of it in private after the game, but I think he respected the fact that somebody stood up for him, even if it should never have happened.

The next game was against Western Province – basically the Western Stormers in Super 15 rugby in everything but name. Newlands was packed that day, and though we lost 12-6, we had a try disallowed after Warren introduced his famous thirteen-man line-out. It was the first time it had been tried on tour but Jonathan Kaplan was a young referee and he disallowed the try, in controversial circumstances. We were raging afterwards because the decision had cost us dearly.

The day before the first Test against South Africa in Bloemfontein I was sitting in the foyer of the hotel when this man came up to me and introduced himself. He had just arrived in off a plane from London. It was the father of Justin Fitzpatrick, who was making his Test debut the next day, along with Justin Bishop.

'Hello,' I said. 'He's playing great stuff and he deserves it.'

'I just had to be here,' he explained. 'I can't believe that himself and Justin Bishop are getting their first caps together on the same day.'

'Great day for London Irish,' I agreed.

'No, no,' he said, 'you don't understand. I just had to be here. I drove the two of them to London Irish U12s when they started playing together on the same day. I brought them to their first ever training session, and now, to have the two of them getting their first caps on the same day, it's an incredible moment.'

Later in the evening another group of Irish supporters

arrived and these eight mad fellas came over to me. They were all from Barnhall and had come over to support Trevor Brennan who had been selected on the bench for the first time and was therefore in with a chance of winning his first cap.

These were such proud moments for the players, their families and friends. We were a long way from home yet here they were supporting them and the team.

The following day we arrived at the stadium an hour and fifteen minutes before kick-off, and as we were pulling up in the team bus we found the gate was locked and we couldn't get into the stadium. Marooned temporarily outside the entrance, all of these South African supporters started coming up and beating their flags off our bus. I said, 'Fuck this,' got out of the bus, went up to the gate and spoke to one of the security fellas.

'What's the story?' I said. 'We're the Irish team – open the gate.'

'Oh,' he said. 'Sorry, we all saw the South African team arrive and we wanted to go and watch them.'

'Well, there'll be no game if we don't get in,' I reminded him rather forcibly.

There were apologies from the South African rugby union about it afterwards, but again it was a sign of how we were being treated. We were just the sideshow to the match.

In the game itself, South Africa were overwhelming favourites. We started quite well, put it up to them physically, but were overwhelmed by their power and lost 37-13. They thought we targeted Gary Teichmann, their captain, for special treatment, which wasn't the case, while Woody appeared to be a certain target for them.

South Africa played well but we showed a huge amount of

resistance. Given where we were coming from and given where South Africa was, we were competitive for long periods of the game but just couldn't sustain it.

We won the last midweek game of the tour in demanding circumstances. It was a boiling hot day and we were playing a North West District side called the Leopards. The surface of the pitch was so hard it was grey. I don't know what temperature it was but we had these big sack jerseys, and when a young and inexperienced John Hayes was substituted in the final quarter, he lay down next to me on the sideline and his jersey was just soaked in sweat. I actually thought he was going to have a heart attack.

John was only four months playing professional rugby and was still learning his trade as a prop, having converted from the second row. Years later, when he became the first Irish player in history to win a hundred caps, I said to him, 'Hayes, on the day I saw you lying on that pitch, on the verge of a heart attack, if somebody told me you'd get one hundred caps . . .'

He was a massive man, naturally strong. What I liked about him was, when he did come under pressure in the scrum in the early part of his Munster and Ireland career, he'd find a way of coping with it. And don't forget, contrary to most props nowadays, Hayes nearly always played the full eighty minutes at Test level as well.

The second Test at Loftus Versfeld in Pretoria was one of the dirtiest games I ever saw. South Africa have this bully mentality, especially at home, and though there were a few incidents in the first Test, the second game just got dirtier and dirtier.

In the first ten minutes Malcolm O'Kelly got a kick in the back from Joost van der Westhuizen, the scrum-half, but the touch judge did nothing about it. It kind of developed from there. Our fellas weren't saints either, and there were all kinds of incidents going on. By half-time there was blood everywhere, with fellas being stitched up to get them through the second half. Then we brought Peter Clohessy and Trevor Brennan on with twenty minutes to go. Let's just say they weren't peace envoys.

In adversity, that game brought the group even tighter together, but it incensed me at the time. In the dressing room afterwards somebody from SARFU came in and said, 'Look, South Africa won't be citing anybody, so I presume you'll do the same?'

'Why are you presuming that?' I said. 'We have twenty-four hours to decide if we want to cite anyone and if it takes twenty-three hours and fifty-nine minutes, we'll take it and decide what we're going to do.'

Then I got a message from the South African management that Alan Solomons, a future coach of Ulster, wanted to see me.

'Look, Donal,' he said, 'I know both teams didn't cover themselves in glory, but we're not going to cite anyone if you won't.'

'That's not the way it works,' I told him. 'We had a fella kicked in the back.'

'Well, we had this and that,' he replied.

'Look,' I said, 'we're playing Georgia in our next game, we're willing to take our chances. I'm telling you that we're taking twenty-four hours to review the video.' I knew they had the Tri Nations coming down the track and I wanted them to sweat it out.

Importantly, the players were aware that all of this was going on; they knew we weren't just going to roll over. Nowadays citings are carried out by independent commissioners which avoids the potential for those tit-for-tat allegations that used to happen.

The last straw that day, however, was when we changed and

dressed for the post-match reception and they served up sausages and boiled eggs for us. It was insulting. Woody just pulled everyone in around him and started to sing.

> When Friday comes around we're only into
>   fighting.
> My ma would like a letter home but I'm too
>   tired for writing.

One by one, the players and staff joined him:

> It's a long, long way from Clare to here,
> It's a long, long way from Clare to here;
> It's a long, long way,
> It gets further by the day,
> It's a long, long way from Clare to here.

We went back to our hotel and got the players some proper grub. At around midnight I agreed with the South Africans that neither side would cite and that was the end of it. At least it was my decision and we were not being railroaded into making it under pressure from them.

'Don't forget, lads,' I told our players. 'This crowd are coming to Dublin in November. Remember how you felt in that dressing room after the game.'

In my first ever tour report to the IRFU I wrote, 'Given the way we were treated, under no circumstances should we be hosting a lavish banquet for these guys in the Berkeley Court.' But, of course, the IRFU were having none of it and said, 'There's no way that South Africa aren't going to be hosted properly.'

What kind of message did that send to the players? We got

treated like second-class citizens and we were going to give them the silver tea service.

Although I never played against South Africa because of the apartheid ban, I wasn't really surprised by their attitude or approach. I played against Transvaal and Western Province on that tour to mark the opening of Ellis Park in 1982 and had been there for the World Cup in 1995, so I knew just how much rugby meant to them.

To finish the tour on a defeat of that magnitude, 33-0, was very disappointing, but Wales played against them the following week, also in Loftus Versfeld in Pretoria, and South Africa put 96 points on them. That helped put things in perspective, but we all had serious catching up to do. There was a real sense of 'This is the new era, and this is the level we need to aspire to in order to survive in professional rugby'.

18
A New Generation

When we came home after the South African tour, Warren and I were appointed as coach and manager respectively for a two-year period. We had served our apprenticeship and satisfied the IRFU that we had something to offer as a team. That time frame incorporated a Five Nations Championship, another summer tour, this time to Australia, the 1999 World Cup and a first ever Six Nations Championship in 2000. We were going to be busy.

Although we started off the 1999 Five Nations with a home defeat to France, we lost by the smallest of margins – a single point, in heartbreaking circumstances. David Humphreys had a kick to win it in the last minute but missed narrowly. As Ireland hadn't beaten France since 1983, I hadn't felt as disappointed after a game since that World Cup quarter-final defeat to Australia in '91. It was another sign, though, that we were heading in the right direction.

On 20 February we beat Wales 29-23 in Wembley. The WRU were redeveloping the Millennium Stadium for the World Cup at the time, and the players got a great kick out of playing and winning in such an iconic arena. Having watched so many FA Cup finals on television as a kid growing up, I really enjoyed the experience myself, even if I couldn't get over how dilapidated the stadium was. I can still see Justin Bishop announcing his arrival in the dressing room when hanging up his gear – 'Bobby Moore, George Best, Pelé, Maradona, and now The Bish!' The room exploded, which helped ease the tension of the moment.

We finished the campaign with two more disappointing defeats, to England and Scotland, but we were never going to light up the tournament that year. We had our eyes on the longer term, on the World Cup in October as well as that tour to Australia in June.

At least on this occasion, unlike South Africa twelve months earlier, I had sufficient time for the planning of the tour. I wanted to get things right, from the quality of gear we were wearing to the itinerary and accommodation. We flew out in May, and for the first week of the trip we stayed in an idyllic setting in a beautiful seaside town called Terrigal, an hour outside Sydney. The pitches were fantastic, we had a great hotel, and there was a beach there so the lads could go and do their post-training cool-downs in the sea.

Many of the squad had been with us in South Africa the year before, but of course the biggest thing to emerge from that tour was the international debut of Brian O'Driscoll. He was only twenty at the time but people were already beginning to notice him. He was certainly on our radar having sat on the bench against Italy at the end of the previous season.

Earlier in the year we'd invited Brian and Gordon D'Arcy to a squad session in Galway. Gordon got a run on the wing with Drico in the centre due to injuries. It was lashing rain but Conor O'Shea approached me after the session and said, 'Who's the number thirteen?' Because a lot of the players were based in England, they had no idea who some of the younger players coming through were.

Gatland was a great man to take a punt on a youngster. And with O'Driscoll, from day one you could see he had something special. We followed our instinct and picked him for the first Test against Australia in Brisbane. The Wallabies had a much more experienced side and were fine-tuning the team that would go on to win the World Cup later in the year.

We went for a walk in the afternoon in the Botanical Gardens, across the road from our hotel, to get a bit of fresh air and let the forwards walk through their line-out permutations. It was just a few hours before the evening kick-off and I remember watching O'Driscoll. He was like one of those kids who stops to have a look at what's going on and just takes it all in. He was juggling the ball, all smiles, without a care in the world.

That night Australia were fantastic; we were poor and got hammered 46-10. Warren had thought we were further down the road than we actually were, and the travelling press had a bit of a pop at him afterwards. He had a hissy fit and wouldn't talk to the Irish media for the week, which meant I was the buffer for that.

In the game, though, Drico did enough for Tim Horan to take note. I played against Horan on the 1989 Lions tour and in the 1991 World Cup and he came up afterwards to say he was really impressed with the guy opposite him. 'He has something,' he said to me.

We transferred to Perth for the second Test a week later, and I'd say Australia were very confident, overconfident perhaps. We played our best rugby in years and lost by just 6 points after Malcolm O'Kelly gave away a penalty at a vital stage late in the game. All things considered, it was a positive end to the tour, running Australia so close. Plus we had unearthed a very promising young talent, and by this stage the players were also far more integrated and settled.

The World Cup was next on the horizon.

The biggest issue we had was that the breed of promising young players like John Hayes and Ronan O'Gara were making real progress, but not quickly enough. When you're playing a World Cup in the autumn, your selections are based primarily on what happened in the latter half of the previous season, with the tour used to see if there are any bolters, like Drico. There were a few beginning to make an impact, especially in Munster; however, the dilemma, as always, is when do you bring them through? Joe Schmidt is experiencing that with Garry Ringrose now. We debated it at length and felt they just weren't ready. You couldn't just throw them in cold into a World Cup.

In August we beat Argentina in a warm-up match and were going well. Our first game in the tournament itself was a straightforward 53-8 win over the United States in Lansdowne Road. Australia were next up, however, and they were flying. The Wallabies were the first team in the professional era to look at the game from a defensive point of view, bringing in a specialist rugby league coach to look after that aspect, and in the game against us they beat us up really. We lost 23-3.

There was an incident in the game when Trevor Brennan was seized around the arms, and though he wasn't an innocent party by any means, it was off the ball and he couldn't defend himself against the blows of Toutai Kefu. Trevor had to come off soon afterwards and that was a setback.

We beat Romania 44-14 in the last pool game and therefore progressed from the pool stage into a quarter-final play-off – the one and only time the tournament hosted such a format – against Argentina five days later in Lens. We had beaten them only two months earlier, and in the late nineties they weren't on the radar to the degree they would be years later, but we couldn't afford to be complacent against anyone.

One of the biggest regrets I had in the run-up to that game was the fact that the hotel we were booked into was crap. The organizers had designated only two hotels in the city in advance, and the Argentinian one was every bit as bad as ours. I wasn't doing the job as manager on a full-time basis and I bitterly regretted not inspecting it in advance of the tournament, though I'm not sure if I could have forced the organizers to change it. That said, had I seen it in advance I would certainly have applied pressure to do so. The food was shite, the place was shite, everything was just wrong. We didn't have our reconnaissance done.

We had a terrible training session the day before the game, too. It was a bit shambolic and I had a bad feeling about things. We also lost Peter Clohessy and Jeremy Davidson, two key forwards, to injury before the match which didn't help either.

As the game progressed, it was like your worst nightmare unfolding slowly in front of your eyes. It was the perfect storm. A couple of things went against us on the day: David Humphreys missed a few kicks and we had try-scoring opportunities that we didn't take. And of course that failed thirteen-man line-out at the end became the stick to beat us with afterwards.

Nobody gave Argentina the credit they deserved either. They were a bloody good team, with a number of that side going on to finish third in the World Cup in 2007. In many ways the Argentinians are very like the Irish. They're a passionate group, and in the professional era, among the top teams, they are the ones who have retained the best attributes of the amateur ethos. They just love playing for their country and bring everything to the cause. They sensed an opportunity that night in Lens and, to their credit, they seized the moment. Fair play to them. We lost our way and lost the game, 28-24.

The scene in the dressing room afterwards was one of utter devastation. The silence was eerie. There was nothing worth saying, so nothing was said. I remember going to the post-match reception after a difficult and challenging press conference. The media wanted blood. They weren't the only ones.

If you were looking for any words of comfort or consolation from the IRFU committee after the match then you were in the wrong place. If you wanted a feeling of utter isolation, like lepers in a colony, you had it there. They were looking at you as if to say, 'Fuck ye, what have ye done?'

Although it was soul-destroying at the time, I think history has shown it was probably the best thing that happened to Irish rugby. If we'd won that play-off we would've gone on to play France in Dublin in the quarter-final. If we'd lost to France, well, that would've been OK because the quarter-final box had been ticked – move on to the next World Cup. If we'd beaten France, which we managed to achieve only a few months later, then that semi-final glass ceiling would have been smashed and all would have been perfect in Irish rugby.

The fall-out from the defeat was just huge, especially in the press. After arriving home I was offered respite in a summer house in West Cork, courtesy of Charlie McCarthy from Skibbereen, just for two days to get away from it all. Walking into a pub or going out for a sandwich, the whole place would fall silent as you came in. 'Am I after slaughtering someone's kids here?' you'd be thinking to yourself.

Despite the green shoots beginning to emerge in the provinces, the profile of Irish rugby had taken a major hit. This was seen as the blackest day in Irish rugby, which is saying something, considering there'd been plenty of pretty black days to that point.

When we came together as a squad a few weeks after the end of the tournament, Gatty and I said to the players that all bets were off and everybody was starting with a blank sheet going into the new Six Nations. We knew there was some good young talent coming through. With the benefit of hindsight, should we have given youth its fling at the World Cup? But then, who knows what kind of a setback it would have been for them if they had played in Lens that night.

Within the management team we knew we had made progress, but they were still only the first steps on the ladder and that World Cup defeat to Argentina was a serious setback. We had come from a place where things, in my view, were pretty shambolic on a number of fronts. From a place of conflict, conflict, conflict, at least things were now starting to be ironed out.

The fact that twenty-three of the thirty-man squad were now based in Ireland represented a major turnaround from where we had been less than two years ago. We'd even pulled a major coup by getting Woody to come back and sign for Munster in the year leading up to the World Cup. We needed to get the majority of the rest back permanently, which we were well on course to achieve, even if we knew and accepted that Woody would return to Harlequins after that season at home.

The defeat also convinced everyone within the IRFU that the national team had to take precedence. The provincial representatives at union level were all competing amongst themselves, trying to get the best deals for their own provinces. As the provinces were playing more games than Ireland and beginning to get more professional in terms of full-time squads and coaches, they were being put under pressure to grow and develop. Lens cemented the view, however, that the national team had to sit at the top of the pyramid. That loss to Argentina was to prove the badly needed shock and catalyst that was to bring us to the next level.

Initially, things got worse: in the opening game of the 2000 Six Nations we went to Twickenham and got torn apart, 50-18. That was the last thing Gatty needed and I knew the IRFU, understandably, were beginning to look at their options. 'If we don't beat Scotland, I'm gone,' Warren said to me after the thumping by England. He was prepared to walk if things didn't change quickly.

It was shit or bust now, and the time had come to summon the young fellas. Ronan O'Gara, Peter Stringer, Shane Horgan, John Hayes and Simon Easterby were all selected for their international debuts. O'Gara would have played against England, but he took a bang on the knee two weeks earlier and wasn't 100 per cent right. With the benefit of hindsight it was probably better that he wasn't fit: he came in against Scotland instead, along with the others. It was always a matter of debate as to when to bring the young fellas in. O'Gara, like any cocky young fella, would say, 'I'm ready.'

Above: The nine Irish Lions in 1983: (*from left*) Hugo MacNeill, Ollie Campbell, John O'Driscoll, Trevor Ringland, myself, Ciaran Fitzgerald, Michael Kiernan, David Irwin and Ginger McLoughlin.

Left and below: Finally, my Lions debut against Hawke's Bay in Napier. A proud moment, having been controversially sent home on medical grounds when the squad assembled in London.

Left: Departing Cork airport for the second time for the Lions tour to New Zealand in 1983. With me in the back row are my brother-in-law Matt McGrath, wife Mary and father Gerald; in the front (*from left*) Michael Kiernan's sister Eileen, my mother Chris, sister Jo and her baby daughter Ciara.

Below: Leading the Lions. Coming from behind to beat ACT 41-25 days after losing the First Test in 1989 helped to get the show back on the road and set up a series victory in Australia.

Above and right: That Lions squad was special, both on and off the field, with the likes of Wade Dooley and Andy Robinson, seen here sampling the local produce on a visit to the Hunter Valley, always great company.

Above: With Paul Dean injured in the opening game in Perth, only three Irish players started and finished the 1989 Lions tour of Australia; Steve Smith, Brendan Mullin and I pose for posterity by Sydney Harbour.

Right: It was always good to come home, though, with my son David eagerly awaiting what Dad had brought from Down Under.

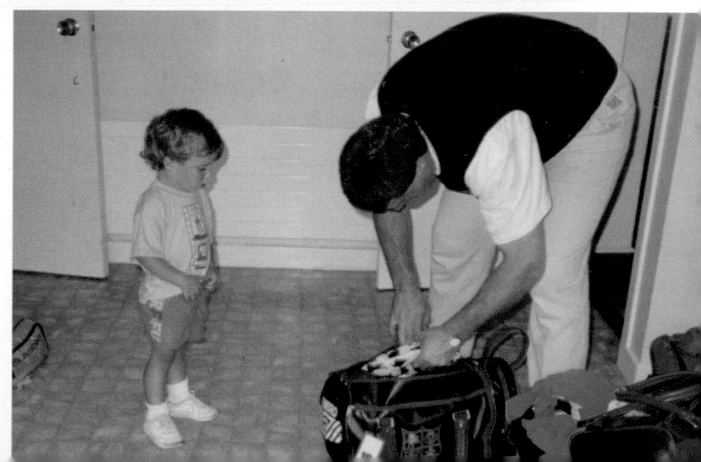

Above left and right: I would return to Australia with the Lions twelve years later, this time as manager. Martin Johnson was an excellent captain and Graham Henry a top coach, but we came up just short in the end.

Above: Thrown in at the deep end. Overseeing the captain's run with Warren Gatland, our excellent media director John Redmond and Philip Danaher before our opening game against Boland Districts in South Africa in 1998.

Below: Turning a corner. All smiles with Eddie O'Sullivan and Warren Gatland as Scotland are put to the sword in February 2000, the day John Hayes, Simon Easterby, Peter Stringer, Ronan O'Gara and Shane Horgan all won their first caps.

Despite rugby dominating my life, my roots are firmly in GAA and it has been a privilege to meet so many great Irish sports stars from other fields. (*From top*) with two legends in Kerry, great Mikey Sheehy and Ireland goalkeeper Packie Bonner; Pat Spillane and Con Murphy; Jimmy Barry Murphy.

Top and above: Staying involved with the game is such a privilege, whether it be acting as MC at a Munster event, or helping to choose the ERC 'Team of 15 Years' with the likes of Michael Lynagh, Ian McGeechan, Ieuan Evans, Stuart Barnes and Lawrence Dallaglio.

Left: Writing for the *Irish Examiner* has also led me to meet people such as Nando Parrado, the Uruguayan rugby player and survivor of the Andes plane crash made famous in the film *Alive.*

Whether in Cork with Ronan O'Gara (**above**) or Dublin with Brian O'Driscoll (**below**), life in the media is always interesting, and seeing that golden generation go on to win the Grand Slam in 2009 was a special moment for all involved with rugby in Ireland.

Left: Twenty-four years after captaining Ireland at the inaugural World Cup, I was back in New Zealand with RTE in 2011, pitchside with Hugh Cahill before the famous win over Australia in Auckland's Eden Park.

Below: Posing with our excellent team of analysts and commentators prior to departure.

Bottom: Family time. On top of Torc Mountain, Killarney, with David, Mary and our dog Holly.

With the team announced for the Scotland game, I got a bang on the door around eight a.m. on the Thursday morning. It was Shane Horgan, and he was upset.

'I just want to tell you there's a story coming out in the *Evening Herald* tonight,' he said. 'I attacked a bouncer in Galway.'

'When did this happen?'

'About six months ago.'

It was an opportunistic story, of course, as Shane, on the verge of his first cap, was now newsworthy. But I was raging because the incident had happened on Leinster's watch, after playing Connacht at the Sportsground, and nobody in Leinster rugby or the IRFU had told us that this issue was hanging over him.

So here was Shane, visibly upset and understandably worried. He didn't need this, and my heart went out to him.

'Do you know with certainty it's coming out in this evening's paper?' I asked him.

'Yeah. I've had a reporter on.'

'Do your parents know about it?'

'No.'

'The first thing you do now,' I told him, 'is you go down, ring them, and tell them that this thing is coming out in the paper tonight.'

At our team meeting before training, I told the players about the impending story. 'You need to know about it,' I said. 'We'll handle it, so go away and train.'

On the coach to training at Greystones rugby club, as usual the grizzled, experienced fellas were down the back of the bus. You have to earn the right to occupy those seats. Then Peter Clohessy stood up and said, 'Right, Horgan, you're down the back with us. Anyone who takes on a bouncer in Galway is good enough to be on our team.'

That lifted the whole atmosphere, but we still had to decide if Shane was in a fit mental state to play. We told him to just go out and train and see how things went. He looked sharp, and afterwards we told him that, whatever happened, we would back him the whole way and that he was definitely playing on Saturday. The relief on his face was palpable.

He then went out and played a blinder on the Saturday, scoring a try for good measure to launch a pretty impressive international career. We won 44-22 – incredibly, the first time Ireland had beaten Scotland since I captained the side to victory all of twelve years earlier. Ireland couldn't buy a win over Scotland in those days.

From that game on, Irish rugby seemed to take off. We played Italy next and put 60 points on them. Then we went to France, who had contested the final of the World Cup only a few months earlier. We were given no chance. Denis Hickie made a brilliant tackle that day on Marc Dal Maso, their hooker, trailing back to cut him down only metres from the line. Plus, of course, there was that historic Brian O'Driscoll hat-trick that really launched him as an international star. We won 27-25, for a first victory in Paris since 1972.

A bit like Tim Horan after Drico's debut in Brisbane, Denis Charvet, who had played for France in my time and was a superb centre and a very flamboyant character – he became an actor for a period after his retirement – approached me outside our dressing room.

'This boy O'Driscoll,' he said excitedly, 'I must meet him. Can you bring me in?'

I'd say that to this day Drico still doesn't know who he was, but I introduced him: 'Brian, this man has played in the centre for France on many occasions and he just wants to shake your hand.'

It's amazing in sport how things can change so quickly. I remember Tommy Kiernan ringing me after the defeat in Lens saying, 'Look, you're doing a good job, stick in there.' After that uplifting win at the Stade de France, I was being interviewed at the side of the pitch when Tommy came down from the stand, shook my hand, and was gone in a flash. After the game many of the IRFU committee who had been giving us the desert stare back in Lens were now all over us.

We finished the campaign on a disappointing note, losing 23-19 at home to Wales. Had we won, we'd have shared a Championship with England. I was happy, though, that Irish rugby had turned a huge corner and things were finally on the up. The seeds had been sown for a revival in fortunes which would result in three Triple Crowns in the 2000s and then the Grand Slam itself in 2009.

Little did I realize, however, that this would be the last time I'd be involved directly with the Irish team. Having acted as a Lions selector for the 1997 tour to South Africa, I was appointed manager for the 2001 expedition to Australia at the outset of that Six Nations campaign and had already decided to step down from the role of Ireland manager in order to focus on that.

19

The Lions Circus

The opening rounds of the 2001 Six Nations confirmed my view that Ireland were going from strength to strength. O'Gara, O'Driscoll, Horgan and the rest of the new blood were finding their feet at this level. Ireland opened with an impressive 41-22 away win in Rome – a Rob Henderson hat-trick propelling him firmly into Lions contention – which was followed by an excellent seven-point victory over France in Dublin.

The team was really going places, but then foot-and-mouth struck. Travel was severely restricted, especially between Britain and Ireland, and Ireland's campaign was put on hold. We didn't know for how long the ban was going to remain in place, but while we sat it out, the other teams in the Championship continued playing. With the squad for the Lions tour to Australia scheduled to be announced in April, that placed the Irish players at an immediate disadvantage. As it transpired, it would be seven months before Ireland could play the first of those remaining three Six Nations games.

As manager of the Lions, one of my most important briefs was to ensure that the Lions made a profit from this tour. They had lost money in 1997, and in the professional era, money was talking more than ever. After the South African tour, you had the RFU's chief executive Francis Baron contemplating whether the Lions concept was even worth the time and expense any more. But the Lions is a fascinating concept in the professional arena. It shouldn't work but it does. Does it have a place? Absolutely.

I was retired from playing when the 1993 Lions tour to New Zealand took place, then four years later I was a selector for the 1997 tour of South Africa, the first of the professional era. Coached by Ian McGeechan for a third consecutive time and captained by Martin Johnson, the Lions were given no chance. Only two visiting teams had ever won a series there – the '74 Lions and the '96 All Blacks. Once again, McGeechan sprinkled his Lions magic in a perfect combination of good cop, bad cop along with my 1983 Lions coach Jim Telfer. The players came together to form a close-knit unit and won the first two Tests to wrap the series up before the final game.

But the Lions as a commercial 'event' really kicked off in 2001. Coached by Graham Henry and captained again by Martin Johnson, the tour was getting bigger and bigger. As a Lions tour only comes around once every twelve years to each of the hosts, it's absolutely huge in that country as well, especially if they can do it right. What's rare is wonderful.

From the thousands of fans who followed the Lions, to the media interest, the colour and the partying around the team and supporters, it was an incredible tour, and it cemented in people's imaginations what the Lions now meant in the modern, professional context.

However, there was trouble brewing right from the outset when I appointed Henry, 'an outsider' in many people's minds, over some home-grown options, including Clive Woodward. I knew Woodward reasonably well because we both represented our countries in the 1980s and had played together on the '83 Lions tour, as well as spending time together on an Easter tour of Bermuda in '84. The reason I didn't involve him in the management team in 2001 was because my brief from the Lions committee was to get the best coach on board. Ian McGeechan was my clear choice, without question. He had been coach in 1989, 1993, and again in 1997 when the Lions won the series in South Africa, and, following my initial approaches to him, it was clear he badly wanted to do it again.

I travelled to Edinburgh on a number of occasions to make it happen, but the problem was he had just been appointed Director of Rugby with the SRU, and Jim Telfer in particular didn't want to release him for the Lions tour as he wasn't long in his new role. I fought and fought, but in the end the SRU made it clear to Geech that they didn't want to release him.

So Woodward was next on the table for investigation as he was the head coach in England. But all the research I did and all the information I had gleaned confirmed that he didn't do any of the on-field coaching. With England he was in more of a managerial role, building up a very good coaching team around him. Phil Larder, Dave Alred and Andy Robinson were doing the hands-on coaching whereas he was more of a manager – and we had one of those!

Of the English players I would have spoken to, they said, in fairness to Woodward, that he was a very innovative guy, very much a forward thinker. But for every five ideas he had, three of them might be daft. The likes of Martin Johnson were strong enough to say, 'No, Clive, that one isn't very good, but this one might work.' But the bottom line was he wasn't a coach – a view subsequently confirmed to me after he took charge of the 2005 Lions to New Zealand by several of the touring Irish players, many of whom were shocked by his lack of input on the field. On those grounds alone I had ruled Woodward out.

When I looked at who else was available, Gatland in Ireland wasn't experienced enough on the international stage, so I was left examining the credentials of Graham Henry, the New Zealander who had gone to Wales and done a brilliant job. Years later in his autobiography Graham stated that his ego got the better of him and that he shouldn't have taken the job, but at the time he was definitely the best coach available.

So I appointed Henry, and Woodward was raging. His nose was out of joint from the outset. There was to be rancour from day one.

The opening game was against Western Australia in Perth. After we'd thrashed them 116-10, I asked James Robson, our excellent team doctor, for an injury update and he mentioned that Scotland No. 8 Simon Taylor had taken a bang on the knee but it was too early to assess. When we returned to the team hotel, Robson feared that Taylor might have done his cruciate but said, 'I won't know definitively until we do a scan on it in the morning.' He was seriously worried, though. This was now after ten p.m. Australian time.

I started to make a contingency plan, should it turn out to be a tour-ending injury for Taylor. Leicester No. 8 Martin Corry was next in line and he was in Canada, preparing for a Test with England that Saturday. Andy Robinson, England's forwards coach, said he would contact Woodward to put Corry on standby, with the possibility he would not be available for the game against their hosts.

Woodward wasn't happy with the prospect of Corry being pulled but we told him to keep it confidential. Next thing, I got a call at one a.m. from one of the English journalists on the Lions tour attacking me because I never told them that Simon Taylor was out of the tour and that Martin Corry was on his way.

'That is not yet the case,' I told him. I admitted that an issue had arisen but we didn't know anything definitively just yet.

It turned out that a member of the English media who was covering the tour in Canada had been told about our request to put Corry on standby and that he might be pulling out to go and join the Lions; he'd then told his sports editor in London, who'd got on to his journalist in Australia wanting to know what was going on. That immediately set the English media in Australia on my back. Having been sent home injured from a Lions tour myself, I'd just wanted to offer Taylor the time to get his scan and find out the extent of his injury before making any statement on the issue. It backfired.

Even after we won the first Test in Brisbane, word was going around the team hotel in Canberra prior to our game against the Brumbies that Woodward was suggesting to some of the English players on the Test side, 'You shouldn't be here, you should be down in Melbourne preparing for the second Test.' He applied that philosophy of splitting the tour party into two when he was in charge in 2005: he had one team at the current match venue and another sent as an advance party to the next venue. That flew in the face of the entire Lions concept, where players from different countries room together and travel together as one. It was to prove a very flawed template on that 2005 tour, when the

Lions image suffered a lot of damage after losing all three Tests against a New Zealand side led by, of all people, Graham Henry.

It probably didn't help things either when I was asked about the Corry situation at a press conference by one of the English journalists who said that Woodward had commented in Canada that it looked like we were panicking. I replied that I thought Woodward had the franchise on panic. England had lost two Grand Slams on the last day of the Championship at that stage and would do so again at Ireland's hands three months later in Dublin. It probably wasn't the most diplomatic of comments to make, but Woodward had been sniping away at Graham and me ever since Henry's appointment. Still, with the benefit of hindsight I shouldn't have made that comment.

In Australia in 2001, one of the biggest issues we had from the outset was trying to familiarize players from different countries with the different coaching requirements and systems being put in place. Players were coming in from varying levels and it was clear from the start that the England players were slightly more advanced in some aspects of professionalism than the Welsh, Scottish and Irish. For example, England had started to go down the route introduced by Australia when winning the 1999 World Cup of having a dedicated rugby league defence coach. Phil Larder was doing an excellent job with England, and we appointed him to do a similar job for the Lions. Problem was, what the English players were able to take for granted under him after nearly two seasons of working together, the rest of the party were having to pick up in a few squad sessions. As a consequence we ended up spending too much time on the training paddock, with all the specialist coaches looking for time to hone their particular area of expertise. The players were put under too much pressure and we didn't offer them as much downtime as they needed after a long, demanding season.

On the flip side, the work that was put in resulted in the Lions starting to produce some really brilliant phases of rugby. Just two weeks out from the first Test we played a Queensland Reds side that had competed in the semi-finals of the Super 12. Queensland had about nine of the Australian team and we scored 42 points in one of the best exhibitions of rugby the Lions had ever produced. That's when Australia thought, 'Shit, we're in serious trouble here and we need to do something to stop them.' That's when things started getting dirty.

There was real momentum building behind us going into the first Test in the Gabba in Brisbane. The Gabba is a noisy old ground used for cricket and Aussie Rules, and when I arrived to inspect things on the Thursday before the game, the dressing room I had agreed upon and signed off on a year previously was not made available to us. It was the dressing room used by the Brisbane Lions AFL side, and the ARU said that the home team didn't want a different breed of Lions in their dressing room. The dressing room now assigned to us was like a shoe box. It just wasn't suitable. We ended up converting another big space into a makeshift dressing room, which worked just fine but it meant that we were togging out at one end of the ground while Australia were at the opposite end.

The pre-match toss of the coin would therefore have to be made on the halfway line, so I accompanied Martin Johnson to meet the match officials. When we came up out of the bowels of the stadium, the noise to welcome us was incredible. We were walking down the middle of the field and Australian captain John Eales had to walk from the other side. He was just looking around the whole time in amazement at the sea of noise and colour, the vast majority of which was red. The Lions support was outnumbering the locals and making so much noise with their songs it was hair-raising to hear it. I remember Johnno looking at me, and when we walked back into the dressing room he told the players, 'Lads, wait till you see what it's like outside.'

Johnson was a fascinating character. Not a demonstrative type of captain with the big rousing speeches, he was someone who just led by example and had an aura about him because of the way he carried himself. He just led with a serious presence. He was tough as nails and did what needed to be done. Nothing would get the better of him because he had this inner strength and determination.

If you go and play underage rugby in New Zealand, as he did, and they want you to stay permanently and potentially become an All Black, you know you have something special. He made the 1993 Lions as a replacement for Wade Dooley before captaining the tourists four years later, and then again in 2001. Johnson, to me, is a bit like the image the English have of Roy Keane in that he probably represents the John Bull stubborn Englishness to us over here. But, I tell you one thing, you would love him on your side.

And we certainly needed his toughness in that series against the Aussies. We lost a whole host of players to injury, including Will Greenwood, Lawrence Dallaglio and Neil Back, on the Saturday before that first Test in a filthy game against the Waratahs. Danny Grewcock received an elbow to the head right from the kick-off while Ronan O'Gara was subjected to a savage assault from Duncan McRae. The Aussies were attempting to set down a marker. It was that kind of series. But with the incredible noise and support behind us in the Gabba we won 29-13 and were never really threatened.

In the second Test in Melbourne a week later we picked up

from where we had left off in Brisbane. For the opening 40 minutes we played outstanding rugby, producing several line breaks but, crucially, failed to convert that dominance on the scoreboard. While we entered the dressing room at half-time leading by 11-6, we should have been further ahead. As reigning World Cup holders that offered Australia something to cling to.

It was crucial therefore that we started the second half well and emphasized the need to dominate territorially. The game and the entire series then turned on two crucial incidents. Firstly we lost England flanker Richard Hill, who was having an outstanding tour, to a cheap shot to the head from Wallaby centre Nathan Grey, who wasn't even cited for the incident. Hill was a huge loss. That decision was every bit as bad, in my opinion, as the failure to cite Tana Umaga and Kevin Mealamu for the spear tackle on Brian O'Driscoll four years later in New Zealand. No wonder it is so difficult to win a Lions series.

The second occurred minutes after the restart when a floated pass from Jonny Wilkinson was intercepted by Joe Roff and he scored against the run of play from 30 metres. He then followed it up with another opportunist try a few minutes later. All of a sudden we were on the ropes.

It didn't help that we then lost our outstanding half-back partnership of Wilkinson and Rob Howley when both were forced off injured. The series should have been put to bed in Melbourne but we offered Australia a lifeline and they grasped it with both hands. It was going to come down to the last game seven days later in Sydney.

In front of 84,188 spectators – a record for a Lions test – in the city's brand-new Olympic Stadium, the final Test and the build-up all week was what the commercial organizers had been praying for. The media interest was unprecedented.

Our injuries had reached crisis proportions with eleven of the original squad now unavailable for selection come that final week. We didn't even have sufficient bodies to prepare properly. Yet the game and the series came down to the final play in the final minute.

It was nip and tuck all the way, the lead switching between both sides before the Aussies opened up a gap with two final penalties to lead 29-23. When we lost the final line-out on the Wallaby twenty-two with time almost up, the series was gone. It was devastating.

There were some fantastic players on that tour playing superb rugby, and Graham Henry deserves huge credit for it. However, when you lose a Test series, that tends to get overlooked. The tour also impacted on his job with Wales, and he resigned after the 2002 Six Nations when Wales lost by a record 54-10 to Ireland and then 50-10 to England. He ended up nearly a broken man.

I know Graham Henry learned a massive amount from that tour and it helped shape his pretty incredible career afterwards. It was fantastic to see him win the World Cup with New Zealand in 2011, especially after their loss in the quarter-finals to France in 2007. The NZRFU had had the balls to stick by him then, and they were proved right in the end.

When Henry was being interviewed for the All Blacks job in 2003 I got a phone call out of the blue from the NZRFU saying Graham had me down as a referee on his CV and was I prepared to take an interview from their chief executive? 'Absolutely,' I said, and four days later I was on the phone for nearly an hour being grilled up and down about Graham Henry and what happened with the Lions.

'Would you back him?' I was asked.

'One hundred per cent, absolutely,' I replied.

They called him the Great Redeemer for what he did with Wales in the late nineties, and he redeemed himself again four years after that France defeat by going on to beat them – just about – 8-7 in that 2011 World Cup final in Eden Park.

If I was to say what I'm most proud of with the Lions, it's when I hear people talking about the 'British and Irish Lions'. Up to 2001 it was just the British Lions, even though Irish players had been involved throughout its history. I sought to change that, correcting people all the time, telling them, 'No, it's the British and Irish Lions.'

It became a bit of a personal crusade, which didn't always sit well with those in authority. At one stage I was a director of British Lions Limited – a company based, of all places, in Dublin. The original Lions blazer had the initials of the British Isles on it, as indeed had our gear bags up to 1983. 'God Save The Queen' was played as the Lions anthem before all three Tests on the 1989 tour which didn't seem right either.

What is it with me and anthems?

I set about trying to influence change on that front in 2000. Slowly, the phrase 'British and Irish Lions' started to enter the rugby vocabulary. People in the print media and on Sky's excellent television coverage of the Lions, like their commentary team of Stuart Barnes and Miles Harrison, were instrumental in helping to embrace the title whenever they were writing/broadcasting. When the Lions jersey came out in 2005 the inside collar was emblazoned with the words 'British and Irish Lions'. That felt good. Irish players had been in Lions tour parties right from the outset, and after over 108 years on the road were at last officially getting recognized for their involvement and contributions to the Lions down through the years.

20

'Beware of what's coming'

The Irish players on that 2001 Lions tour had to pick themselves up after the final Test defeat to Australia as they still had a Six Nations campaign to finish in September and October after the postponements due to foot-and-mouth earlier in the year.

But the first game back, against Scotland, caught them cold and Ireland were well beaten 32-10 in Murrayfield. While the Grand Slam and Triple Crown might have been off the table, the players made up for it by destroying Wales in Cardiff 36-6 and finishing up with a 20-14 home win over England to deny them a Grand Slam.

That brave and gutsy performance showed how far the new talent in the side was progressing. Two years on from Lens and Irish rugby looked to have a bright future, helped in no small part by the rise of the new generation and the strides being taken by the provinces – especially Munster – in Europe.

Just twelve months previously Munster had suffered the heartbreak of a European final defeat to Northampton, but the Munster bandwagon was growing and building its own myths all the time, threatening to be the defining Irish rugby story.

What was it about Munster, though, that captured the hearts and minds of Irish people at home and even beyond?

The first thing that's worth saying about Munster is there's a perception out there that they're about the collective spirit being stronger than the sum of the parts and all of that. But the truth is it's the club rivalry and intensity that made Munster what it is. However, historically speaking anyway, that had often been the very thing holding Munster back on a domestic level.

Looking back at the old inter-pros, Munster were usually a good third behind Leinster and Ulster in terms of number of titles won. The problem was, it always took time to build the type of trust required to perform to the maximum of your abilities, and with so few matches, that wasn't always forthcoming. Everybody got on great but there was that feeling that the Shannon contingent would be reluctant to disclose any state secrets to the Cork Con crowd, and vice versa. You could hear the whispers – 'Don't tell them anything' – and you always felt there was something being held back in reserve.

The only time that all came together was when we played the touring teams because there was a historical responsibility on you to perform. There was a recognition that if we all don't pull together here, we're in trouble.

The reality in Munster is that there is a natural divide between Cork and Limerick, a rivalry built up over years of internal competition when it was the club scene that mattered most. That intense rivalry came to the fore most prominently with the advent of the All Ireland League in 1990.

From the outset, the favourites, at least from a media perspective, were Ballymena and Wanderers. Wanderers had done the double in Leinster the previous year and nobody took any notice of the Munster clubs. But on the opening weekend, Garryowen played Wanderers on the main pitch at Lansdowne Road and travelled in strength, on and off the field. Garryowen promptly went out and stuffed the favourites.

Leinster rugby didn't know what hit them. Afterwards, the fans were celebrating wildly in the quaint old Wanderers clubhouse bar in the corner of Lansdowne Road and the place was jam-packed. The Wanderers crowd weren't used to this at all. A long-term female Wanderers supporter, resplendent in her fur coat, was sitting in the corner, observing what was going on around her. The Garryowen crowd were roaring and singing, knocking back a few pints, when one of their supporters spilled a bit of his drink on top of her. She went ballistic.

'Garryowen, you're an absolute disgrace!' she shouted at him. 'Look at you, roaring and shouting, coming up here and spilling your drink all over us.'

The Garryowen faithful turned round, apologized, and said, 'Look, ma'am, where we come from, we're the snobs. So, beware of what's coming.'

Welcome to the AIL.

Cork Con played St Mary's on that opening day at Temple Hill and beat them. They too were shocked. Nobody had prepared themselves for what the Munster clubs were capable of delivering.

They simply didn't know what hit them. The Young

Munster supporters would arrive in their thousands. They were the most colourful of all. They'd come into the clubhouse beforehand and set up base camp. They'd have the sandwiches ready and one massive communal picnic would break out. They'd have their pig's feet and a few pints and they'd be saluting everyone. This was a big culture shock if you were from Wanderers or Lansdowne.

The All Ireland League instantly took off for all the Munster clubs. The crowds were huge and the après-match in the clubhouses of Garryowen, Shannon, Young Munster or Cork Con was mighty. They would be hopping for hours after the game.

Now that clubs around the country were being exposed to the competitive animal that was the Munster clubs, the other Irish players began to understand. 'Lads, I told you for years. You have no idea what Munster club rugby is all about.' They did now!

We didn't always get the best out of what we had as a collective with Munster, but there was that natural ingredient, that competitive spirit and that bit of hardness that existed between us. It was something I identified straight away on tour in New Zealand. Every place you went in that country, no matter who we were playing, it was hard and competitive. In the bar afterwards, mixing with some of the opposition players, you'd be saying, 'That was a tough game.'

They'd ask, 'Who are you playing next?'

'Oh, we're going to Hamilton to play Waikato.'

'Jesus, if you think today was bad . . .'

It was always the same.

That's what Munster was like for touring teams coming to Ireland – all those pictures of people down the Mardyke in Cork, hanging off trees or peering in through the railings to get a glimpse of the famous All Blacks, or on the packed terraces at the old Thomond Park.

As a result of the AIL, the standard was raised right across the province. The numbers of people following the game increased and there was much more of a buzz around every match. Every game you were playing, the teams were of a higher standard.

When they started the All Ireland League, there were only nine teams in Division 1. That was eight games of sustained intensity. Two defeats and you were toying with relegation; two wins and you were in with a chance of winning it. It was cup rugby every week, and it was brilliant. From the outset, Munster clubs dominated, winning the first nine AILs in a row and seventeen of the first twenty. That was the foundation for what was to follow, the launch pad for Munster in Europe.

Apart from the touring sides, which came only every few years anyway, what finally brought Munster together as a province was the Heineken Cup. It took the advent of European competition to bring things to that level on a consistent basis. Instead of the touring teams you now had famous English and French club sides coming to Limerick and Cork. Again, it was brilliant, and it brought the best out of the Munster team and their supporters.

Munster's maiden voyage in Europe was against Swansea in Thomond Park on 1 November 1995. For a Wednesday afternoon, a decent crowd of 6,000 turned up. The fact that Munster won (17-13) against a famous Welsh club added a bit of colour to the occasion. Castres were also in Munster's pool, which added a bit of the unknown.

I would never have played against a French club side in my time with Munster, and when the team travelled to Castres they were introduced to a whole new world. There were fireworks going off, big wire fences surrounding the pitch, and the crowd were baying for blood. Welcome to French club rugby.

Even in those early stages there was a recognition that this was a whole new level. Culturally, on and off the field, it was opening people's eyes. I travelled to Toulouse as an Irish selector for the first time the following season when they put 60 points on Munster. I was sitting in the stand looking at this demolition job thinking, 'Jesus, what have we got ourselves into . . .' If you'd told me that day that within four years Munster would be beating Toulouse in a Heineken Cup semi-final on French soil, I'd have said, 'No way.' You just couldn't see it happening back then, at least not that qucikly. We weren't that far behind, but at the very top level, the All Ireland League was a million miles from French club rugby at the time.

Munster (and the other Irish provinces) were also caught between two stools. The clubs in Ireland were having to get used to the fact that their players – at least that is how the clubs saw them – were now contracted to the IRFU and they dictated when they were available.

All the clubs were interested in was winning the AIL, but at least Munster weren't playing that many games. The Celtic League hadn't yet come into the equation so even the full-time professional players were playing more often for their clubs than for their provinces. The ground rules were changing rapidly, though, and the clubs were having grave difficulty coming to terms with this.

The problem was, for the club people, the real die-hards, they just couldn't get it into their heads that the provincial management teams could turn round and tell them Ronan O'Gara and Donncha O'Callaghan couldn't play for Cork Con in the AIL next Saturday. They'd go ballistic. But Munster was now their employer; clubs didn't control these players any more.

It took about five years for things to work themselves out between club and province – although you could say it's still an issue today. The modern player may still have a club in brackets after his name but the reality is he might never have played for them. It's still important, though, for the modern professional to align himself with a club. I would always encourage players to go to the odd club match when they can. Take some training sessions, go to the underage games. Have an identity, a place to hang your hat when it's all over. Munster don't have a clubhouse; you can't go and watch them train. When you're finished, you're finished. You might play for Munster for ten years if you're lucky but you could be involved with a club for a lifetime. For the future of the clubs, to get those players back into their environment post-retirement is a massive boost, because clubs are struggling on all fronts.

It was a toe in the water for Irish sides that first year in Europe but they liked what they saw – Munster especially. Although the first few seasons were a struggle to get up to speed with the top French and English teams, especially away from home, the myths surrounding Thomond Park and how difficult it was to win there quickly grew legs. It was like preparing for the international touring sides again: the big boys were coming and you weren't going to be the ones to surrender on home turf.

Thomond Park only had a capacity of 12,000 but regularly attracted up to 10,000 for the big Munster Cup matches. The European games were starting to attract a much wider audience and getting your hands on tickets was becoming increasingly difficult. There were loads of fanatical rugby supporters in Munster whose club might never get to a Munster

Cup final or win the Munster Senior League. Now, all of a sudden, they could follow a team that was playing some of the biggest sides in Europe.

At the time they weren't thinking they were going to win the European Cup, but it's like playing Barcelona: you might not think you have a great chance, but everyone wants to be there to see it. All of a sudden, the demand for tickets went through the roof. I now had more people looking for tickets for Munster matches than I ever had for international games.

In the old Thomond Park, two-thirds of the supporters were packed into the terraces so you had to be at the ground early to secure your slot. People started to take ownership of their spot on the terrace, standing in the same place game after game. Then, when the visiting teams started doing their warm-ups on the pitch you'd have all these characters hanging over the wall, shouting at the opposition. The bigger the name, the greater the slagging. You could see the opposition players scratching their heads, wondering, 'What the hell is this all about?'

All of this helped to feed into the monster that Munster was becoming. That fed down to the players on the pitch as well, who never knew when they were beaten. They were seeing off everyone at home. It didn't matter who it was: Wasps, Stade Français, Harlequins, Bourgoin with Anthony Foley bagging a hat-trick of tries, even Toulouse.

While all of this was going on, the players were still immersed in their respective clubs, trying to win the All Ireland League – after all, winning the Heineken Cup didn't appear all that realistic at first. Some of the players might only have been getting a match fee for playing in Europe and were holding down a day job at the same time. The club was still an integral part of the rugby scene, but this European thing was becoming increasingly more attractive.

It was well into 1998/99 before the provinces were enabled to sign an entire squad on a full-time contractual basis. At the time, Cork's Musgrave Park was getting some Heineken Cup matches, but they were becoming few and far between. There were some very good people running the clubs who saw European games in Limerick as a great way to raise revenues for their clubs. So you had Shannon putting up a big marquee behind their clubhouse, Garryowen taking over the Green Hills Hotel for pre-match lunches before the big Munster games, packing the place out. Soon, if you wanted a match ticket, you had to go to a corporate event beforehand.

So this Munster thing was now helping to generate huge money for a lot of the clubs. Because the game was now professional, many of the top clubs were paying match fees and win bonuses to their players, and the animal Munster was becoming in Europe was helping to fund that. It was beneficial, but still you were trying to satisfy two monsters. The clubs were getting a smell of this and they were getting more money than they'd ever had, particularly the Limerick clubs because the vast majority of the games were in Thomond Park. It was inevitable that something had to give.

Club v. province? In the professional era there was only ever going to be one winner.

21

Anyone but Munster

The game that really set Munster on the road to European greatness and changed the course of their history was the encounter with Saracens in Vicarage Road on 26 November 1999. Even then, Saracens were a team packed with stars. Up front they had British and Irish Lions present and future in Julian White, Paul Wallace, Tony Diprose and Danny Grewcock, one of the best back-row forwards of the professional era in Richard Hill, and South Africa's World Cup-winning captain François Pienaar completing that magnificent back row alongside Hill and Diprose.

That said, the atmosphere during that game appeared slightly manufactured. Saracens had moved grounds a few times, and were struggling to find an identity. They were developing a good support base, but nothing extraordinary. Their fans were wearing these fez hats and they had this motorized car that brought the kicking tee out on to the pitch for their out-half Thierry Lacroix. It all felt a bit superficial really.

Saracens raced into a decent lead but made a number of substitutions early in the second half, thinking they had the game in the bag. Munster being Munster hung in there and bounced back spectacularly with two tries. 'We started the second half the way we had wanted to start the first half,' hooker Keith Wood said afterwards. 'We just took off. I think we were more surprised than anyone.'

'A raging inferno in defence and in attack' was how the *Independent* in England described it, and three minutes from time Jeremy Staunton stormed over the line, Ronan O'Gara's conversion making it 35-34 to Munster. It was incredible stuff. I was at the game with Warren Gatland, and coming just a few months after the World Cup defeat to Argentina in Lens, it was a badly needed shot in the arm for Irish rugby.

The *Independent* hit the right note in its summation of the game: 'The smouldering fires of Munster, whose tradition encompasses historic wins over the All Blacks and Australia, blazed brightly.' The Munster movement was starting. It was a huge result, but then Saracens also had to come back to Thomond Park and were keen to teach Munster a lesson.

On 8 January 2000, I'd say the 12,000 fans were in the ground by breakfast time. The build-up to the game was incredible. Saracens had been forewarned after what had happened in London and weren't going to be caught by surprise this time. Pienaar led them out to a typically respectful reception but Munster just left them there to stew for a while. The roar when Mick Galwey led Munster out was deafening.

Again, Saracens were on top early. Munster staged a comeback but were losing 30-24 heading into injury time. John

Langford won the line-out, the forwards drove on, and Woody scored in the corner. Still one point behind, and with the last kick of the game Ronan O'Gara, his arse almost touching the perimeter wall as he stepped back from the ball, landed the conversion from the touchline.

The place went ballistic. The Munster legend was born.

Pienaar came in afterwards and was extremely gracious in defeat. In all his rugby days, I'd say he'd never experienced anything like that.

I think the thing that registered most with him was that it was all natural, nothing manufactured. There was nothing stage-managed. There were no dancing girls. There was no motorized car. There were no fez heads. This was just raw emotion and support. Allied with that, you had the respect for the kickers, the total silence around the ground for the opposition kicks. Despite all the experience they had on board, they were slightly freaked by this.

The thing that really got them was, when it was all over and Pienaar led his side off the field, everybody stood and applauded them and him in particular. In the post-match reception afterwards, Grewcock and Pienaar were asking themselves, 'What in the name of Jesus was that? What just happened?'

At that time I was involved in the Ireland management set-up and would also have been at several of the Leinster games in the Heineken Cup. Friday nights in Donnybrook were great nights too. I remember when they beat Leicester in a cracking game in similar circumstances. Everybody was patting themselves on the back saying, 'Isn't this brilliant? Isn't this great?'

And it was, but I said to them, 'Lads, you're missing a trick here. Seven thousand is the maximum you can get into Donnybrook but Leinster's target audience should be at least 20,000. If

55,000 turn up to the old Lansdowne Road for an international then at least 20,000 of those must be from Leinster. That has to be your target audience. If 12,000 are begging to get in the door in Thomond Park, with a population in excess of a million people in Dublin, 20 to 25,000 has to be your target audience.'

Now it's happened. Their move to the RDS was an inspired decision, and with the proposed redevelopment there they should now achieve that target of 25,000. I've watched the evolution of the RDS as Leinster's new home base over the last few years. It's a brilliant setting, in the middle of Ballsbridge with loads of pubs and restaurants. Donnybrook is on the other side with the tradition of Kielys and all that. The Leinster support has grown and grown and, of all the Irish provinces, they're the one best positioned to rival the big-money clubs in England and France.

They've also got a massive advantage in being able to access the Aviva Stadium two or three times a year. They'll use it for a pool match in Europe and a home quarter-final if they get that far. Ironically, Munster have become the cash cow for them also. For a few years now they have been attracting over 45,000 people for their Pro12 match against Munster in Dublin and netting close to €1 million out of that.

Back to that 1999/2000 season, and despite losing the final game, away to Pontypridd, Munster topped the pool and that unforgettable season just rolled on. There was the 27-10 defeat of Stade Français in the quarter-final and a first ever semi-final appearance, away to Toulouse.

Here we were in Bordeaux just a few years on from that 60-19 thrashing in Toulouse, but massive strides had been made. Trailing 15-11 at half-time and 18-17 when down to fourteen men, Munster's belief finally shone through when O'Gara went over for a try that had started from their own 22.

Another try and conversion just four minutes later and Munster were all but through. It finished 31-25. Munster were into a European Cup final, and what a way to get there.

The final against Northampton in Twickenham was the place to be and Munster fans were going mad to get there. The scenes in Cork airport on the morning of the final were incredible with a number of chartered aircraft lined up on the tarmac. There were people in red jerseys everywhere. The *Irish Examiner* were handing out their special supplement on the game and the team sponsor, Bank of Ireland, had their marketing people handing out hats and flags in their thousands. I wasn't that long finished playing myself and to see this fanaticism for Munster that had never existed before, certainly not on this scale, I was astounded. Where had it come from? Everybody on the plane was reading about the match, talking about the match, as excited as a bunch of kids on Christmas morning. There was a big event for the Munster supporters at the Harlequins ground, the Stoop, beforehand and you were bumping into people you hadn't seen for years.

After a morning of thunder and rain, the sun shone through that afternoon and it seemed destiny was in Munster's hands when David Wallace scored the first try before half-time. Ultimately, though, it was a day for the kickers, and for once Ronan O'Gara didn't deliver, missing all four penalties including one to win it in the final minute. Munster lost 9-8.

I've spoken to Ronan about it many times in the years since and he believes that the kick he missed in some ways made him, but he will always say, 'Look, I missed it when it mattered most.' The animal in him made him realize that he had to make sure that never happened again.

He had a work ethic that he thought was professional, but a

year later he was on the Lions tour to Australia, and observing Jonny Wilkinson, who is six months younger than him, just blew him away. Missing that kick and seeing Wilkinson's work ethic and level of preparation made him realize what he had to do. They were two key events that made O'Gara the player he became.

I often think of what might have happened if O'Gara had got that last-minute penalty and Munster were crowned champions. I'm not so sure the province would have developed to the extent that it did. Munster's story became all about this quest for Heineken Cup glory and the gut-wrenching journey towards achieving that. I'll never forget Mick Galwey coming up the steps of Twickenham that day as the losing captain. It was heartbreaking. All the Munster supporters stayed beyond the presentation, however, and started singing 'The Fields Of Athenry'. In the years after that, the chase to win the competition turned into an obsession.

Two years later Munster made the final again, at the Millennium Stadium against Leicester Tigers. Heartbreak again, losing 15-9. There was the 'hand of Back' controversy with the scrum at the end, but that was all bullshit. He did something, he got away with it. It was blown up out of proportion. Munster thrived on the persecution complex. They thrived on the chip on the shoulder. The Neil Back incident only served to fuel that. If the roles had been reversed and Alan Quinlan or David Wallace had done the same, they'd have been hailed as 'cute hoors' and gone down in folklore.

And if you thought getting to London in 2000 from Cork airport was bad, in 2002 the crowds following Munster had quadrupled. Cardiff was just manic, and their airport couldn't cope. There were people everywhere. As if losing a second final wasn't bad enough, the journey home was shambolic. They had marquees set up outside the airport in an attempt to control the flow of people going through the terminal, but it didn't work. There were delays for hours and hours. There were just bodies everywhere, total chaos. They'd never seen anything like this in Cardiff airport. They didn't know what hit them.

I finally got on a charter after someone I know who was involved with Cork airport literally rounded up people he knew. It was like the Americans getting out of Vietnam. 'I can get you on a plane. Get your family, get your belongings, get out now while you can.'

Two finals, two defeats. The persecution complex continued. The quest would go on.

There was that epic semi-final against Wasps at Lansdowne Road in 2004. It was Warren Gatland's first time back in Ireland since getting the sack from the IRFU. I had been in contact with him a lot and he'd done a brilliant job at Wasps, but this game was always going to be extra special for him. The night before we met up for a few drinks. Warren is a good man to have a few pre-match pints with and I said to him, 'Regardless of what happens tomorrow, win, lose or draw, don't let yourself down. I can see you coming out with some rubbish. Don't rake up the past. You've got to take the moral high ground.'

He's nodding away, saying, 'Yeah, you're right, you're right. No, I accept that.'

Lansdowne Road was heaving, over 49,000 people, and most of them screaming for Munster. Wasps targeted O'Gara and he was gone after half an hour. Munster were leading 32-22 on the hour mark but Wasps forced their way back into it, and then Trevor Leota scored a try in the corner in the final minutes. It was a very questionable try – shouldn't have been allowed in my view – but they won by 2 points.

Despite the game being hailed as a classic, it was Munster's third semi-final defeat in four years. Of course Gatty comes out afterwards and says, 'Sure it's easy for Munster. They qualify automatically every year.' I could have choked him!

If you take the period from that first final in 2000 to finally winning it in 2006, Munster had four world-class players – players who would challenge for a place on a World XV. Keith Wood played in the 2000 final, and though he was only with Munster for that season, he had a massive influence in terms of his professionalism, attitude, approach and will to win. He was carrying that mantle on his own with both Munster and Ireland for a while but his influence gradually began to seep through.

Around this time you had the emergence of Ronan O'Gara as a serious international-quality player, and he too became a massive influence. You also had David Wallace, who for me was just a freak of an athlete. He was the amalgam of his two brothers, Richie and Paul, both of whom, of course, played for Ireland and the Lions, on the wing and in the front row. David had Richie's pace and Paul's strength, and more football than both of them. His speed over 10 metres was phenomenal while his power and leg drive made him very difficult to contain. In many ways he was Munster's most potent attacker. Munster often used him to good effect in midfield, withdrawing him from the line-out and using him as a trail runner, feeding off the centres.

Then in 2002 Paul O'Connell burst on to the scene. He was an extraordinary player who had an unbelievable will to win. The older he got, the better he became. He learned the basics in the club game with Young Munster and was offered a glimpse of the old amateur ethos. He emerged from all of that with the self-belief and the restraint to ignore the bad habits while also cherishing and embracing the importance of identity and playing for where you come from – old school with a professional gold star.

Anthony Foley, too, was a very intelligent player, and it's no surprise he has now gone down the coaching route. Also crucial was the introduction of some quality overseas players. You had Jim Williams straight out of a World Cup-winning Australian team adding to the back-row strength, with the likes of Alan Quinlan and Denis Leamy competing for places. Williams and Aussie lock John Langford quickly bought into the ethos of the place.

Langford was some athlete. On the first day he arrived, he wasn't feeling well and didn't want to train. Declan Kidney had a team-building exercise organized and wasn't impressed. 'We don't want any prima donnas here,' he said. 'Look, you'll have to train.' They did some distance running, and Langford left them all for dead. He was a greyhound breed. He was a big guy, but he wasn't a heavy guy. They picked the wrong discipline that day to check him out.

Declan was great for Munster. He was never the most technical coach, but his man management skills were excellent, along with his ability to think outside the box. Declan was a better coach than a player. He would have been on the periphery of a lot of good teams, and I think he appreciated the challenges facing players on the fringe of the team more than others. In a tactical sense he was excellent in that he recognized his shortcomings and he listened to people – particularly the players. He was very good at playing the underdog card and he would always have an angle to go on. Declan managed to get the best out of every resource he had and would create or invent a cause which suited the Munster psyche.

Many different things go into the make-up of a successful team, but if the chemistry in your dressing room is wrong you have no chance, regardless of how talented and how fit you are. Rugby is a game where everybody depends on everybody else. If John Hayes isn't holding up the scrum, O'Gara's under pressure. If O'Connell isn't dominating the line-out, you can't implement the plays that get Wallace into the areas you want in midfield.

While numbers 1 to 10 were more often than not involved with Ireland, the ones outside of O'Gara also played their part. The likes of Anthony Horgan, Dominic Crotty, John Kelly and Ian Dowling were incredibly effective, honest players who always played above themselves and gave everything to the cause.

It was the small things that you wouldn't see with any other team. That umbilical cord between the supporters and the team, for instance. Even though the players might not always have won, they always turned up and always gave everything. If you're not good enough, people accept that and move on. The atmosphere on those trips around England and France in particular was amazing in that, normally, the team charter would depart for home within four hours of the final whistle. It was always a manic rush to make it. People would have their night out before the game, and mixing with home fans in Clermont and Toulouse in particular was great.

For some, the exodus begins straight after the game. There's thousands of people in their queues, waiting in the airport, and then the Munster team arrives and everybody stands back. There's this massive round of applause, the sea opens, and the players stroll through and head straight for the departures lounge. The front of the plane is held for the squad and everybody else has boarded by the time the team steps on board, usually to another massive round of applause. It's a close bond. Who wouldn't want to play in that environment?

There would always be two or three younger fellas in the squad, just to let them experience what it's like playing away in France and everything that goes with that. Their jaws would be hitting the ground when they saw how the fans treated them. The likes of Peter O'Mahony and Conor Murray tell stories of growing up, watching Munster from the terraces in Cork and Limerick, dreaming of being there too one day.

For the overseas contingent, players like Doug Howlett, who had experienced it all in world rugby terms, seeing the support that Munster got, away from home especially, was something special. In New Zealand, the Auckland Blues could be travelling to the South Island to play Canterbury but nobody from Auckland travels down to see them. They go to play the Queensland Reds in Brisbane, but nobody flies over to see them. If you're going to South Africa, forget about it. Dougie makes his debut for Munster against Clermont in France in 2008 and he sees all these people in red and the respect they have. On the way back from this maiden Heineken Cup adventure, the charter stops in Cork airport first to let all the Cork- and Waterford-based supporters off. Dougie comes in to collect his bag off the carousel and everybody just stands back and applauds him. He just can't get over the warmth of the supporters – and this after Munster have been beaten! Of course, he's on to his fellow players in New Zealand, saying, 'Jesus, this crowd, this is amazing. You have to come over.'

Yes, you have mad, enthusiastic and passionate fans at clubs across Europe, but the main difference is they don't travel in any great numbers. Clermont are the best French supporters of all. They have that respect, they're hugely vocal, and when you come out on to the pitch, the colour, noise and atmosphere at the Stade Marcel Michelin is fantastic.

But in terms of travelling support, there was nothing to compare with Munster at the height of their powers. Munster became the rugby equivalent of Jack's Army, though we should also remember that this was back in the Celtic Tiger days so there was a lot more money around, and Munster was the gig to be at.

It almost became a cult to show the extremes to which you were prepared to go to follow the team. You didn't count unless you'd endured some hardship; you were no one unless you could show that you'd run from Cork to Rosslare and then swum from there to Southampton. You had all these stories floating around about the lengths people had gone to in order to get to an away match. The more difficult, the better. Fellas on motorbikes who travelled thousands of miles, that sort of thing. If you boarded a plane, you weren't a real supporter. You had to endure pain, some sort of a pilgrimage or crusade that took you a week to get there. It all fed into the myth.

For a long time other teams didn't rate Munster, but by the early 2000s that had changed. I was over in Bath once just before the quarter-final permutations were clarified and it was clear who they didn't want to face. They were like, 'Jesus, not Munster.' When you'd arrived at a stage where none of the English or French clubs wanted to play you, you knew Munster had come a long way.

22
Empty Seats in Thomond

I'm often asked, 'Would you like to have played in the professional era?' The only thing I would love to have experienced is playing in the Heineken Cup with Munster. I played against the Leicester Tigers for the Barbarians in Welford Road and got a little taste of being in that type of environment, but having that week after week, playing against Toulouse or Clermont? I would have loved that.

Don't get me wrong, international rugby is still the pinnacle. There's no question about that. There was a period for the professional players when the Irish side wasn't going well, and it was probably more enjoyable to be involved with your province. Loads of the international players have said that after a bad Six Nations campaign they couldn't wait to get back into their provincial set-ups in order to get up and running again. To have this as your staple diet is great, and Europe is a phenomenal level to play at.

It also helps that all the club grounds around Europe are smaller than the international venues and thus when packed to capacity can be far more atmospheric. I've been to the Stade Marcel Michelin in Clermont on five different occasions to see Munster and Leinster play and witnessed the same fanaticism, passion and colour from their supporters as for the Irish teams. The night before the game you're in the heart of Clermont and everybody's talking about the match. You go into the stadium where the stands are right on top of the pitch. You can almost touch the players. Contrast that to international rugby which is generally held in a massive stadium in the middle of a big city where, unless you're in Cardiff, the occasion can be lost in the midst of all the other things going on.

If you're a young kid in Dublin you can go to the RDS on a Friday night. You can see your heroes warming up. They're within 10 yards of you. The fact that the Irish players, by and large, have stayed in Ireland has also helped to create that fanaticism and hopefully contributes to the next generation of supporters beginning a long association with their chosen side.

Brian O'Driscoll had several opportunities to go abroad but recognized from an early stage that winning a Heineken Cup medal with Leinster would make that achievement ten times more meaningful for him. I can clearly identify with that. He had the opportunities to go, but he stuck in there. The fact that he won his medals with Leinster just means so much more. It's your team. Very few professionals in any sport get to play for the team they grew up supporting, or in the area where they were born and raised. Professional rugby in Ireland affords you the opportunity to do that.

If you're talented, there aren't that many rugby players in Ireland so the dream is slightly more attainable than the fella who thinks he is going to play for Manchester United. You have young rugby players growing up now who know nothing other than going to the RDS, Thomond Park, the Sportsground or Ravenhill to watch their team competing and winning against the best in Europe.

You get moments in sport when all the stars align. With Munster, a great generation of players came through together. They got battle-hardened and learned how to win in the All Ireland League. It was Munster's time.

World-class players in Wood, O'Connell, O'Gara and Wallace gives you a great starting point. Add in proven overseas players such as John Langford, Jim Williams, Doug Howlett, Trevor Halstead and Rua Tipoki. Then you have the next layer: Anthony Foley (an outstanding leader), Alan Quinlan, Donncha O'Callaghan (the workhorse who operated so effectively in tandem with O'Connell for so long), John Hayes (who was monumental) and Peter Stringer (who played ninety-eight times for Ireland).

Without the Heineken Cup they wouldn't have made the same impact at international level. I have no doubt about that. The competition was the catalyst. The consistent exposure to top-quality opposition engendered the do-or-die attitude to keep hanging in there when you're beaten in horrific circumstances. Beating Saracens home and away in the 1999/2000 season, that first semi-final win over Toulouse in Bordeaux – and of course the 'Miracle Match' against Gloucester in 2003 when the leaders of the Premiership came to town with Munster needing to score four tries and win by 27 points to get through to the quarter-finals.

Munster had been well beaten by Perpignan the previous week and heads were down on that journey home – one of the quieter charters. The whole focus of that Gloucester game was on maintaining their unbeaten Heineken Cup record in Thomond Park. Not for a minute did Munster think they were going to qualify. O'Gara didn't even know he needed that conversion at the end to seal it. Nobody had worked out the permutations. Even Gloucester hadn't worked out that if they lost by a margin of 23 points they'd still go through. Why else would they pass up on a straightforward penalty opportunity with only a few minutes to go?

I was sitting in the stand next to Peter Clohessy that day. We were all starting to get excited. What's the points differential? What's going on? We think this kick is important – is it? You couldn't have written the script.

The best sporting occasion I ever witnessed, for a variety of reasons, was the 1995 World Cup final between the hosts South Africa and New Zealand. The only thing to rival it, as a Munster man, was the 2006 Heineken Cup final when Peter Stringer scored that memorable solo try and the big screen showed Limerick's O'Connell Street jammed to the rafters with people going crazy.

Beating Biarritz that day was special in itself, but the noise, colour, singing, good humour and passion that seeped out from the stands on to the field was wondrous. No other team brought anything like that to a Heineken Cup final. As an entity, Munster rugby was elevated to another level. The match was broadcast all around the world, and in a rugby context the province had reached an all-time high. The scenes afterwards were just incredible. One wonders now if we will ever witness days like that again.

The rise of the provinces in Europe has proved the best thing that has ever happened to Irish rugby. It provided the belief that great things could be achieved. Now I fully respect that the beleaguered club man would differ and vehemently argue that professionalism has been at the root of the demise of the club game in this country – a challenge that, should the IRFU fail to recognize, grasp and rectify it, will ultimately cost the professional game, with Munster the biggest potential victim. In truth, I think that has already started to happen.

It is proving very difficult for the current Munster squad to escape from the shadow of their illustrious predecessors, who eventually landed two Heineken Cups in three years after years of pain and disappointment. It is a bit like the Welsh players of the 1980s who were constantly being unfavourably compared to all-time greats such as Gareth Edwards, Gerald Davies, J. P. R. and J. J. Williams, Barry John and Phil Bennett. They had no chance.

It might never be the same, but you still see glimpses of that backs-against-the-wall, never-say-die Munster mentality. There was J. J. Hanrahan's last-minute try against Perpignan in 2013 when Munster refused to be beaten. They should never have won the game. Even the quality of the build-up play was sloppy, but Denis Hurley then made this brilliant break and offload and they were through.

That night, in line with tradition, the players were the last to board the plane. All of the fans were already seated, and when the players stepped through the door at the front of the plane, the applause and cheers were as rapturous as ever. For the likes of Hanrahan, Peter O'Mahony, Conor Murray and their generation, this was the first time they'd done something special away from home in a Munster jersey. It was their moment.

But the cracks are appearing. Time moves on. The big guns are all retired, and the best and brightest are looking at their options outside Munster. Hanrahan's departure to Northampton in 2015 was a major body blow.

Thomond Park is becoming harder and harder to fill. Questions are being asked as to why Cork, a county with a population of 550,000, wasn't chosen for the new development. There's 180,000 in Limerick City and County, yet that has the 26,000-capacity modern stadium. I'll tell you why: all they could come up with in Cork were reasons why you couldn't rebuild on the site in Musgrave Park or at a greenfield location out in Curraheen, just off the link road. Planning issues and obstacles. In Limerick, those charged with the responsibility knocked their heads together and got it done. Planning permission was seen as an obstacle that would and could be overcome because the will was there to make it happen. That will didn't exist in Cork, and now the bird has flown.

At the outset of the Heineken Cup when Munster started to develop a head of steam, Thomond Park could only hold 12,000. When the demand started to increase, tickets became as rare as hen's teeth, and that fuelled people's interest. Soon everybody wanted to be in Thomond Park on matchday. Now, with success hard to come by and a 26,000-capacity stadium to fill, it's getting harder to attract the crowds. The scheduling of games is controlled by television interests and that doesn't help, given that Munster attracts people from all over the province and beyond. If Munster are playing in Limerick on a Friday night, are you going to make it up from Cork after work? No chance.

Between my involvement with RTE and Setanta Sports, I'd say I've probably covered as many Celtic League/Pro12 games as anyone since their inception, and the crowds travelling to Thomond Park for the vast majority of those games have fallen off significantly. People just aren't travelling any more. They certainly won't travel on a Friday night, and they're not taking their kids on a Saturday either, especially for a 7.45 p.m. kick-off. After a game there is little or no traffic on the road back to Cork.

There's been a sea change, and I think people are pissed off that the vast majority of games are in Limerick. It will be very interesting to see what happens when the ten-year tickets come up for renewal in 2017. It will be very difficult to get the same people to bite again. When those tickets were originally sold we were in the midst of the Celtic Tiger. You can get tickets now for the matches very easily if you want them so why would you splash out for a ten-year ticket?

In reality, our expectation levels have grown too high. After the Wales v. Ireland game in 2015, a former Welsh player asked me, 'I'm in Thomond Park next week covering the game between Munster and Cardiff Blues for BBC Wales. What kind of a crowd will it be?'

'You won't get a huge crowd,' I told him. 'You'll be lucky to get ten thousand.'

He looked at me as if I had two heads. 'Ten thousand? Bloody hell!'

Cardiff, who back in the amateur days boasted one of the best club sides in the world and were regularly attracting crowds in excess of 10,000, are now getting less than half that for the professional game.

Sometimes we're victims of our own success. Munster, Leinster and Ulster regularly average crowds of 15,000-plus for Pro12 games but there's nobody else in the league getting anywhere near that. Glasgow Warriors made a big announcement that they're expanding their stadium to 6,000!

If you look at the Aviva Premiership in England, there are a lot of games where they're lucky to attract crowds in excess of 12,000 from a much bigger population base. The problem with Thomond

Park, though, is it needs to be near full capacity to rock. The atmosphere at that All Blacks game in 2008 was electric, and the new Thomond was absolutely brilliant. Unfortunately those occasions are becoming few and far between.

The way the Celtic League was initially structured, you never had to worry about qualifying for the Heineken Cup, so the model suited the requirements of both the provincial and national management teams perfectly in that you could rest key players at certain key times in the season. You could blood younger players without the worry of relegation or qualification for Europe, and the Irish sides were nearly always good enough to make the top four. It was a bit like Wasps under Warren Gatland, who made an art form out of finishing fourth in the regular Premiership season, thus ensuring qualification for the play-offs before winning it outright.

The ground rules for all the Pro12 sides have changed now, of course. The advent of the Champions Cup and the fact that the pools are based directly on your finishing position in your domestic league, coupled with the reduction in the number of teams competing from twenty-four to twenty, has made the pool stages far more competitive. If you don't finish in the top four of your domestic league at the very least, you can be assured of a very tough Champions Cup pool.

The success of Munster and Leinster in winning five Heineken Cups in seven years definitely caused consternation amongst the European elite, especially when the 2012 final in Twickenham was an all-Irish affair, Leinster beating Ulster. Something had to change.

Many of the private benefactors pouring money into the game in England and France had become totally frustrated by the governance offered by their respective rugby unions, especially as the primacy of contract for the players rested with the clubs. That is the big difference here, with all the Irish players directly contracted to and under the control of the IRFU. Wales are finally looking to emulate that system and are now offering central contracts to all their top players.

The club game in France and England is growing in strength, as evidenced by their recently upgraded television deals for their domestic leagues. The most recent three-year deal negotiated for the Top 14 in France commencing in 2019 increases from €73 to €97 million having been €33 millon as recently as the 2014/15 season. When you add the European money on top of what some club benefactors are putting in, there is a real danger now that the French and English leagues will end up attracting all the top players in the game.

Just look at Toulon's dominance in Europe in recent years, winning an unprecedented three-in-a-row. They've become the Real Madrid of European rugby. Is it sustainable? Saracens have been declaring losses averaging £5m annually for some time now; their accumulated losses are close to £45m. For how much longer can they live with that? And yet Saracens won the 2016 Champions Cup at a canter.

For the traditional club game in this country, the death knell came with the establishment of the Celtic League. In the early days of the Heineken Cup, if a Munster player was injured, the provincial management would be pleading with the club to pick him to give him some game time. Problem was, there wasn't a full enough playing calendar to sustain the provinces and maintain their competitiveness for the big games in the Heineken Cup. It was no different in Wales and Scotland. The Celtic nations recognized they needed something. France and England had huge domestic leagues; Irish, Welsh and Scottish regions needed revenue and more games if they were going to sustain professional teams. You have to play at least twenty games a year to get sufficient funds, and they had to find another way of generating money to pay the players.

From an Irish perspective, we had the history and tradition already there with the four provinces. We hit the jackpot because we already had a structure in place that would have been the way forward if you'd started with a blank sheet of paper. When the game went professional the pathways were already there, and that was our saving grace. We didn't have to manufacture teams like they did in Wales and Scotland. That was a huge help. Even today the Principality League in Wales, which houses most of the old traditional clubs like Llanelli, Newport, Bridgend, Pontypridd and Ebbw Vale, regularly attracts bigger crowds than the Scarlets or the Ospreys.

That's not to say we don't have problems with the structure of the game in Ireland. To me, the British and Irish Cup competition for the provinces' A sides offers little or nothing. I have no issue whatsoever with the Celtic League and Champions Cup, but I think for young provincial academy and development players, the All Ireland League still has a role to play with Division 1A and 1B acting as a filter for players to get into the professional game. To me, your academy players and your developing players will learn far more playing in the AIL than from going over to play Doncaster on a Wednesday night with little or no appetite shown by the host team. I would have an A team fixture list. I'd have a proper inter-provincial series played home and away, with a trophy. I'd put it on Wednesday nights and play the games under lights on club grounds. I guarantee that if it was promoted and marketed properly you would get a couple of thousand people out to watch them.

In a way, the clubs were always filters for the bigger stage. They're proud to be able to produce or at least to be associated with an international or provincial player. What irks them is that they feel they still have an important role to play. While clubs all around the country introduce lads to the game at mini and youth level, why can't that continue all the way through?

At the moment you have academy and development players sitting around every Saturday, not playing a match. But you train to play. If I'm a tight-head prop, I have to play every weekend. I need to go up against a wiry thirty-year-old loose-head who has been around for years and get screwed. If I'm an out-half, I need to play regularly. I need to develop, understand and learn what game management is all about. You will only get that from playing a game every weekend.

J. J. Hanrahan, to me, is a typical example of what is wrong with the modern game. He was recognized at fifteen years of age from a GAA background in Castleisland. He seemed to be very promising and was approached with the offer: 'Are you interested in developing as a rugby player? Would you be prepared to go to boarding school to follow the dream?'

'Yes, I will,' he said, and off he went to Rockwell.

He was a star for Rockwell. He got on the Irish Schools team and was a burgeoning talent, signing for Munster. But then he was left hanging there without sufficient game time to sustain his development. He would be introduced off the bench and attempt to prove himself by doing something brilliant every time he was in possession, like that chip he tried against Edinburgh in 2013 which led to a try by Tim Visser and cost Munster a game they should never have lost. To see him go to Northampton, to me, is a failure on Munster's part.

Dusty Hare is Northampton's chief scout. He was with

Leicester for years and years, played with England and the Lions. Ireland were playing England's U20s in Donnybrook and he was over for the game. But he was over for one reason. It wasn't to run the rule over the English players – he knew them intimately at that stage. He was looking at the Irish players.

'I have one question for you: J. J. Hanrahan?'

'Yeah,' he said, 'we've been tracking him for a while. We see ourselves building our back line around him.'

I will follow that one with interest.

The system in Ireland continues to produce some very talented players and unfortunately not all can be accommodated in the professional game. The fact that there is a bottleneck is a good thing in some ways, because it means the quality and the standard are high enough that they can't all make it, but we need to be able to facilitate the management and development of these players better.

Academies produce individuals and the clubs can still play a role in shaping them in terms of what is required to become a functioning part of a team. You've got to learn how to fit into a system. You have to understand the importance of identity and history. These were the things that made Munster.

Munster are having problems in maintaining the quality of the production line. They don't have the volume of schools they have in Leinster, who appear to be churning out a cross-section of talented players every year. That is a major challenge for Munster, and if the club game in the province is allowed to go down the toilet any further, the chances of emulating past glories are certain to become slim.

23

Rugby from the Other Side

After the 2001 Lions my rugby management career was at a crossroads. I was keen to take a break as I had been heavily involved in the game ever since my retirement from playing. To be honest, I didn't think at that stage that I wouldn't get back in some capacity at some point in the future; all I knew was that I definitely needed to take a back seat for a while. Things were getting spiky within the Irish set-up in any case, and despite Warren Gatland's success with the team, his relationship with the IRFU was breaking down and his contract wasn't renewed at the end of 2001.

Defeat to New Zealand in Dublin that November, when Ireland were leading 21-7 in the second half before Jonah Lomu went into overdrive and they scored a handful of tries to make it 40-29 at the final whistle, sealed Gatland's fate. Some within the squad felt that he was too slow to change and adapt things – having no defence coach was one charge laid at him. For others who had experienced a different level of structured coaching and game management with the Lions, Gatland was seen to be behind the curve.

But I knew Gatty well from having worked with him and was taken completely by surprise when I heard the news that his contract wasn't being renewed. I rang him immediately, and he was shell-shocked. He explained how it happened, how he was going up to renegotiate his contract and was told, 'Well, it's not being renewed.' Did I think it was the wrong decision? Yes, I did, and he has subsequently proved what an outstanding coach he is. But I am also pretty certain that it proved to be the kick in the arse Gatty may have needed at the time. Had he stayed with Ireland he wouldn't be the same coach he is today.

Eddie O'Sullivan, Gatty's assistant at the time, was also very ambitious and saw himself ready for the role. I had to remind him on a few occasions when I was manager that his function was to support Gatty in every way he could, but at the same time I had no doubt that Eddie would make a top-class head coach when the time was right.

It was no surprise, then, when he was appointed as Gatland's successor. With Brian O'Brien doing a good job as Ireland team manager and Munster going very well under Declan Kidney, Jerry Holland and Niall O'Donovan, neither of those was an option for me to go to in any case after the Lions tour ended.

Around the same time I had finally decided to set up my own business in commercial and residential mortgage finance, and that was going to be my main focus. Things were taking off, the economy was booming, and there were huge opportunities. I was only in my early forties and at the back of my head I thought if I didn't go out on my own and work for myself now, I wouldn't ever do it. It seemed like the natural cut-off point for me to move on from rugby and throw myself fully into the next challenge.

I might not have been involved directly with a rugby team but it wasn't long before I was to find myself back in the thick of it, albeit on the other side of the fence, when I got a call from the *Irish Examiner*'s sports editor, Tony Leen, about the possibility of writing a weekly column. I had done a piece for them on crisis management in sport during the 2002 soccer World Cup in Japan and South Korea when the issue between Roy Keane and Mick McCarthy raised its head in Saipan, and Keane was sent home.

The first column I did was supposed to be done in consultation with a ghost writer, but when I read it before submission I just didn't like the way it came out and ended up rewriting the whole thing myself. It was the best thing to have happened. Fourteen years and hundreds of columns later, I've written them all myself since then.

Once I got into the rhythm of things, I surprised myself. I actually enjoyed it. Then both Setanta Sports and RTE contacted me as well. RTE had approached me loads of times over the years to get involved, but when you were in management it wasn't an option. I started doing analysis and commentary for RTE on the radio while doing the same with Setanta Sports TV. It proved the perfect mix. I was getting to comment on the games and still be involved, which was the best of both worlds. When the TV rights for the Celtic League transferred from Setanta to RTE in 2010, I moved there to work across all their outlets. I have really enjoyed my time there working on the Six

Nations, Pro12, Heineken Cup, a number of World Cups and two Lions tours.

Radio and television commentaries are two different animals and I enjoy the variety that comes with doing both on a regular basis, working with the likes of Ryle Nugent, Michael Corcoran and Hugh Cahill. One of the things I never really thought about was the vast audience of ex-pats who rely on digital radio in order to follow their favourite teams from all around the world. That was brought home to me in earnest after the famous Munster-All Blacks game in 2008.

Michael Corcoran and I did that on radio, and RTE gave us a copy of these emails that came in from all over the globe. It was phenomenal because you had people as far afield as South America, New Zealand and Australia writing in to tell you where they were listening and what they were doing. One guy described sitting in a Starbucks café in Chicago, listening to the game, hanging on to every word as Munster looked like they were going to create another Thomond miracle. He was jumping up and down and went on to describe this local fellow sitting opposite him, reading his book, thinking he was crazy. It was hilarious.

With minutes to go, Joe Rokocoko gets over the line and it finishes 18-16 to New Zealand. The tears are rolling down his face while his fellow coffee drinker is wondering what the hell is up with this guy.

Describing himself as a Munster fanatic, he wrote, 'I just want to thank Michael and Donal for putting me in Thomond Park last night even though I was thousands of miles away in Chicago.' You don't really appreciate it when you're doing your job just how much of an impact it can have on people, especially those ex-pats living so far from home.

Another highlight for me was when I got to meet and interview an extraordinary man, someone I had known from a distance for over thirty-five years – Nando Parrado, the Uruguayan who, with his rugby team-mates and their friends and supporters, was stranded on the frozen Andes for seventy-two days in 1972 after their plane crashed. Every living moment of those two and a half months brought with it an invitation to die. Miraculously, he and fifteen others survived, and the famous film *Alive* was made about their story.

Nando's story was one that had fascinated me since the day in October 1972 when my CBC school principal, Brother John 'Dicey' O'Reilly, summoned our class to pray for the missing victims of a plane that had disappeared on the border between Argentina and Chile with a Uruguayan rugby team on board. The majority of the players had been pupils of Brother O'Reilly when he taught at the Stella Maris College in Montevideo. The school had been founded by the Christian Brothers in 1955 who then introduced rugby to its pupils in an effort to promote teamwork and discipline.

In December, the astonishing news came through that sixteen of the original forty-five passengers and crew had survived an incredible ten-week ordeal in the mountains. We again gathered to pray, this time in thanks.

The story of these rugby players' survival on the mountains stayed with me, especially Parrado, who after sixty-one days decided, along with team-mate Roberto Canessa, to try and climb over the Andes and look for help.

In 2006 Parrado revisited the story in his book *Miracle in the Andes*, and he spoke about his life and that of his fellow survivors in the years that followed. Parrado's mother and sister were also on board the plane, and he explained that throughout the ordeal his drive to survive was fuelled by the thought of his father at home mourning the loss of his wife and two of his children. He thought that if he could return it would provide a fresh reason for his father to rebuild his life. He made a vow to him: 'I will not die here, I will come home'.

I read the book in a few days while on holiday and was captivated. I turned to Mary one evening and declared, 'I'm going to interview Nando Parrado.'

With Ireland heading on a two-Test tour of Argentina in 2007 I smelt an opportunity for me to try and make contact with Nando and sold the idea to Tony Leen. Both he and the *Irish Examiner* backed my proposal, and on 30 May at the Emperador Hotel in Buenos Aires, I sat down for breakfast and interviewed the man who had survived this incredible ordeal all those years ago. It was an emotional and inspiring experience that taught me so much about appreciating life.

Coverage of rugby was really starting to expand at this time – you had online social media, TV3 beginning to get involved, and Setanta starting up as well. There are just so many different outlets now, and it's incredible the impact they can have, social media in particular. People like Brian O'Driscoll can tweet something and it's all over the place in seconds. He mentions Garry Ringrose and all of a sudden it becomes a national issue.

Each to its own, but you also have to be prepared to take the negative stuff too. With Twitter, it's like inviting people to a party in your house: you get all sorts turning up and you can't complain when you open the door and they're there.

The problem with social media is it's instantaneous. There are times when you might come out immediately and react to something, whereas if you sat back and thought about it for twenty-four hours you might respond a little differently. And once it's out there, that's it. The message is clear: think before you tweet.

I enjoy meeting up with and chatting to the modern-day professional players. Every year in the media room there's another new arrival who's just come out of the game, though it can be difficult being asked to comment on players you shared a dressing room with.

Alan Quinlan came in for a lot of criticism in January 2016 for what he said about Munster in the aftermath of their 20-point defeat to Stade Français in the Champions Cup. 'Embarrassing, humiliating, disgraceful, these are words that spring to mind,' he told Sky Sports after the game. 'Munster have no divine right to win these games . . . It's embarrassing. This whole organization needs to be dissected.' Maybe he could have been a little more measured, but to be fair he thought about exactly what he was going to say. I don't think it was a rant, I think it was just born out of pure frustration from somebody who was in the dressing room for fifteen years. There was a sense that Munster had thrown in the towel, and I could understand fully where he was coming from.

If you're straight and honest in your analysis, it's not an issue. It isn't as if you're not telling the players anything new: behind closed doors they are even more critical of their own performances. If you have a criticism and it's valid or you've given an honest opinion, well, for me it's not an issue. I don't believe in saying something for the sake of saying it. I need to say it because I believe in it.

The one thing I've noticed, whether you're doing television, radio or print media, is there are a lot of people out there who have a blurred interest in the sport. They love the game and follow their sides passionately without any clear understanding of the specific nuances of the game. If you have never played rugby, it can appear complicated at times, especially when it comes to the laws of the game. A lot of the professional players coming out of the game have grown up in a very specialized, unitized environment which is a different culture, and they can talk in a different language even. Their analysis can be brilliant but I keep saying, 'Look, if 80 per cent of the people out there don't understand what you're talking about, then you're only satisfying 20 per cent of the audience.' I always feel a duty, during match commentary especially, to make things as simple and straightforward as possible. That said, trying to interpret some of the refereeing decisions made in games can prove quite challenging.

When I was a player I was cognizant of media stories and criticism, but it's a different era now in which media interest has ratcheted up ten-fold. When I started out playing, the worst that could happen to you if you had played poorly was journalists like Edmund Van Esbeck, the *Irish Times*' highly respected rugby correspondent, not mentioning you in his copy. That changed pretty quickly with the advent in the mid to late eighties of the specialist Sunday newspaper columnists whose analysis and nose for a story went far beyond what had gone before. Given that Irish rugby was beginning to experience some difficult times around then, the level of criticism aimed at the players escalated to new heights, with our former coach Mick Doyle very much in the vanguard.

Initially I thought the media work I had fallen into might only last for a few years before I'd consider getting involved in the management game again, but I was finding it so interesting and rewarding that I didn't feel any great desire to get back involved. Ireland were doing very well and Munster were flying. I'd spent a long time either playing or in management and it was actually great to just sit back, observe and enjoy.

Now, it would have been great if my timing had been a bit better and I'd been involved as a manager in the heady times Irish rugby has enjoyed from 2000 onwards. I would love to have been involved in the Munster set-up to see them in full flow behind closed doors when they were flying in Europe, to observe Paul O'Connell operating up close and the influence he had along with Ronan O'Gara at his peak. Instead, though, I was involved in the transitional period, and to some degree there is nearly more satisfaction in seeing the outcome of that come to fruition. In any event, I enjoyed the best seat in the house to witness the exploits of Munster, Leinster and Ireland in what proved a brilliant time to be commentating on and analysing rugby in this country.

I'm sure if I had really put myself out there I could have gotten back involved in the game. I did act as chairman of the Munster academy board for a number of years from its inception, which was great because it enabled me to follow the development of young players like Conor Murray, Peter O'Mahony, Donnacha Ryan, Keith Earls, Tomás O'Leary and Tommy O'Donnell, to mention just a few, from their induction as promising youngsters to becoming integral parts of the Munster and Ireland set-up. I was pleased to be invited by Munster rugby on to the interview panel to find a replacement for Tony McGahan, but having discussed it with RTE, the feeling was that it would compromise my position and they couldn't put me commentating on Munster games, so I said fine and turned down the opportunity.

That, I suppose, was the final closing of the door, and I have remained on the outside looking in ever since. I have learned over the years, however, that when one door closes another one usually opens, so who knows what opportunities lie ahead for me in this great game? Never say never.

24

The Golden Generation and Beyond

In the last few years the Irish rugby supporter has been brought up on a massive degree of success. We have won back-to-back Six Nations Championships and we've beaten top teams in the autumn internationals. At provincial level we've also seen a lot of success with Munster and Leinster's five Heineken Cups in seven years. The 'golden generation', the likes of O'Connell and O'Driscoll, can look back on titles won, knowing they played in a side that was in the top three in the world at one point. We've come a long way as a rugby nation since the first ever World Cup in 1987. In '91 we were gallant quarter-final losers but now we don't accept that any more. The '99 tournament was a low point, but at the same time there was change happening.

But O'Connell is gone; O'Driscoll is gone; O'Gara is gone.

We're now at the stage where we don't really have marquee names any more. Johnny Sexton is still Europe's leading out-half and Sean O'Brien is an outstanding player, but there are so many outstanding back-row forwards currently plying their trade worldwide, with Australia's David Pocock leading the charge now that Richie McCaw has retired.

That golden generation was exceptional; it was unprecedented for Ireland to have so many world-class performers all involved at the same time. You had Mike Gibson and Willie John McBride playing together for long periods in the sixties and early seventies but with nothing like the same quality in support. I would imagine that when the main players from that golden generation look back on their achievements, the one criticism is that they should have delivered a Six Nations Championship long before 2009, when they also achieved a Grand Slam for good measure. They might have been winning Triple Crowns, but without Championship success that achievement is somewhat devalued. The fact that Ireland won more Championships in the 1980s than throughout that golden period in the noughties is a misrepresentation of that group's talent, especially as management of our resources by the IRFU was streets ahead of any of the other European nations. We got the maximum return out of what we had, whereas the likes of the French were, and still are, generating the minimum out of their vast playing resources.

England won the 2003 World Cup with a world-class management team and some world-class players in Martin Johnson, Jonny Wilkinson, Lawrence Dallaglio and Richard Hill, but went on to struggle to reproduce that sort of form. Given that in June 2016 Eddie Jones took his England squad to Australia and won a series over there for the first time in England's history, 3-0, what odds now that he might just match that achievement in the 2019 event in Japan?

Then take Wales. They reached the semi-final of the 2011 tournament along with consecutive Six Nations in 2012 and 2013, Gatland sticking with a core of ten to twelve players and allowing them to gain experience. It's incredible to think that at twenty-three years of age George North had won over fifty caps. Jamie Roberts, Jonathan Davies and North could, injury permitting, be together for another four or five years.

In Ireland, at the advent of professionalism, the priority was geared more towards the provinces, whereas now the balance has gone the other way, possibly too far, to the national team. Provincial success was the foundation that enabled the national side to reach unprecedented heights. For that to happen again, our provincial sides must become a force in European competition once more.

So if we want the national team to be winners again, the provinces are the starting point. You can talk about TV money and billionaires in France and England, but I strongly believe that Leinster, with the right structures in place, can compete with the big guns overseas. Munster and Ulster, however, face a tougher fight, while it remains to be seen if Connacht can continue to compete on their limited resources after their heroics in the 2015/16 season.

The next part is the hardest part, though, because now the national side is vying for a consistent slot in the world's top four. We've made unbelievable progress and have been incredibly consistent, up to last season. The litmus test, however, is always the World Cup, when everybody is looking to peak at the same time. Autumn internationals and summer tours have to be taken in the context of the season and what coaches want to get out of them.

Why is Ireland still the only major nation not to have reached a World Cup semi-final? I don't know – that's the honest answer. We've had opportunities in the past and not taken them. In 2011 we should have been in the semi-final. We should have beaten Wales in Wellington. Unfortunately, our World Cup campaigns have always flattered to deceive. In 2007 we were definitely in the best position ever to compete for a semi-final place, but Eddie O'Sullivan will put his hand up now and say that preparation on a number of fronts was wrong.

Tournaments also take on a life of their own. Take France, who reached the final in 2011 despite losing to Tonga in the pool stage. France were so bad they reached a point where the players just said, 'We've got to take this on ourselves.'

The same happened to England in 2007. They got beaten 36-0 by South Africa in their second game. They were in such a shambolic state that the senior players just pulled the whole thing together, and the side progressed against all the odds. They ended up getting to the final before losing to the same Springbok side by just 9 points.

The problem with the 2015 World Cup was that Ireland were no different than ever before in that we were reliant on four or five key players and managed to lose all of them before the quarter-final against Argentina – O'Connell, Sexton, O'Brien and O'Mahony – in an extraordinary sequence of events. Argentina were an excellent side, but somehow, by beating France in our pool and thus avoiding New Zealand, that was supposed to make our path to the semi-final easier. I had been concerned about the quality of that Argentinian team from the start, having followed their progress in the Rugby Championship, and even more so after watching them live in their opening pool game against New Zealand at Wembley. Despite that 10-point defeat, I saw enough to know that, at their best, they would cause Ireland a lot of problems. Going into that match without the four lads was a complete game changer. I think we're realistic to know that, while we have a very competitive side, all the stars would have to align for us to win a World Cup.

The most striking thing, sitting in the stand and looking down on the pitch at the Irish team at that World Cup, was that we lacked lightning pace across the back line to open things up and score from deep. That is why we are dependent on Joe Schmidt's power plays from certain phases, to do something to break the line. Simon Zebo doesn't have out-and-out pace. Tommy Bowe was never a sprinter. Jared Payne isn't one, nor is Robbie Henshaw. Our back line just doesn't have the searing pace and stepping ability that the likes of Milner-Skudder offer New Zealand, while up front, we're not going to be beating anybody up in the knockout phase to win a World Cup. We need to be able to find an edge to open teams up. To be fair to Schmidt, I think he's maximized everything we have, but even that put us right to the wire to win those two Six Nations Championships. Both of them went down to the last play in the last game.

The big question now is, have we reached a wall in terms of what we're capable of? Schmidt has achieved massively with the players at his disposal. The challenge facing him now is that the opposition know what to expect from Ireland and have worked on countering the effectiveness of our kicking game in particular. There was a lot of truth in what Warren Gatland said about us prior to the last World Cup, about being narrow and predictable. Our players are workmanlike. They're extremely vigilant. They're fitter than they've ever been. They're students of the game, and Schmidt offers them a very detailed framework to play off.

Schmidt has been labelled a conservative coach, which is nonsense when you consider what he achieved with Leinster. There's a huge difference, though, when you train a team every day: you can concentrate on skill development and you can work them hard and use repetition to perfect the process. Unfortunately you just don't get that at international level.

Our breakdown work when everybody's up to speed is outstanding in that everybody knows his role. Whether you like it or not, the fact that players know that the ball carrier isn't going to offload means they can commit to cleaning out and therefore generate a quicker recycle. Joe Schmidt is in complete control, and the players are in no doubt as to who has the final word. Contrary to public opinion, he is not set against offloading. Problem is, if you're going to do it, you'd better make sure the pass sticks. Fine if it works, but the players' starting point now is, 'I'm not going to make that mistake, I'm going to recycle.' It's the easier option. That's where we're at.

Don't get me wrong, I have no doubt that Schmidt was the reason why we won the Six Nations Championship in consecutive years. The subtlety that he brought, the attention to detail, those were the things that got us over the line. He always sees a chink. He will always emphasize the things that make the opposition vulnerable, so that you go into a game, even against the best of teams, knowing that if you can do A, B and C, you can score and you can beat them. That always changes the mindset going into a big game, and Schmidt provides that time after time as we saw to good effect in that captivating series against South Africa in June 2016.

The basic ingredients are there: talented players with successful backgrounds, particularly the Leinster guys who would have been involved in multiple Heineken Cup successes, even if 2012 seems a long time ago now. The thing is, there are lots of different ways to play rugby and we can't all do what New Zealand do. We've got to do what suits our skill set and resources best.

The challenge now is that Argentina will only get better, with a regional side involved in Super Rugby to complement the promotion of the national side to the Rugby Championship. I think there's a real danger that Argentina could pull away from Ireland by the time we go to Japan in 2019, that the gap could by then be even wider. In fact, given their age profile, they are well worth a few bob to go all the way. They have always thrived in the tournament environment. The only danger here, with so many of the Pumas squad now playing regularly and travelling the world with the Jaguares in Super Rugby, is that the players get stale, and the inspirational buzz of coming together to represent their country is diminished as a result. Either way, having provided all four teams for the semi-finals of the 2015 World Cup, the southern hemisphere sides will still be leading the charge come Japan, even if South Africa appear to be slipping somewhat.

Let's be honest, the 2016 Six Nations, as a spectacle, was poor, especially when you compare it with the World Cup three months earlier. In Europe, the range of attacking options and skills is limited in comparison. If you look at the way France are playing, it's ten years behind, but I think England under Eddie Jones could develop to a stage where they will challenge for the next World Cup because he's got young talent there, they're accumulating a lot of experience, and he's got players with that explosive pace that Ireland just don't have at present.

Jones also cuts through all the crap. He doesn't care. He changed the mindset of his players in his first three months from everything that Stuart Lancaster went on about – 'We're humble, we're this, we're that.' Eddie Jones doesn't give a shit.

Ireland still have a very good base to work from with promising talent coming through, as we saw on that recent South African series. We'll be competitive with England, that's for sure. Criticisms of the team and Joe Schmidt in the 2016 Six Nations campaign were completely misplaced in the context of the players who were missing.

The way Connacht performed in 2015/16 has been a pleasure to watch, and I think has the capacity to change the Irish mindset in terms of showing that we are capable of playing multi-phase rugby. Now, to do that, a key element is searing pace. You have to have that in abundance. Their back three of Tiernan O'Halloran, Matt Healy and Niyi Adeolokun all have it, and it was no coincidence that all three contributed the tries on the greatest day in Connacht's history when they landed the Guinness Pro12 trophy against Leinster at Murrayfield on that emotionally charged day in May 2016. That day, when Connacht lifted their first ever trophy, was when all the elements of the game that coach Pat Lam had been working on for three years came together.

People ask, why can't Ireland play this way? The big issue here is that it has taken Lam three years with a team that's training together five days a week for it to be perfected. You simply don't have that facility at international level. The only way you could make that happen is if all provinces had the same approach and playing philosophy. In New Zealand it works because all their Super Rugby sides play, more or less, the same way. They all play that offloading, all-encompassing game. We don't. If the provinces aren't doing it collectively, then it's very hard for the national team to do it.

While it has taken Lam three years to perfect, he has killed the notion that Irish teams can't develop the skill levels to effect that type of rugby. Now we know that with perseverance, quality skills coaches and the right attitude, it can be done. In fact there are parallels here with what Mick Doyle achieved with Ireland back in 1985. I am sure he would have enjoyed and approved of what Lam has delivered in the West.

At provincial level we're definitely at a crossroads now. There's a seismic shift happening with the changes in Europe as well as the millions being pumped into the English and French clubs through huge TV deals and wealthy benefactors. The Heineken Cup seeding system that once made us great is no longer in vogue, and apart from the one Italian club, there are very few gimmes now in the pool stage. Glasgow Warriors winning the Pro12 in 2015 has also put our sides on notice, and we'll have to watch the Welsh districts at some stage, if they ever manage to get their act together. We will be competitive, but I think in a European context, the future is uncertain.

It's the natural evolution of the game. We're only twenty years into professionalism. The inevitable conflict with the growing influence of the wealthy clubs looking to take on the respective rugby unions for the control and ownership of the players has started. The question is, what degree of interference is that going to have in the international game in ten years' time?

For our provinces, the question is, will we become the equivalent of those mid-table soccer teams, consistently competitive but always short of the big players? This is sport all over the world, however. There are only a chosen few dominant teams in every league, usually driven by money, even if Leicester City's Premier League success has offered hope to everyone. But can it be sustained? Remember Blackburn Rovers.

I fear that in European rugby terms we're in danger of slipping back into the middle of the pack. Leinster have the resources, in both playing and financial terms, to challenge the big boys, and they represent our best chance of staying the pace and competing for European silverware. To do so, however, will also require a Joe Schmidt-type presence at the helm. Unfortunately, Joe Schmidts don't grow on trees.

25

Robotic Games

The big opportunity for Irish rugby is that there's a rugby club now in almost every area of the country. Driving around Ireland, one of the most striking aspects is that almost every parish has a GAA pitch. While rugby isn't quite at that stage, and never will be, it's likely that if you really want to play rugby there is a club of some shape or form within a manageable distance. From Ceann Sibéal in the Dingle peninsula to the Liberties in inner-city Dublin, clubs are springing up everywhere.

That said, we need to encourage kids to keep playing all types of sports, from Gaelic football to hurling, soccer, rugby and basketball. It's that wide range of skills that will ultimately feed into their athleticism and ability. They can then focus on rugby, or whatever leisure activity they choose, later on.

Kids at ten, eleven, twelve should be trying their hands at all sports, be it rugby, soccer, Gaelic football or hurling.

I think if a player can develop his eye for a game, his eye-hand coordination, his competitive spirit, you don't need to specialize too early. It's the development of your overall sporting skills from twelve to sixteen that will stand to you.

The John Hayeses of this world – he only took up rugby in his late teens – are few and far between. Yes, of course you can turn a big strong man into a prop forward, but the most effective team is one whose players are contributing in all aspects of play, not just at set-pieces.

In an Irish context, given our population base, if we have kids who've played a multiplicity of sports in their teenage years, that will prepare them better when they come to specialize. It is a strength, most definitely. There are things we do naturally in our indigenous sports that other countries are still striving to try and match, such as our ability to catch a ball above our head.

Everything is so programmed nowadays. Everybody is doing the same training, same drills, same thinking, even at underage level. Spontaneity is severely lacking in modern sport. Maybe the coach who is brave and innovative will end up winning silverware. At the top level of sport, a programmed style of game plan does prove effective. A lot of players welcome it because it takes the on-pitch, split-second decision-making away from them. It's almost like, 'If I've my homework done, this is all I need to do. I know what my function and my role is within the context of the team.' Simon Zebo is probably one of the few that has spontaneity, but that hasn't always endeared him to his coaches. It is all about getting the balance right.

You take away some of that spark and you have to ask, is the Irish team as a collective better with players doing what they're doing in the system, with everybody singing off the same pre-ordained script? Recent successes would suggest that to be the case. It's probably far more entertaining to have spontaneity, but you're judged on whether you win or lose. Like all sport nowadays, particularly professional sport, there is only one measure: did you win or lose? We might not like it, but that's the case.

To be consistently successful, however, you need players who have the ability to make the right decisions at the right time. That is what sets New Zealand rugby apart. Coaches can't make all the decisions for players. Joe Schmidt puts a framework together that enables the team to get into specific positions on the field. By and large they are playing to pattern; but that doesn't mean that if a gap is on you can't take it. The problem for some players is recognizing it. There is danger in players getting too caught up in a formulaic way of thinking.

Maybe that's just the way the game has gone. Not so long ago, as a forward you were told to go out and get stuck into every ruck, all together. You were encouraged to hunt as a pack of eight. Now only three players are designated to go and hit it. Other players are running off into pre-ordained positions so that when the ball is recycled you have at least two different lines of attack. Teams have formulated four or five plays ahead and players know exactly where they are supposed to be and what's coming down the line.

Don't get me wrong, the professional game is so much better in so many ways. It's more exciting, it's faster, and there's more ball-in-play time, but a lot of it is repetitive. You could be watching any game or any team and they all appear to be playing the same way.

Technology also plays a massive role in the game now. The amount of analysis that's been done, the amount of time that's spent studying the opposition, trying to pick up calls, listening to the audio because you might pick up a few triggers off the referee's mic – it's incredible. Every team gets a dossier on the referee – what he's hot on and what he's more inclined to let go. Where can you push the boundaries under his watch? Everything is scrutinized to the nth degree.

Kilkenny's hurling manager Brian Cody has been a great one for empowering his players to make decisions on the field. It is a huge benefit if the players are the ones who can shake things up by themselves. Thankfully that hasn't been taken completely away on the rugby pitch.

At half-time there are only two or three key messages you can get across, and they could be things that coaches see from above. The players will always be given their voice for something that's specific to them. After all, they are the ones in the thick of the action and the ones best placed to sense the mood and weaknesses of the opposition. But the days of shouting and roaring in the dressing room are definitely gone. It's now far more clinical. All teams do a well-thought-out warm-up on the field and then take just three or four minutes to go back into the dressing room, take off the training top and put on their playing jersey before hitting the pitch once again. It's very much down to every player to get his individual mindset prepared. In times past you might be waiting for your captain or coach to deliver something or press the right buttons to give you that final boost before taking to the field. Now the responsibility to get ready is very much down to yourself.

That's one of the reasons why the role of captaincy is different now and you've so many different leaders on the field, so many people who take responsibility for different aspects of the game in different areas of the pitch, which means the captain can concentrate more on just delivering an influential personal performance, affecting the outcome of the game directly. That is what made Brian O'Driscoll and Paul O'Connell such effective captains.

The make-up of the modern rugby player's personality is different, too. They are shaped by the environment. Every modern player is a product of the professional system. There's very little individualism in terms of background, lifestyle or life experience. Go into a dressing room in the amateur days and one fella was a doctor, one a banker, the other an electrician. That brought a different mindset together, a totally different dynamic. As a result of that you had diverse characters, all shaped and influenced by their everyday lives. Nowadays the make-up of a dressing room is very much of a type, the only difference being that one player might have a New Zealand accent and another could be from Kerry. They're all products of the same system so that individualistic streak is lacking. It's become a different sport, with everything mapped out for you on a daily basis.

That's why academy players are encouraged to do things outside rugby, to do some form of skill training or college degree or *something*, because in many respects there's a robotic element to making it as a professional athlete. You're constantly being told what to do. You're given advice to do this, do that. Your coaches and fitness advisers give you a sheet and there's a multiplicity of things to do and if you do all those things there's a fair chance you're going to improve, get bigger, stronger and faster. It's the things outside the gym that interest me the most: the skill development, that ability to make decisions under pressure – that's the personality.

That's what Paul O'Connell brought to the game. He had something in him. When he was training for swimming in his teens at half five in the morning, he had a drive in him. Without that special ingredient, that X factor, everybody would be the same, but there is something innate in an O'Connell, an O'Driscoll or a Martin Johnson; in an O'Gara or a Roy Keane. You're very lucky now if you've one or two of those in the make-up of your squad. Jamie Roberts from Wales qualified as a medical doctor and was that bit different. He's obviously a very intelligent guy, and that intelligence is a key part of his make-up as a rugby player. You'd be thrilled to have somebody who brings that special something to the table.

As a result of professionalism and the robotic nature of the game and their lifestyles, life after professional rugby can be a big challenge for retired players. A lot of them struggle for a while to find their feet again. You start off as a professional rugby player and you're earning money on a high level while your non-rugby peers are down at the bottom of the salary scale. But as your career is winding down or ending, they pass you out. Your earning capacity is diminishing at a time when they are establishing themselves in their chosen careers or professions.

Having said that, would any of them give up the chance to do it all again, to play for their country, win Championships and medals, perform in front of thousands of people, experience the highs and the lows, going through it all with your team-mates, bonding in situations that 99 per cent of the population never get to experience? I doubt it very much. You'd be tying up your bootlaces in a heartbeat to get that opportunity again.

26

Too Big, Too Fast, Too Strong?

Rugby as a sport is at a crossroads. It was never meant to have the physical shapes playing the game that it has now. For the first time, I think we're going into an era where many parents would be happier *not* to have their kids playing rugby. That is a worry.

With all the talk surrounding concussion, I've had mothers and fathers approach me worried about their kids playing the game and wondering what they should do. After that revealing documentary *Hidden Impact* on RTE exploring the increasing incidents of concussion and the potential side effects, the questions kept coming from people I had never met before. Former Scotland and Lions No. 8 John Beattie produced a similarly revealing programme for the BBC.

'But rugby was always a physical game,' people will say. Yes, if you look back at old footage of games, some were filthy. But the difference is, a lot of the damage inflicted was only superficial. It is the hidden damage now, the effects of some of the big hits going in these days that might not manifest themselves until a few years down the road, that is more a cause for concern.

Just look at the tackles going on in modern rugby. There's no comparison with previous eras. I was covering France v. Ireland in Paris in the 2016 Six Nations for RTE when Mike McCarthy was concussed after a clash of heads. While the match moved on, I watched him closely as he tried to get up off the ground three times. He lifts his head up so far, but can't get up; he goes back down and tries again but still can't get up. It reminded me of when you catch a fish and throw it on its side and it's just flapping around as the life drains from it. Mike McCarthy was flapping out on the pitch in front of me. It was no surprise when the IRFU announced that he would play no more rugby for the remainder of the season.

Who knows what the long-term consequences will be of all these hits? In training, in matches, hit after hit after hit. How much longer can it be sustained?

The game in the northern hemisphere has to evolve. In the southern hemisphere it's about evasion, whereas we seem more intent on the collision. Players are told 'win the collisions', but the smart teams such as New Zealand look to keep the ball alive, looking outside your weak shoulder for the space to open up and offload. The All Blacks in recent years have actually downsized their forwards, opting instead for more mobility and higher skill levels. Crucially, they have achieved that without any major concession to set-piece effectiveness and are still able to compete at their effective best at the breakdown.

There was a stat that came out recently from the French Top

14 which revealed that number 10s suffered the highest proportion of incidents of concussions. But are we surprised? Look at Johnny Sexton and Ronan O'Gara, who was targeted throughout his career; when you're in the thick of it and they're piling into you, what are you going to do? You have to stand there and take what's coming towards you.

There isn't a back-row forward now, I'd say, who will go through his career without a reconstructed shoulder. That is the result of all these collisions. Rugby was supposed to be a game for all shapes and sizes. It was logical that once it transformed into a professional sport the ground rules would change, but I think we're only just coming to terms with the implications of having players that are bigger, stronger and faster than ever before. The game is only two decades old in the professional sense but we're having to react in the same way American football is after having their heads in the sand for years and years around the issue of concussion. I think we are going to have to look at ways of safeguarding the players.

It was Sean O'Brien who said in relation to the much-touted Garry Ringrose, 'They were right not to pick him for the Six Nations because he would have been injured.' Garry doesn't have the bulk to compete in the midfield areas just now. He's currently 10kg lighter than the average midfield back, and by definition that changes the ground rules.

When we introduced Brian O'Driscoll as a twenty-year-old in 1999, at no stage did we look at each other and say, 'Is there a possibility he could get smashed to death?' It wasn't an issue seventeen years ago. It is today.

The size of players, even in Schools rugby, is getting ridiculous. Because of the competition that exists, especially in Leinster, you hear of annual budgets now of €100,000-plus for school teams. Ultimately, though, the focus on size and bulk has been to the detriment of skill development. After all, it's easier to measure muscle and weight mass: you can put a fellow up on a weighing scale and see if he's 2kg heavier than he was six months earlier, or if he can bench-press 10kg more in December than he could in October. But how do you measure if his passing off his left hand is improving?

You're also going up against a Schools Senior Cup model that is over 125 years old. With the tradition and history associated with it, winning is always going to be the bottom line.

While there's been a huge focus on the game and its evolution in recent years with a lot of scaremongering surrounding concussion, I'd say we're in a better place now than we were even two years ago. The authorities have now accepted the issues and have begun to take remedial action. The most appalling incident I have seen in the modern era was the George Smith/Richard Hibbard clash of heads in the third Test on the Lions tour in 2013. Smith was carried off right underneath where I was sitting doing commentary for RTE, and I thought, 'That's it for him.' But he was back on the field within ten minutes. It was almost a dereliction of duty on the part of the Australian Rugby Union to let that happen. Thankfully, I think we've moved on hugely from that point.

I think a reduction in the number of substitutions from the current level of eight to five – with some allowance for independently vouched front-row injuries – would make a difference. It would immediately negate the prospect of carrying 23-stone behemoths on the bench who only have the aerobic capacity to play for thirty minutes. On so many occasions it is those types being introduced in the final quarter against fatiguing players that have created the biggest problems. When you are tiring, your technique suffers, and if you don't effect the perfect tackle with your head in the right position against opponents of that size, then you are asking for trouble. It is important that the lawmakers continue to look at ways of reducing the ever-increasing injury count the game is currently inflicting.

Having said that, there has always been an element of danger in rugby, as there is in all sports, be it cricket, hockey, boxing or F1. I have a friend who played rugby all his life and now his daughter does showjumping and he's nervous as hell every time she goes out on the horse. I know from first-hand experience that serious accidents can happen in our sport with devastating consequences.

My worst day on the rugby field was during a colours match for UCC against UCD in the Mardyke. Ironically it was Valentine's Day 1981 – the same day as the Stardust nightclub tragedy in Dublin. Those two events will always be linked in my head.

During the game a ruck formed, but my close friend and team-mate in the centre, Fergus Barrett – Gus – got caught in a very poor position when, at the same time, one of the UCD players came in and hit the ruck.

Gus never got off the ground. I can still see him there, his face turning blue as we stood looking at him, stricken. Mick Molloy, who was our coach and also the Irish team doctor at the time, rushed on to the field and basically saved his life. I clearly remember standing on the pitch and we knew there was something badly wrong. I got a tap on the shoulder and somebody said, 'Is he OK?'

'I think he's in serious trouble,' I replied, then turned round to see that it was Gus's brother Aylmer, who was watching the match with his dad from the sideline.

Gus was a team-mate of mine from the very first game of

rugby I ever played – CBC U13s against Rockwell. We won a Junior Cup and two Senior Cup medals together with CBC, and both of us went to UCC at the same time.

I remember that night vividly as we gathered after the match in the Western Star, which was like a morgue because we were all awaiting news on Gus. We just didn't know how things were going.

He was transferred to the national rehabilitation centre in Dún Laoghaire in Dublin, and his injuries were serious. A month after the incident, we played Terenure in Dublin and it was arranged that we would visit Gus afterwards. We were counselled as to what to expect, what we were going to see and how to deal with it. We were driven to the hospital by members of Terenure, and their captain said he'd come in with us.

I'll never forget going into that room, seeing Gus lying there in a rotating bed with a mirror a foot over his head to enable him to look around. He was paralysed from the neck down, a quadriplegic. It was so hard to take. Only the fact that we'd been counselled and advised in advance allowed us, just about, to deal with it. The Terenure captain, who hadn't been prepared, fainted on the spot.

A massive amount of fundraising went on and Gus returned to Cork's University Hospital where he remained in care until he passed away in March 1989. The thing that struck me most was that he had been a dental student in UCC and the dental hospital was also based in the CUH where he was invalided. That must have been very difficult for him.

While he was still in Dublin, I tried to drop in to see him as much as possible when up for games or squad sessions. After winning my first cap for Ireland I arranged with Mick Molloy to call out to him on the day after the game.

Lying in his bed, he looked at me through this mirror and said, 'Do you remember Wales?'

'What do you mean?' I said.

'Do you remember the school tour with Christians?'

'I do, of course.'

'Do you remember your man who said you'd get twenty caps for Ireland?'

Five years earlier, when we were in sixth year in CBC, we'd both gone on our first ever rugby tour, to Wales. After one of the games we went into the clubhouse and I was sitting down with Gus when this man came up to me, asked my name, and said, 'I'll make a note of that. You'll get twenty caps for Ireland.' I did recall the incident, and was shocked that Gus brought it up. It brought it home to me for the first time just how perfect and unaffected his mind was. I just couldn't get it out of my head that Gus was reliving that moment in his head. He was lying in that hospital bed every day with little or no movement and his thought process was absolutely perfect.

The strange thing was, Gus's accident never once made me or the majority of the other players who were playing that day stop and think about the dangers of what might happen to us on the rugby field. We were young, and we just continued with rugby and life. You talk about parents nowadays and the worries they harbour with their kids playing, but all our parents would have been invested in the teams at that stage as well and they would have gone to all those matches. Yet it wasn't something that was discussed. It never crossed my mind that I might get seriously injured, even after that incident. The dangers are there, as they are in all sports – they always have been – but sometimes you can just be in the wrong place at the wrong time. Yet, like all young students, we felt immortal, that life couldn't harm us. We were ready for whatever it wanted to throw at us, and for the next decade I made sure that I gave everything I had on the rugby field. I got the chance while Gus never did.

Rugby has given so much to me. It's a huge part of who I am, and I couldn't imagine my life without it. I've experienced the highs of winning Five Nations Championships and Triple Crowns and the lows of wooden spoons and being sent home from the Lions after only one day. I've seen Munster and Ireland struggle, and I've also seen them bounce back.

Life is no different, as I know only too well from personal experience. Rugby has helped to shape the person I am today, but I often wonder what might have happened if my parents had sent me to one of Cork's famous GAA nurseries instead. After all, I wanted to join my friends in going to Coláiste Chríost Rí or the North Monastery. Would rugby have discovered me, or would I have been drawn to it? Who knows! All I know is that it has been the major influence in my life, shaping who I am, and for that I am grateful.

As for my grandfather, Jacko, I wonder what he would have made of my future sporting career . . .

Acknowledgements

I have been approached on a number of occasions over the years to document my life's journey through rugby, but never really gave it any serious thought. That changed primarily due to the persistence and persuasive skills of Daire Whelan. He was the one who convinced me that I had a story to tell and his professionalism and dedication made it a thoroughly enjoyable experience over the year of collaboration it took to complete this project.

Five minutes into my initial meeting with Eoin McHugh I knew that, with him at the helm, Transworld would be my publisher of choice. That gut instinct was fully justified with Eoin offering invaluable support and a fountain of common sense from the moment we agreed to work together. That support continued to the conclusion of the project, especially when Giles Elliott, Transworld's excellent editorial director, came on board. Suffice to say our final marathon session in Cork proved invaluable.

In relation to the events surrounding my grandfather Jacko Lenihan, I would like to thank Listowel historian Vincent Carmody for his help and support in compiling the background information and for facilitating a number of key meetings. My thanks also to the Brosnan family for their help and cooperation.

In order to tell this story properly, the views and recollections of a number of my playing colleagues had to be accessed, and I am particularly grateful to Des Fitzgerald and Brian McCall for agreeing to sit down in front of the dictaphone and place their experiences on record. In addition, I would like to acknowledge the contribution of another great international team-mate in Jimmy McCoy, who agreed to be interviewed by me for the *Irish Examiner*, extracts of which are included in this book.

The fact that I had a story to tell in the first place is down to the effort and commitment of countless talented players both from Ireland and further afield, many of whom have become lifelong friends, and coaches who helped shape my playing career from the day I came under the profound influence of Brother Philip O'Reilly in Christian Brothers College in Cork back in 1971.

I would like to thank all the members of the various selection committees and management teams I was privileged to work with through several Five/Six Nations campaigns and on various tours around the globe with Ireland and the British and Irish Lions.

That my journey took a detour through the world of the media back in 2003 is due in no small measure to the *Irish Examiner*'s excellent sports editor Tony Leen for persuading me to commit my thoughts on the game in print. In doing so he unearthed in me a love for writing that I might never have discovered.

I also owe a debt of gratitude to John D. O'Brien at Setanta Sports and to Glen Killane and Ryle Nugent at RTE for affording me the opportunity to sit in the best seats in the house across a plethora of rugby stadia around the world, working in television and radio.

To my parents, Gerald and Chris, who were so supportive

in every way without ever being interfering, and to my sisters Jo and Audrey, I apologize for hogging the limelight in the Lenihan household for so long. I would also like to thank a large circle of friends who continue to be there when needed.

And to David, who has provided nothing but pleasure since the day he was born and continues to make his parents proud.

Finally, I owe the biggest debt of gratitude to Mary for her unwavering love, support and friendship through the good and challenging times that define everyday life. She is unquestionably the rock of our family.

Picture Acknowledgements

All images have been supplied courtesy of the author unless otherwise stated.

First section

Page 2 (Ireland debut), page 7 (press conference; Australia game 1991) all © INPHO/Billy Stickland

Page 3 (attacking philosophy), page 5 (only try), page 6 (Wales game), page 7 (Australia game 1987) all © Colorsport

Page 4 (line-out in colour) Getty Images © Mike Brett/Popperfoto

Page 5 (linking arms) © Irish Times/Peter Thursfield

Second section

Page 9 (Hawke's Bay action shots) both Getty Images: line-out © Mike Brett/Popperfoto; running © Bob Thomas/Getty Images

Page 10 (Lions captain), page 11 (Three Lions), page 12 (Gatland/Redmond/Danaher) all © INPHO/Billy Stickland

Page 11 (Lions action), page 12 (Lions defeat) both © Colorsport

Page 12 (Lions manager) © David Rogers/Getty Images

Page 12 (O'Sullivan and Gatland) © Damien Eagers/SPORTSFILE

Page 14 (Munster awards), page 15 (Brian O'Driscoll) both © INPHO/Dan Sheridan

Page 16 (Hugh Cahill) © Brendan Moran/SPORTSFILE

Page 16 (RTE team) © INPHO/James Cromble

Index

About the Author

Donal Lenihan was born on 12 September 1959 and educated at St Patrick's National School, Christian Brothers College and University College Cork. A loyal servant of UCC, Cork Constitution and Munster, Lenihan won the first of his fifty-two Ireland caps against Australia in November 1981 and took part in eleven Five Nations Championships and two World Cups, captaining his country seventeen times, before playing in his final Test match against Wales in January 1992. He went on to manage both Ireland and the British & Irish Lions and is now a much-respected analyst of the game for RTE and columnist with the *Irish Examiner.*